ORACLE8

PROGRAMMING:

A PRIMER

ORACLE8 PROGRAMMING: A PRIMER

Rajshekhar Sunderraman
Georgia State University

An imprint of Addison Wesley Longman, Inc.

Reading, Massachusetts • Menlo Park, California
New York • Harlow, England • Don Mills, Ontario
Sydney • Mexico City • Madrid • Amsterdam

Acquisitions Editor: Maite Suarez-Rivas
Project Manager: Trillium Project Management
Composition: Windfall Software, Paul C. Anagnostopoulos
Copyeditor: Donald Lafferty
Proofreader: Trillium Project Management
Cover Designer: Lynne Reed

Access the latest information about Addison-Wesley books from our World Wide Web site: http://www.awl.com/cseng

Library of Congress Cataloging-in-Publication Data

Sunderraman, Rajshekhar.
Oracle8 programming : a primer / Rajshekhar Sunderraman.
p. cm.
ISBN 0-201-61258-5
1. Oracle (Computer file) 2. Relational databases. I. Title.
QA76.9.D3 S2953 2000
005.75′85—dc21 99-047984

This book was composed with the ZzTEX typesetting system on a PC. The text is set in ITC Berkeley Oldstyle and the open-face titles in Monotype Old Style Bold Outline. The monospaced computer program font is ZztexMono-Regular. The book was printed on Lynx Opaque Plus.

3 4 5 6 7 8 9 10—CRS—03020100

To

My mother
`Saraswathi Sunderraman`
for her love and hard work

My father
`Sqn. Ldr. Rajagopala Sunderraman`
for his love and encouragement

My wife
`Radhika`
for her love and caring

My children
`Nandita` and `Naveen`
for their love and innocence

PREFACE

Oracle is the most widely used database system in the world. It runs on virtually all platforms ranging from the PC to mainframes. It also comes with an array of programming tools and environments and provides access to the database from a variety of high-level programming languages.

In recent years, more and more universities in the United States and elsewhere are using Oracle in their database courses as the primary vehicle to illustrate database concepts and principles. This has resulted in the need for a concise book on Oracle programming to supplement the traditional texts in the database courses. The main motivation for writing this book is to satisfy this need. This book can also be used by a non-academic professional who is interested in learning about SQL, PL/SQL, embedded-SQL programming, JDBC, and SQLJ.

The topics discussed in this book are Oracle SQL, PL/SQL, embedded programming with Pro*C/C++, JDBC, and SQLJ. A brief introduction to the object features of Oracle8 is also presented in the book. To work with Oracle, it is absolutely essential to learn about SQL and PL/SQL, the two languages at the core of the Oracle database engine. Embedded-SQL (Pro*C/C++), JDBC access to Oracle, and the relatively new SQLJ standard are some of the important environments in which to develop applications. Java is an emerging language that will have a significant impact on computing in the coming years and Oracle is investing in this technology by providing JDBC drivers, SQLJ translators, and other related tools to develop applications, expecially on the Web. Embedded-SQL is part of the SQL standards and is also an important technique for database programmers to learn.

Three sample databases are introduced early in the book and most of the chapters use these databases for illustration purposes. Several application programs are developed in their entirety in the different programming environments discussed in the text[1].

Book Use

This book is suitable as a supplemental text for an introductory database course which covers the relational model and uses Oracle as the database system for the course projects and assignments. Course projects can be developed using embedded-SQL (Pro*C/C++), JDBC, or SQLJ. An entire chapter is devoted to suggestions for course projects. These course projects are typically assigned in introductory database courses where a team of students start with a problem statement, write the problem specifications, design the database, create the database in Oracle, and write application programs that access the database. Some of the chapters also have review problems for the reader to go over to consolidate their understanding of the concepts presented in these chapters.

This book is also appropriate for a non-academic individual who is interested in learning about Oracle. He or she can find materials on SQL, PL/SQL, Pro*C/C++, JDBC, and SQLJ, all in one text. This book can be considered a starting point in the exploration of what Oracle has to offer.

World Wide Web Support

Most of the code presented in the book can also be found at the following `World Wide Web` site:

`http://www.awl.com/cseng/titles/0-201-61258-5`

In addition, the author will attempt to include other related materials to be developed in the near future at this Web site.

1. The programs and the applications presented in this book have been included for their instructional value. They have been tested with care but are not guaranteed for any particular purpose. The publisher does not offer any warranties or representations, nor does it accept any liabilities with respect to the programs or applications.

Acknowledgments

First of all, I would like to acknowledge Katherine Harutunian at Addison-Wesley for working with me closely and diligently to get this book out in time. The staff at Addison-Wesley is always a pleasure to work with. The reviewers, Akira Kawaguchi (City College of New York), Louis Mazzucco (SUNY Cobleskill), Mark Barnard (Marquette University), Willie Favero (Professional) and Ashesh Parekh (Professional) deserve special mention, as they made very useful and critical observations to improve the presentation and content of the book.

I would also like to acknowledge all my students who have diligently worked on various projects using Oracle over the past several years at Wichita State University and Georgia State University. In particular, I would like to acknowledge the effort put forth by Krissy Echols, Veena Pujari, and Radhika Venkataraman in designing and implementing the investment portfolio database application introduced in this edition of the text.

Finally, I would like to acknowledge the support my family has shown to me during the writing of this edition of the book. Thank you, Radhu, for all the hard work and understanding and thanks, Nannu and Nammi, for encouraging me to write this book so that I can buy you candy and toys from the money I get!

CONTENTS

CHAPTER

1

The Relational Data Model

The relational data model presents a logical view of a database in which the user perceives the data to be organized in tabular form. This is a simple and intuitive view of data that hides all the complex details of how the data are actually stored and accessed within a computer. Moreover, over the years, very sophisticated and efficient structures and algorithms have been developed to implement database systems based on the relational model. As a result, relational databases are being used overwhelmingly in the industry and anywhere else there is a need to manage large amounts of data.

In this chapter, the basic concepts and foundations of the relational data model are presented. The chapter also presents three sample relational databases that will be used throughout this book.

1.1 The Relational Database

The relational data model has a strong mathematical foundation based on set theory. We thus begin here a brief mathematical definition of a relational database.

A *relation scheme* is a finite sequence of unique attribute names. For example,

```
EMPLOYEES = (EMPID, ENAME, ADDRESS, SALARY)
```

is a relation scheme with four attribute names.

Each attribute name, `A`, is associated with a *domain*, dom(`A`), a set of values. This domain includes a special value called *null*. For example, dom(`EMPID`) could be the set of all possible integers between 1000 and 9999 and the special null value.

Given a relation scheme `R = A1, . . . , An`, a *relation* `r` on the scheme `R` is defined as any finite subset of the Cartesian product

dom(`A1`) × · · · × dom(`An`).

Assuming appropriate domains for the `EMPLOYEES` relation scheme, a sample relation under this scheme could be

```
{ (1111,'Jones','111 Ash St.',20000),
  (2222,'Smith','123 Elm St.',25000),
  (3333,'Brown','234 Oak St.',30000) }
```

Each of the elements of a relation is also referred to as a *tuple*.

A *relational database scheme*, `D`, is a finite set of relation schemes,

`{R1, . . . , Rm}`.

A *relational database* on scheme `D` is a set of relations

`{r1, . . . , rm}`,

where each `ri` is a relation on the corresponding scheme `Ri`.

1.2 Integrity Constraints

In addition to the data content, a relational database consists of *integrity constraints*, a set of conditions that must be met or satisfied by the data content at all times. The relational database is referred to as a *valid* database if its data content satisfies all the integrity constraints specified in its definition. Individual relations are referred to as *valid* if they satisfy all the constraints imposed on them. Three basic and important types of constraints are discussed here.

Primary Key

A *key* for a relation scheme `R` is any subset `K` of `R` that satisfies the property that in every valid relation under the scheme `R`, it is not possible to have two different tuples with the same values under `K`. A *candidate key* for `R` is any key for `R` such that none of its proper subsets is also a key. In all cases, a relation scheme must have at least one candidate key. The *primary key* for a relation scheme `R` is one of the candidate keys chosen by the designer of the database. For the `EMPLOYEES` relation scheme, the `EMPID` attribute by itself is the primary key. It is not always the case that the primary key is a singleton. In many situations, the primary key consists of more than one attribute. The primary key attributes are required to satisfy the **`not null`** constraint—i.e., that no tuple can have a **`null`** value under the primary key attributes. This property of primary keys is often referred to as the *entity integrity rule*.

Referential Integrity Constraint-Foreign Key

The *referential integrity constraint* is a condition that is specified across two relations. During the design of a relational database, the designer may create a relation scheme R that includes the primary key attributes of another relation scheme, say S. In such a situation, the referential integrity constraint specifies the condition that the values that appear under the primary key attributes in any valid relation under scheme R *must* also appear in the relation under scheme S. The attributes in scheme R that correspond to the primary key attributes of scheme S collectively are referred to as a *foreign key* in scheme R. Unlike the primary key attributes, the foreign key attributes do not have to satisfy the **not null** constraint.

As an example, consider the **EMPLOYEES** relation scheme and the two additional relation schemes

```
PROJECTS = (PROJID,PROJNAME,LOCATION)
WORKSIN = (EID,PROJID,HOURS).
```

The **PROJECTS** relation scheme presents information about different projects, and the **WORKSIN** relation scheme presents information about which employee works for which projects and how many hours they work. It is clear that the primary key for **PROJECTS** is the lone attribute **PROJID**. The primary key for the **WORKSIN** relation scheme, which represents a relationship between **EMPLOYEES** and **PROJECTS**, is the combination of the **EMPID** and **PROJID** attributes. We can assume that a single employee can work for multiple projects, and that a project certainly can have many employees. The relation scheme **WORKSIN** includes primary key attributes from the **EMPLOYEES** and the **PROJECTS** relation schemes. The referential integrity constraint in this situation dictates that if an **EMPID** value is present in a valid relation under the **WORKSIN** scheme, then the same value must also be present in the relation under the **EMPLOYEES** scheme. In a similar manner, a **PROJID** value in a valid relation under the **WORKSIN** scheme must also be present in the relation under the **PROJECTS** scheme.

Not Null *Constraint*

This constraint specifies the condition that tuple values under certain attributes (specified to be **not null**) cannot be **null**. This condition is almost always imposed on the primary key attributes.[1] Other attributes may also be constrained to be **not null** if the need arises. In the **EMPLOYEES** relation scheme, the attributes **EMPID** and **ENAME** are likely candidates on which the **not null** constraint should be imposed.

1. In Oracle, primary key attributes are automatically constrained to be **not null**.

1.3 Tabular View of a Relation

A relation, as defined earlier, can also be informally viewed as a table made up of rows and columns. The columns are labeled with the attribute names of the relation scheme and the rows correspond to individual tuples of the relation. For example, the sample relation under the **EMPLOYEES** relation scheme can be arranged in a tabular format:

EMPID	ENAME	ADDRESS	SALARY
1111	Jones	111 Ash St.	20000
2222	Smith	123 Elm St.	25000
3333	Brown	234 Oak St.	30000

The four columns are labeled with the attribute names in the relation scheme, and the three rows correspond to the three tuples in the relation. Since the relation scheme and the tuples are defined to be sequences, it is important that the order of the components within a row correspond with the column names.

1.4 Sample Databases

Three databases are described in this section. The first represents information that is typically recorded in the grade books of university instructors. The second represents information that is usually maintained in the records of mail-order companies. The third represents information that is ordinarily kept in an investment portfolio tracking system.

Grade Book Database

The grade book database consists of the relations defined in the six schemes shown in Figure 1.1.

- The **CATALOG** relation contains information about course numbers and titles of courses taught by a particular instructor. **CNO** is the primary key for the **CATALOG** relation.
- The **STUDENTS** relation contains information about the students of a particular instructor. The **SID** attribute is the primary key for the **STUDENTS** relation.
- The **COURSES** relation contains information about the various courses that have been taught by a particular instructor. The **TERM** attribute corresponds to the term (such as Fall97 or Spring98) in which the course was taught; the **LINENO**

Figure 1.1 Grade book database schemes.

```
CATALOG(CNO,CTITLE)
STUDENTS(SID,FNAME,LNAME,MINIT)
COURSES(TERM,LINENO,CNO,A,B,C,D)
COMPONENTS(TERM,LINENO,COMPNAME,MAXPOINTS,WEIGHT)
ENROLLS(SID,TERM,LINENO)
SCORES(SID,TERM,LINENO,COMPNAME,POINTS)
```

is a unique section number assigned by the registrar of the university within a term. The combination of `TERM` and `LINENO` is the primary key for this relation. The `CNO` attribute is a foreign key in this relation as it appears as a primary key in `CATALOG`. The attributes `A`, `B`, `C`, `D` are attributes that represent numerical values that correspond with each letter grade (for example, `A = 90, B = 80, C = 70, D = 60`).

- The `COMPONENTS` relation contains information about the various grading components (such as homework, quizzes, and exams) for a particular course taught by the instructor. For each course taught, identified by the attributes `TERM` and `LINENO`, this relation records information about the grading component, the maximum points assigned to this component, and the weight of this component relative to the other components. Since each course may have multiple components, the combination of the attributes `TERM`, `LINENO`, and `COMPNAME` forms the primary key. Since the combination of `TERM` and `LINENO` appearing in this relation is a primary key for the `COURSES` relation, it is classified as a foreign key.

- The `ENROLLS` relation records information about which student was enrolled in which course taught by the instructor. The combination of all three attributes (`SID`, `TERM`, and `LINENO`) forms the primary key. There are two foreign keys in this relation: `SID` referring to the `STUDENTS` relation and the combination of `TERM` and `LINENO` referring to the `COURSES` relation.

- The `SCORES` relation records the grading component scores (or points) for each student enrolled in a course. The combination of the attributes `SID`, `TERM`, `LINENO`, and `COMPNAME` forms the primary key for this relation. There are two foreign keys in this relation: the combination of `SID`, `TERM`, and `LINENO` referring to the `ENROLLS` relation and the combination of attributes `TERM`, `LINENO`, and `COMPNAME` referring to the `COMPONENTS` relation.

A sample from a grade book database is shown in Figure 1.2.

Figure 1.2 A sample from a grade book database.

Catalog

CNO	CTITLE
csc226	Introduction to Programming I
csc227	Introduction to Programming II
csc343	Assembly Programming
csc481	Automata and Formal Languages
csc498	Introduction to Database Systems
csc880	Deductive Databases and Logic Programming

Students

SID	FNAME	LNAME	MINIT
1111	Nandita	Rajshekhar	K
2222	Sydney	Corn	A
3333	Susan	Williams	B
4444	Naveen	Rajshekhar	B
5555	Elad	Yam	G
6666	Lincoln	Herring	F

Courses

TERM	LINENO	CNO	A	B	C	D
f96	1031	csc226	90	80	65	50
f96	1032	csc226	90	80	65	50
sp97	1031	csc227	90	80	65	50

Components

TERM	LINENO	COMPNAME	MAXPOINTS	WEIGHT
f96	1031	exam1	100	30
f96	1031	quizzes	80	20
f96	1031	final	100	50
f96	1032	programs	400	40
f96	1032	midterm	100	20
f96	1032	final	100	40
sp97	1031	paper	100	50
sp97	1031	project	100	50

Figure 1.2 —Continued

Enrolls

SID	TERM	LINENO
1111	f96	1031
2222	f96	1031
4444	f96	1031
1111	f96	1032
2222	f96	1032
3333	f96	1032
5555	sp97	1031
6666	sp97	1031

Scores

SID	TERM	LINENO	COMPNAME	POINTS
1111	f96	1031	exam1	90
1111	f96	1031	quizzes	75
1111	f96	1031	final	95
2222	f96	1031	exam1	70
2222	f96	1031	quizzes	40
2222	f96	1031	final	82
4444	f96	1031	exam1	83
4444	f96	1031	quizzes	71
4444	f96	1031	final	74
1111	f96	1032	programs	400
1111	f96	1032	midterm	95
1111	f96	1032	final	99
2222	f96	1032	programs	340
2222	f96	1032	midterm	65
2222	f96	1032	final	95
3333	f96	1032	programs	380
3333	f96	1032	midterm	75
3333	f96	1032	final	88
5555	sp97	1031	paper	80
5555	sp97	1031	project	90
6666	sp97	1031	paper	80
6666	sp97	1031	project	85

Figure 1.3 Mail-order database schemes.

```
EMPLOYEES(ENO,ENAME,ZIP,HDATE)
PARTS(PNO,PNAME,QOH,PRICE,LEVEL)
CUSTOMERS(CNO,CNAME,STREET,ZIP,PHONE)
ORDERS(ONO,CNO,ENO,RECEIVED,SHIPPED)
ODETAILS(ONO,PNO,QTY)
ZIPCODES(ZIP,CITY)
```

Mail-Order Database

The mail-order database consists of the relations defined in the six schemes shown in Figure 1.3.

- The `EMPLOYEES` relation contains information about the employees of the company. The `ENO` attribute is the primary key. The `ZIP` attribute is a foreign key referring to the `ZIPCODES` table.
- The `PARTS` relation keeps a record of the inventory of the company. The record for each part includes its number and name as well as the quantity on hand, unit price, and the reorder level. `PNO` is the primary key for this relation.
- The `CUSTOMERS` relation contains information about the customers of the mail-order company. Each customer is assigned a customer number, `CNO`, which serves as the primary key. The `ZIP` attribute is a foreign key referring to the `ZIPCODES` relation.
- The `ORDERS` relation contains information about the orders placed by customers, the employee who took the order, and the dates the order was received and shipped. `ONO` is the primary key. The `CNO` attribute is a foreign key referring to the `CUSTOMERS` relation, and the `ENO` attribute is a foreign key referring to the `EMPLOYEES` table.
- The `ODETAILS` relation contains information about the various parts ordered by the customer within a particular order. The combination of the `ONO` and `PNO` attributes forms the primary key. The `ONO` attribute is a foreign key referring to the `ORDERS` relation, and the `PNO` attribute is a foreign key referring to the `PARTS` relation.
- The `ZIPCODES` relation maintains information about the zip codes for various cities. `ZIP` is the primary key.

A sample from a mail-order database is shown in Figure 1.4.

Figure 1.4 A sample from a mail-order database.

Employees

ENO	ENAME	ZIP	HDATE
1000	Jones	67226	12-DEC-95
1001	Smith	60606	01-JAN-92
1002	Brown	50302	01-SEP-94

Parts

PNO	PNAME	QOH	PRICE	LEVEL
10506	Land Before Time I	200	19.99	20
10507	Land Before Time II	156	19.99	20
10508	Land Before Time III	190	19.99	20
10509	Land Before Time IV	60	19.99	20
10601	Sleeping Beauty	300	24.99	20
10701	When Harry Met Sally	120	19.99	30
10800	Dirty Harry	140	14.99	30
10900	Dr. Zhivago	100	24.99	30

Customers

CNO	CNAME	STREET	ZIP	PHONE
1111	Charles	123 Main St.	67226	316-636-5555
2222	Bertram	237 Ash Avenue	67226	316-689-5555
3333	Barbara	111 Inwood St.	60606	316-111-1234

Orders

ONO	CNO	ENO	RECEIVED	SHIPPED
1020	1111	1000	10-DEC-94	12-DEC-94
1021	1111	1000	12-JAN-95	15-JAN-95
1022	2222	1001	13-FEB-95	20-FEB-95
1023	3333	1000	20-JUN-97	null

Odetails

ONO	PNO	QTY
1020	10506	1
1020	10507	1
1020	10508	2
1020	10509	3
1021	10601	4
1022	10601	1
1022	10701	1
1023	10800	1
1023	10900	1

Zipcodes

ZIP	CITY
67226	Wichita
60606	Fort Dodge
50302	Kansas City
54444	Columbia
66002	Liberal
61111	Fort Hays

Figure 1.5 Investment portfolio database schemes.

```
MEMBER(MID,PASSWORD,FNAME,LNAME,ADDRESS,EMAIL,BAL)
SECURITY(SYMBOL,CNAME,CURRENT,ASK,BID)
TRANSACTION(MID,SYMBOL,TDATE,TTYPE,QTY,PRICE,COMM,AMOUNT)
```

Investment Portfolio Database

The investment portfolio database consists of relations defined in the three schemes shown in Figure 1.5.

- The `MEMBER` table contains information about the members of the investment portfolio tracking system. `MID` is the primary key for the `MEMBER` table. The table includes other attributes such as `PASSWORD`, used to sign in to the application program, and `BAL`, which contains the cash balance in the member's account. The members can buy shares of securities only if they have enough cash in their account to cover the cost of the shares.
- The `SECURITY` table contains information about the various securities available for the members to invest in. The attribute `SYMBOL`, the ticker symbol for the security, acts as its primary key. The table includes other attributes such as `CNAME`, the company name, and `CURRENT`, `ASK`, and `BID`, the price per share of the most recent sale, the current asking price per share, and the current bidding price per share respectively.
- The `TRANSACTION` table contains entries for every buy or sell transaction executed by a member. The table contains `MID` and `SYMBOL` attributes as foreign keys referring to the `MEMBER` and `SECURITY` tables respectively. In addition to these, the table contains attributes for transaction date (`TDATE`), transaction type (`TTYPE`), number of shares (`QTY`), price per share of the security (`PRICE`), and commission (`COMM`). The transaction type is either `buy` or `sell`. The table also has a derived attribute, called `AMOUNT`, which is computed from the `QUANTITY`, `PRICE`, and `COMM` attribute values. The `COMM` attribute is assumed to be 1% of the total transaction amount. The `MID`, `SYMBOL`, and `TDATE` attributes combine to form the primary key for the table.

A sample from an investment portfolio database is shown in Figure 1.6.

Figure 1.6 A sample from an investment portfolio database.

Member

MID	PASSWORD	FNAME	LNAME
10000	1111	Quigon	Jinn
10001	2222	Obiwan	Kenobi

Member (continued)

MID	ADDRESS	EMAIL	BAL
10000	12 Star Avenue, Moon City, KS	qj@abc.com	10000
10001	22 Star Avenue, Moon City, KS	ok@abc.com	20000

Security

SYMBOL	CNAME	CURRENT	ASK	BID
AMZN	Amazon.com	119.06	119.18	119.06
EBAY	eBay Inc	174.00	174.25	174.00
KLM	KLM Royal Dutch Air	29.93		
MSFT	Microsoft Corp	78.50	78.56	78.50
ORCL	Oracle Corp	23.25	23.25	23.18

Transaction

MID	SYMBOL	TDATE	TTYPE	QTY	PRICE
10000	ORCL	20-MAY-99	buy	100	26.81
10000	SEG	20-MAY-99	buy	100	32.12
10000	ORCL	09-AUG-99	buy	50	30.00
10000	ORCL	14-AUG-99	sell	20	32.00

Transaction (continued)

MID	SYMBOL	TDATE	COMM	AMOUNT
10000	ORCL	20-MAY-99	26.81	2708.05
10000	SEG	20-MAY-99	32.12	3244.61
10000	ORCL	09-AUG-99	15.00	1515.00
10000	ORCL	14-AUG-99	15.00	625.00

1.5 Relational Algebra

Relational algebra is a set of algebraic operations that takes as input one (for unary operators) or two (for binary operators) relations and returns as output a relation. Using these operations, we can answer ad hoc queries about the content of any database. A good understanding of relational algebra makes the task of phrasing complex queries in Structured Query Language (SQL) much easier. The relational algebraic operators are briefly introduced here, and then some queries related to the sample databases are answered using these operations.

The relational operators are usually classified into two categories: set-theoretic operations and relation-theoretic operations.

1.5.1 Set-Theoretic Operations

The *set-theoretic operations* include *union, difference, intersection,* and *Cartesian product*. These operations are borrowed from mathematical set theory and are applicable in the relational model because relations are nothing but sets of tuples.

The union, difference, and intersection operators are binary operators that operate on two *union-compatible relations*—which means that they have the same number of attributes and that the domains of the corresponding attributes in the two relations are the same. Consider two relations r and s that are union-compatible. The set-theoretic operations are defined as follows:

- *Union:* $r \cup s = \{t \mid t \in r \text{ or } t \in s\}$. In other words, the union of two union-compatible relations contains all the tuples from each of the relations.
- *Difference:* $r - s = \{t \mid t \in r \text{ and } t \notin s\}$. The difference between two union-compatible relations contains all those tuples in the first relation that are not present in the second relation.
- *Intersection:* $r \cap s = \{t \mid t \in r \text{ and } t \in s\}$. The intersection of two union-compatible relations contains all the tuples that are contained in both relations.
- *Cartesian product:* The Cartesian product is a binary operator that takes as input two relations (r and s on any scheme) and produces a relation on the scheme that is the concatenation of the relation schemes of the input relations. The tuples in the Cartesian product are constructed by concatenating each tuple in the first input relation with each tuple in the second input relation. Formally,

  $$r \times s = \{t1.t2 \mid t1 \in r \text{ and } t2 \in s\},$$

  where $t1.t2$ is the concatenation of tuples $t1$ and $t2$ to form a larger tuple.

Figure 1.7 Set-theoretic operations.

r

A	B
a	b
a	c
b	d

s

A	B
a	c
a	e

$r \cup s$

A	B
a	b
a	c
b	d
a	e

$r - s$

A	B
a	b
b	d

$r \cap s$

A	B
a	c

$r \times s$

r.A	r.B	s.A	s.B
a	b	a	c
a	b	a	e
a	c	a	c
a	c	a	e
b	d	a	c
b	d	a	e

Examples of the set-theoretic operations are shown in Figure 1.7.

Since the attribute names in a relation scheme must be unique, the scheme of the Cartesian product of relations r and s in the example contains attribute names prefixed by $r.$ and $s.$.

1.5.2 Relation-Theoretic Operations

The relation-theoretic operations include *rename*, *select*, *project*, *natural join*, and *division* among others.

- *Rename:* The rename operator takes as input a relation and returns the same relation as output, but under a different name. This operation is useful and necessary for queries that need to refer to the same relation more than once.

The symbolic notation for the rename operator is $\rho_s(r)$, where r is the input relation and s is the new name.

- *Select:* The select operator acts as a horizontal filter for relations. Given a selection condition, the select operator produces an output relation that consists of only those tuples from the input relation that satisfy the selection condition. Symbolically, the select operator is written as $\sigma_F(r)$, where F is the selection criterion and r is the input relation. Formally, the select operator is defined as follows:

$$\sigma_F(r) = \{t | t \in r \text{ and } t \text{ satisfies } F\}.$$

- *Project:* The project operator acts as a vertical filter for relations. Given a sublist of attribute names of a relation, the project operator keeps only those values that correspond to the sublist of attribute names and discards other values in tuples. Symbolically, the project operator is written as $\pi_A(r)$, where A is a sublist of the attributes of r. Formally, the project operator is defined as follows:

$$\pi_A(r) = \{t[A] | t \in r\},$$

where $t[A]$ is a tuple constructed from t by keeping the values that correspond to the attributes in A and discarding other values.

- *Natural join:* The natural join operator takes as input two relations and produces as output a relation whose scheme is the concatenation of the two schemes of the input relations with any duplicate attribute names discarded. A tuple in the first input relation is said to *match* a tuple in the second input relation if both have the same values under the common attributes. The tuples in the natural join are constructed by concatenating each tuple in the first input relation with each *matching* tuple in the second input relation and discarding the values under the common attributes of the second relation. Symbolically, the natural join is written as $r \bowtie s$, where r is a relation on scheme R and s is a relation on scheme S. Formally, the natural join operation is defined as follows:

$$r \bowtie s = \{t | (\exists u \in r)(\exists v \in s)(t[R] = u \text{ and } t[S] = v)\}$$

- *Division:* The division operator takes as input two relations, called the dividend relation (r on scheme R) and the divisor relation (s on scheme S) such that all the attributes in S also appear in R and s is not empty. The output of the division operation is a relation on scheme R with all the attributes common with S discarded. A tuple t is put in the output of the operation if for all tuples u in s, the tuple tu is in r, where tu is a tuple constructed from t and u by combining the individual values in these tuples in the proper order to form a

Figure 1.8 Relation-theoretic operations.

r

A	C	D
a	c	d
a	e	f
a	g	h
b	c	d
b	g	h
c	c	d
c	e	f

s

C	D
c	d
e	f

t

B	C	D
b	c	d
b	e	f

$\sigma_{A='b' \text{ or } C='c'}(r)$

A	C	D
a	c	d
b	c	d
b	g	h
c	c	d

$\pi_A(r)$

A
a
b
c

$r \bowtie t$

A	C	D	B
a	c	d	b
a	e	f	b
b	c	d	b
c	c	d	b
c	e	f	b

$r \div s$

A
a
c

tuple in r. Symbolically, the division operation is written as $r \div s$ and is defined as follows:

$$r \div s = \{t | (\forall u \in s)(tu \in r)\}.$$

Examples of the relation-theoretic operations are shown in Figure 1.8.

Among the relational operators presented so far, there are six basic operators: union, difference, Cartesian product, rename, select, and project. This basic set of operations has the property that none of them can be expressed in terms of the others. The remaining operators presented—namely, intersection, natural join, and division—can be expressed in terms of the basic operators as follows:

- *Intersection:* $r \cap s = r - (r - s)$.

- *Natural join:* $r \bowtie s = \pi_{R \cap S}(\sigma_F(r \times s))$, where F is a selection condition that indicates that the tuple values under the common attributes of r and s are equal.
- *Division:* $r \div s = \pi_{R-S}(r) - \pi_{R-S}((\pi_{R-S}(r) \times s) - r)$.

Even though relation schemes are defined as sequences, they are treated as sets in these equalities for simplicity.

An explanation for the equality for division is in order. First, all candidate tuples for the result are calculated by the expression

$$\pi_{R-S}(r).$$

Second, these candidate tuples are combined with all tuples of s in the expression

$$\pi_{R-S}(r) \times s$$

to give a relation containing all combinations of candidate tuples with all tuples of s. Since we are looking for tuples under the scheme $R - S$ that combine with all tuples of s and are also present in r, we see that if we subtract r from the previous expression, we will get all the combinations of tuples that are "missing" in r. By projecting these tuples on $R - S$, we get all those tuples that should not go to the result in the following expression:

$$\pi_{R-S}((\pi_{R-S}(r) \times s) - r)$$

Finally, we subtract this set from the set of all candidate tuples and obtain the output relation of the division operator.

1.5.3 Queries in Relational Algebra

The following is a list of queries related to the two sample databases and the corresponding relational algebraic expressions that compute the answers to the queries. The relational algebraic expressions are broken up into smaller parts and are assigned to temporary variables. One could easily write one whole expression from these individual parts and thereby not require the assignment primitive (`:=` in the following).

Grade Book Database Queries

Query 1.1 Get the names of students enrolled in the `Assembly Programming` class in the `f96` term.

$$\begin{aligned}
t1 &:= \sigma_{CTITLE=\texttt{'Assembly Programming'}}(catalog) \\
t2 &:= \sigma_{TERM=\texttt{'f96'}}(courses) \\
t3 &:= t1 \bowtie t2 \bowtie enrolls \bowtie students \\
result &:= \pi_{FNAME,LNAME,MINIT}(t3)
\end{aligned}$$

Query 1.2 Get the `SID` values of students who did not enroll in any class during the `f96` term.

$$\pi_{SID}(students) - \pi_{SID}(\sigma_{TERM=\texttt{'f96'}}(enrolls))$$

Query 1.3 Get the `SID` values of students who have enrolled in `csc226` and `csc227`.

$$\begin{aligned}
t1 &:= \pi_{SID}(enrolls \bowtie \sigma_{CNO=\texttt{'csc226'}}(courses)) \\
t2 &:= \pi_{SID}(enrolls \bowtie \sigma_{CNO=\texttt{'csc227'}}(courses)) \\
result &:= t1 \cap t2
\end{aligned}$$

Query 1.4 Get the `SID` values of students who have enrolled in `csc226` or `csc227`.

$$\begin{aligned}
t1 &:= \pi_{SID}(enrolls \bowtie \sigma_{CNO=\texttt{'csc226'}}(courses)) \\
t2 &:= \pi_{SID}(enrolls \bowtie \sigma_{CNO=\texttt{'csc227'}}(courses)) \\
result &:= t1 \cup t2
\end{aligned}$$

Query 1.5 Get the `SID` values of students who have enrolled in *all* the courses in the catalog.

$$\pi_{SID,CNO}(courses \bowtie enrolls) \div \pi_{CNO}(catalog)$$

Mail-Order Database Queries

Query 1.6 Get part names of parts that cost less than `20.00`.

$$\pi_{PNAME}(\sigma_{PRICE<20.00}(parts))$$

Query 1.7 Get pairs of CNO values of customers who have the same zip code.

$$\begin{aligned}
t1 &:= \rho_{c1}(customers) \times \rho_{c2}(customers) \\
t2 &:= \sigma_{c1.ZIP=c2.ZIP \text{ and } c1.CNO<c2.CNO}(t1) \\
result &:= \pi_{c1.CNO,c2.CNO}(t2)
\end{aligned}$$

Query 1.8 Get the names of customers who have ordered parts from employees living in `Wichita`.

$$\begin{aligned}
t1 &:= \pi_{ENO}(employees \bowtie \sigma_{CITY=\texttt{'Wichita'}}(zipcodes)) \\
result &:= \pi_{CNAME}(customers \bowtie orders \bowtie t1)
\end{aligned}$$

Query 1.9 Get CNO values of customers who have ordered parts only from employees living in **Wichita**.

$$t1 := \pi_{ENO}(employees \bowtie \sigma_{CITY \neq \texttt{'Wichita'}}(zipcodes))$$
$$result := \pi_{CNO}(orders) - \pi_{CNO}(orders \bowtie t1)$$

Query 1.10 Get CNO values of customers who have ordered parts from all employees living in **Wichita**.

$$t1 := \pi_{ENO}(employees \bowtie \sigma_{CITY = \texttt{'Wichita'}}(zipcodes))$$
$$result := \pi_{CNO,ENO}(orders) \div t1$$

Investment Portfolio Database Queries

Query 1.11 Get company names of securities whose current price is greater than \$100.00.

$$\Pi_{CNAME}(\sigma_{CURRENT>100.00}(security))$$

Query 1.12 Get names of members who have purchased **ORCL** shares.

$$\Pi_{FNAME,LNAME}(member \bowtie \sigma_{SYMBOL=\texttt{'ORCL'} \text{ and } TTYPE=\texttt{'buy'}}(transaction))$$

Query 1.13 Get names of members who have purchased **ORCL** shares but not **SYBS** shares.

$$t1 := \Pi_{MID}(\sigma_{SYMBOL=\texttt{'ORCL'} \text{ and } TTYPE=\texttt{'buy'}}(transaction))$$
$$t2 := \Pi_{MID}(\sigma_{SYMBOL=\texttt{'SYBS'} \text{ and } TTYPE=\texttt{'buy'}}(transaction))$$
$$result := \Pi_{FNAME,LNAME}((t1 - t2) \bowtie member)$$

Query 1.14 Get names of members who purchase *only* **ORCL** shares.

$$t1 := \Pi_{MID}(\sigma_{TTYPE=\texttt{'buy'}}(transaction))$$
$$t2 := \Pi_{MID}(\sigma_{SYMBOL<>\texttt{'ORCL'} \text{ and } TTYPE=\texttt{'buy'}}(transaction))$$
$$result := \Pi_{FNAME,LNAME}((t1 - t2) \bowtie member)$$

Query 1.15 Get company names of securities whose shares are purchased by *all* members.

$$t1 := \Pi_{MID,SYMBOL}(\sigma_{TTYPE=\texttt{'buy'}}(transaction))$$
$$t2 := \Pi_{MID}(member)$$
$$result := \Pi_{CNAME}(security \bowtie (t1 \div t2))$$

CHAPTER

2

Oracle SQL

Oracle SQL is a powerful implementation of the SQL-92 standard Structured Query Language, a universal language that can be used to define, query, update, and manage a relational database. This chapter introduces Oracle SQL and its syntax and semantics along with numerous illustrative examples. Topics covered in this chapter include Oracle SQL*Plus, Oracle SQL, Oracle Data Dictionary, and Oracle8 objects. SQL*Plus is Oracle's interactive interface to the database server. SQL statements can be issued at the **SQL>** prompt, and files containing SQL statements can be executed from within SQL*Plus. Oracle SQL topics discussed in this chapter include creating, dropping, and altering tables, creating and dropping views, querying the database using the select statement, and modifying the database using the insert, delete, and update statements. Chapter 2 also introduces Oracle8 objects and covers SQL statements to access and manipulate these objects.

2.1 Oracle SQL*Plus

Oracle's SQL*Plus program provides a convenient interactive environment with the Oracle database server. The user may type the commands directly at the **SQL>** prompt or have SQL*Plus execute commands residing in operating system files.

2.1.1 Entering and Exiting SQL*Plus

To enter the SQL*Plus environment, the `sqlplus` program should be executed in one of the following three ways, where `<userid>` is the Oracle user identification and `<password>` is the associated password:

- `sqlplus <userid>/<password>`
- `sqlplus <userid>`
- `sqlplus`

The Oracle **userid** and **password** are different from the **userid** and **password** required to get access to the operating system. If the **sqlplus** program is invoked with only **<userid>**, the program prompts the user for the password; if it is invoked without any parameters, the program prompts for the **userid** and **password**.

To exit the SQL*Plus environment, the **exit** command must be entered at the **SQL>** prompt.

2.1.2 Executing Commands in SQL*Plus

Once the user is within the SQL*Plus environment, the system will usually display the prompt **SQL>** and wait for user commands. The user may enter three kinds of commands:

- SQL statements, to access the database.
- PL/SQL blocks, also to access the database.
- SQL*Plus commands, for editing and storing SQL statements and PL/SQL blocks, setting options, and formatting query results.

SQL statements can be entered on the **SQL>** prompt. The statement may be broken into multiple lines. SQL*Plus displays a line number (starting at 2) after the user presses the **RETURN** key to go to the next line. The SQL statement may be terminated in one of three ways:

- With a semicolon, indicating to SQL*Plus that it should execute the statement immediately.
- With a slash (/) on a line by itself, also indicating to SQL*Plus that it should execute the statement.
- With a blank line, indicating that SQL*Plus should not to do anything with the statement. The statement is stored in a buffer and could be executed at a later stage.

The following is a screen capture of an SQL statement executed in SQL*Plus.

```
SQL> select pno,pname,price
  2  from parts;
```

```
       PNO PNAME                          PRICE
---------- ------------------------------ ----------
     10506 Land Before Time I                  19.99
     10507 Land Before Time II                 19.99
     10508 Land Before Time III                19.99
     10509 Land Before Time IV                 19.99
     10601 Sleeping Beauty                     24.99
     10701 When Harry Met Sally                19.99
     10800 Dirty Harry                         14.99
     10900 Dr. Zhivago                         24.99

8 rows selected
```

You can also enter PL/SQL anonymous blocks at the **SQL>** prompt for execution and issue statements such as **create function** and **create procedure** at the **SQL>** prompt to create PL/SQL stored objects. The details of working with PL/SQL within SQL*Plus are given in Chapter 4.

Besides SQL and PL/SQL, users can also enter SQL*Plus commands at the **SQL>** prompt. These commands can manipulate SQL commands and PL/SQL blocks, format and print query results, and set various options for SQL*Plus. SQL*Plus commands must be entered in one line. If the command is long, it may be continued to the next line by typing the hyphen symbol (-) at the end of the line before pressing the **RETURN** key. Here is an example of an SQL*Plus command that formats a column of the SQL query:

```
SQL> column price format -
> $99.99 heading "Sale Price"
SQL> run
  1  select pno,pname,price
  2* from parts

       PNO PNAME                          Sale Price
---------- ------------------------------ ----------
     10506 Land Before Time I                 $19.99
     10507 Land Before Time II                $19.99
     10508 Land Before Time III               $19.99
     10509 Land Before Time IV                $19.99
     10601 Sleeping Beauty                    $24.99
     10701 When Harry Met Sally               $19.99
```

```
    10800 Dirty Harry                        $14.99
    10900 Dr. Zhivago                        $24.99

8 rows selected
```

The **column** command formats a particular column in the current query (in this case, the column is formatted and given a different name for display purposes). SQL*Plus commands need not be terminated with a semicolon.

The following are a few of the more commonly used SQL*Plus commands.

- **describe**: Lists the column definitions for a database table. The following is an example of the **describe** command:

```
SQL> describe customers
 Name                     Null?    Type
 ------------------------ -------- ------------
 CNO                      NOT NULL NUMBER(5)
 CNAME                             VARCHAR2(30)
 STREET                            VARCHAR2(30)
 ZIP                               NUMBER(5)
 PHONE                             CHAR(12)
```

- **execute**: Executes a single PL/SQL statement. The syntax is

```
SQL> execute statement
```

  PL/SQL statements are covered in Chapter 4.

- **help**: Gets online help for SQL*Plus commands. For example,

```
SQL> help column
```

  will list the description of the **column** command. To get a list of all commands, use the following command:

```
SQL> help commands
```

- **host**: Executes a host operating system command without leaving SQL*Plus. For example,

```
SQL> host ls *.sql
```

  will list all the files in the current directory with a **.sql** extension. The exclamation key (**!**) may be used instead of the **host** command to achieve the same effect. If the **host** command is entered without a parameter, an operating system shell is entered. The user may manipulate operating system files or perform any operating system–related activity and return to the SQL*Plus session by logging out of the shell (usually by pressing CONTROL-D). This is a particularly useful command when working with a file containing a large collection of statements that are to be executed. You can go back and forth between the operating system shell and SQL*Plus to edit the file and execute the file repeatedly.

- remark: Used for comments. Any line beginning with the keyword remark or rem or two hyphens (--) is treated as a comment and is ignored by SQL*Plus.
- run: Executes the SQL statement present in the buffer. The run command works the same as the slash command, except that it also displays the buffer contents before executing the statement in the buffer.
- set: Sets SQL*Plus system variables. Some of the more useful system variables include:

```
SQL> set pause on
SQL> set autoCommit on
SQL> set echo on
```

  Setting pause to on causes SQL*Plus to pause at the beginning of each page. The user must press RETURN to see the next page. Setting autoCommit to on informs Oracle to commit any changes to the database immediately after the SQL statement that has caused the change is executed. Setting echo to on causes SQL*Plus to list each of the commands in a file when the file is run with the start command. The names of other system variables along with explanations can be obtained by using help on the set command.

- spool: Stores the query results in an operating system file. The syntax of the command is

```
SQL> spool filename
```

  To disable spooling to file, use

```
SQL> spool off
```

- start: Executes commands stored in an operating system file. This is a useful command and is preferable to entering commands directly on the SQL> prompt. If a file called comm.sql contains several statements/commands, these can be executed by using the start command as follows:

```
SQL> start comm
```

  The file extension .sql need not be specified.

Some of the remaining SQL*Plus commands are discussed next.

Figure 2.1 SQL*Plus buffer editing commands.

Command	Abbreviation	Explanation
`append` *text*	`a` *text*	Add *text* to the end of a line
`change` */old/new*	`c` */old/new*	Change *old* to *new* in a line
`change` */text*	`c` */text*	Delete *text* from a line
`clear buffer`	`cl buff`	Delete all lines
`del`		Delete a line
`get` *file*		Load contents of file named *file* into buffer
`input`	`i`	Add one or more lines
`input` *text*	`i` *text*	Add a line consisting of *text*
`list`	`l`	List all lines in buffer
`list` n	`l` n or n	List one line and make it the current line
`list` *	`l` *	List the current line
`list last`	`l last`	List the last line
`list` m n	`l` m n	List lines m through n
`save` *file*	`sav` *file*	Save contents of buffer to file named *file*

2.1.3 Buffer Manipulation Commands

The most recent command that is entered on the SQL prompt is stored in the SQL*Plus buffer. It is possible to access, change, append to, and save the contents of this buffer. The SQL*Plus buffer editing commands are listed in Figure 2.1. All the editing commands (except for the `list` command) affect only one line, the current line. To make a particular line the current line, simply list that line by typing the line number. The following SQL*Plus session illustrates some of the editing commands.

```
SQL> select cno,canme
  2  from customers
  3  where cno > 2000;
select cno,canme
           *
ERROR at line 1:
ORA-00904: invalid column name
SQL> 1
  1* select cno,canme
SQL> change /can/cna
  1* select cno,cname
```

```
SQL> list
  1  select cno,cname
  2  from customers
  3* where cno > 2000
SQL> /

       CNO CNAME
---------- ------------------------------
      2222 Bertram
      3333 Barbara

SQL> clear buffer
buffer cleared
SQL> input
  1  select eno,ename
  2  from employees
  3
SQL> /

       ENO ENAME
---------- ------------------------------
      1000 Jones
      1001 Smith
      1002 Brown

SQL> 1
  1* select eno,ename
SQL> append ,zip
  1* select eno,ename,zip

SQL> /

       ENO ENAME                       ZIP
---------- -------------------- ----------
      1000 Jones                     67226
      1001 Smith                     60606
      1002 Brown                     50302
```

The buffer contents can also be edited by using the command

```
SQL> edit
```

The `edit` command invokes a default operating system editor and loads the buffer contents into that editor. After editing, the buffer contents can be saved. Upon exiting the editor, control returns to the SQL*Plus program, which sees the new buffer. The default editor can be changed to `vi` or any other editor by

```
SQL> define _editor = vi
```

2.1.4 Formatting Query Results

SQL*Plus provides commands to format query results that will produce a finished report.

The `column` command can be used to change the column heading and to reformat column data in a query. The syntax is

```
column <column-name> heading <column-heading>
  format <format-model>
```

Some examples of the `column` command are

```
column sid heading "Student ID" format 99999
column lname heading "Last Name" format A15
column price format $9,99.99
```

When the `order by` clause is used in the query to display the results in some sorted order, the `break` command can be used to create subsets of rows in the result, each of which corresponds to a particular value of the sort column. Space can be added after each subset of rows using the `skip` clause within this command. The `compute` command can be used to display summary information for each of the subsets of rows of the results.

The `ttitle` and `btitle` commands can be used to print titles on the top and bottom of each page.

These query formatting commands are illustrated in the example that follows.[1] The command file creates a report of grades for students in the `Fall 1996` term of the course with line number 1031.

```
spool report.dat
clear columns
clear breaks
clear computes
set headsep !
```

1. The online help section for each of these commands provides additional information about them.

```
ttitle 'Student Report!Fall 1996!CSc 226'
btitle 'Report prepared by R. Sunderraman'

column sid heading 'SID' format a5 word_wrapped
column lname heading 'Last Name' format a12 word_wrapped
column fname heading 'First Name' format a10 word_wrapped
column compname heading 'Component' -
       format a10 word_wrapped
column points heading 'Points' format 9990

break on sid skip 2 on lname on fname
compute sum of points on sid

set linesize 79
set pagesize 50
set newpage 0

select E.sid, S.lname, S.fname, C.compname, T.points
from   enrolls E, students S, components C, scores T
where  S.sid = T.sid and
       S.sid = E.sid and
       E.term = C.term and
       E.lineno = C.lineno and
       E.term = T.term and
       E.lineno = T.lineno and
       C.compname = T.compname and
       E.term = 'F96' and
       E.lineno = 1031;
spool off
```

The report generated is shown in Figure 2.2.

2.1.5 Screen Capture of an SQL*Plus Session

This section presents a simple way to capture the screen of an SQL*Plus session involving execution of several SQL queries. The following command file containing SQL queries, when executed within SQL*Plus, will capture the SQL*Plus session in the file `capture.dat`.

Figure 2.2 SQL*Plus report.

```
Fri Mar 20                                 page    1
            Student Report
               Fall 1996
                CSc 226

SID   Last Name    First Name Component  Points
----- ------------ ---------- ---------- ------
1111  RAJSHEKHAR   NANDITA    EXAM1          90
                              QUIZZES        75
                              FINAL          95
***** ************ **********            ------
sum                                         260


2222  CORN         SYDNEY     EXAM1          70
                              QUIZZES        40
                              FINAL          82
***** ************ **********            ------
sum                                         192


4444  HOLMES       ZACK       EXAM1          83
                              QUIZZES        71
                              FINAL          74
***** ************ **********            ------
sum                                         228

        Report prepared by R. Sunderraman
```

```
spool capture.dat
set echo on
-- (1) list cno and cname of customers
select cno,cname
from   agents;
-- (2) List cno and cname of customers
--     living in "Wichita"
```

```
select cno,cname
from   customers,zipcodes
where  customers.zip = zipcodes.zip and
       city = 'Wichita';
set echo off
spool off
exit;
```

2.2 Creating, Dropping, and Altering Tables

Oracle SQL provides the **create table**, **drop table**, and **alter table** statements to create and drop tables and to alter their structure. The syntax of these statements is discussed in this section.

Consider the usage of the **create table** and **drop table** statements for the grade book database shown in Figure 2.3. Each **create table** statement has been preceded by a **drop table** statement. This is a practice that many database programmers and administrators follow to drop any previous version, if there is one, of the table being created.

2.2.1 drop table

The syntax for the **drop table** statement is quite trivial.[2] The simplest form of this statement is

```
drop table <tablename>;
```

If there are any foreign keys in other tables referring to the primary or candidate keys of the table being dropped, this simple form of the **drop table** statement will cause an error situation, and the table will not be dropped by Oracle.

To force a table drop in cases where the table has other tables referring to its keys, the following version of the **drop table** statement can be used:

```
drop table <tablename> cascade constraints;
```

In this case, Oracle drops all referential integrity constraints that refer to primary and unique keys in the dropped table and then drops the table from the database. Note that the **drop table** statement ends with a semicolon, as does every SQL statement.

2. The following notation is used for describing the syntax of statements in this book: square brackets ([and]) enclose optional items; curly brackets ({ and }) enclose items that could be repeated zero or more times; angular brackets (< and >) enclose a variable item; the vertical bar symbol (|) is used to separate options.

Figure 2.3 Creating tables for the grade book database.

```
drop table catalog cascade constraints;
create table catalog (
  cno       varchar2(7),
  ctitle    varchar2(50),
  primary key (cno));

drop table students cascade constraints;
create table students (
  sid       varchar2(5),
  fname     varchar2(20),
  lname     varchar2(20) not null,
  minit     char,
  primary key (sid));

drop table courses cascade constraints;
create table courses (
  term      varchar2(10),
  lineno    number(4),
  cno       varchar2(7) not null,
  a         number(2) check(a > 0),
  b         number(2) check(b > 0),
  c         number(2) check(c > 0),
  d         number(2) check(d > 0),
  primary key (term,lineno),
  foreign key (cno) references catalog);

drop table components cascade constraints;
create table components (
  term      varchar2(10),
  lineno    number(4) check(lineno >= 1000),
  compname  varchar2(15),
  maxpoints number(4) not null check(maxpoints >= 0),
  weight    number(2) check(weight >= 0),
  primary key (term,lineno,compname),
  foreign key (term,lineno) references courses);
```

Figure 2.3 —Continued

```
drop table enrolls cascade constraints;
create table enrolls (
  sid       varchar2(5),
  term      varchar2(10),
  lineno    number(4),
  primary key (sid,term,lineno),
  foreign key (sid) references students,
  foreign key (term,lineno) references courses);

drop table scores cascade constraints;
create table scores (
  sid       varchar2(5),
  term      varchar2(10),
  lineno    number(4),
  compname  varchar2(15),
  points    number(4) check(points >= 0),
  primary key (sid,term,lineno,compname),
  foreign key (sid,term,lineno) references enrolls,
  foreign key (term,lineno,compname) references components);
```

2.2.2 create table

The **create table** statement has a more complicated syntax:

```
create table <tablename> (col-def, ..., col-def,
                           tab-constr, ..., tab-constr);
```

It begins with the keywords **create table**, followed by the name of the table and then by a list of definitions enclosed within parentheses. The list of definitions consists of two parts:[3] *column definition* and *table constraints*. These individual definitions are separated by commas.

3. Actually, Oracle's **create table** statement provides for several other properties of the table to be defined in the list of definitions—for example, in which tablespace the table should be located, how much space should be allocated, how should space be allocated when table grows. These details are left out of the discussion here.

Figure 2.4 Common Oracle data types.

DATA TYPE	DESCRIPTION
`char(n)`	Fixed-length character string of length **n**. Maximum value of **n** is 255. If **(n)** is not specified, the default length is 1. If the value stored is a string of a length less than **n**, the rest of the string is padded to the right by blanks. String constants are specified within single quotes such as `'abc'`.
`varchar2(n)`	Variable-length character string having a maximum of **n** characters. The maximum value of **n** can be 2000.
`date`	Holds a date field. Usually specified in string format, such as `'12-DEC-1997'`.
`number`	Integer and real values occupying up to 40 spaces.
`number(n)`	Integer and real values occupying up to **n** spaces
`number(n,d)`	Real values occupying up to **n** spaces with **d** digits after the decimal point.
`integer`	Same as **number**, but does not allow decimal digits.
`integer(n)`	Same as **integer**, but occupying **n** spaces.

Column Definition

The syntax for a column definition is

```
<column-name> <data-type> [default <expr>] [<column-constraints>]
```

There are four parts to a column definition. The first two, the *column name* and its *data type*, are mandatory, and the remaining two parts, the *default clause* and the *column constraint* clause, are optional. The most commonly used data types are shown in Figure 2.4.

The default clause, if used, specifies the default value needed for the column when a row is inserted without a value for this column. For example, the **courses** table could have the column named **a** defined as

```
a number(2) default 90 check(a > 0)
```

indicating that the default value of the column is 90.

If the column being described has a constraint associated with it (such as column value cannot be **null**, or column value is further restricted, or column is a primary, candidate, or foreign key), the constraint could be specified as the last part of the column definition. The syntax for a column constraint is as follows:

```
[constraint <constraint_name>]
  [not] null |
  check (<condition>) |
```

```
unique |
primary key |
references <table_name>[(<column_name>)] [on delete cascade]
```

After giving an optional name for the constraint, one of the five possible column constraints is specified. The **not null** constraint may be specified if **null** values are to be prohibited for the column; the **check** constraint can be specified to impose further restrictions on the column values; the **unique** and **primary key** constraints can be specified if the column by itself is a candidate key or a primary key respectively; the **references** clause may be used in case the column is a foreign key and it refers to a unique key or primary key in another table. If the column is a foreign key referring to a unique key in another table, the **table_name** must be followed (within parentheses) by the unique key attribute name of the other table. The optional **on delete cascade** clause, if specified, will inform Oracle to automatically delete all the dependent rows when a referenced row (containing a unique or primary key) is deleted.

In the grade book database example, several column constraints have been defined. For example, in the **components** table, the column

```
maxpoints number(4) not null check(maxpoints >= 0)
```

has both the **not null** and the **check** constraints defined, indicating that the column cannot assume a **null** value and that its value must also be greater than or equal to 0. If a particular column is by itself the primary key for the table, the primary key constraint could be specified in the column definition itself. For example, the **cno** column in the **catalog** table could have been defined as

```
cno varchar2(7) primary key,
```

If the particular column is a candidate key by itself, the candidate key constraint can be expressed using the **unique** keyword at the end of the column definition. For example, if the **ctitle** column of the **catalog** table were a candidate key, then it could be defined as

```
ctitle varchar2(50) unique
```

If the particular column is a foreign key by itself, the constraint can also be expressed as part of the column definition using the **references** clause. For example, if the **ctitle** column in the **catalog** table were a candidate key and were to be included in the **courses** table under a different name—say, **cname**—then the **cname** column in the **courses** table would be defined as follows:

```
cname varchar2(50) references catalog(ctitle)
```

However, as a common practice, the primary key, candidate key, and foreign key constraints are all expressed as table constraints (discussed next) even if they could be expressed in the column definition.

Table Constraints

After all the columns of the table have been described, any constraints that apply as a whole to the table are described in the table constraints part of the definition list. The three most commonly used table constraints are the primary key, the foreign key, and the candidate key. The syntax for a table constraint is as follows:

```
[constraint <constraint_name>]
  unique (<column> {, <column>}) |
  primary key (<column> {, <column>}) |
  foreign key (<column> {, <column>})
     references <table_name> [(<column> {, <column>})]
       [on delete cascade]
```

Table constraints become necessary if the primary, candidate, or foreign keys consist of more than one attribute.

For example, in the **courses** table definition of the example, the primary key constraint is defined as

```
primary key (term,lineno)
```

and the foreign key constraint is described as

```
foreign key (cno) references catalog
```

Any candidate key constraints could be expressed as a table constraint using the keyword `unique`.

The SQL code to create the tables for the mail-order database are shown in Figure 2.5. Note that wherever possible, the primary and foreign key constraints are defined in the column definition itself, unlike the previous example. This has been done just to be different. It does not matter where you define these constraints. Of course, if the primary, foreign, or candidate keys contain more than one attribute, they have to be defined as table constraints.

The SQL code to create tables for the investment portfolio database are shown in Figure 2.6.

Figure 2.5 Creating tables for the mail-order database.

```
drop table zipcodes cascade constraints;
create table zipcodes (
  zip      number(5) primary key,
  city     varchar2(30));

drop table employees cascade constraints;
create table employees (
  eno      number(4) primary key,
  ename    varchar2(30),
  zip      number(5) references zipcodes,
  hdate    date);

drop table parts cascade constraints;
create table parts (
  pno      number(5) primary key,
  pname    varchar2(30),
  qoh      integer check(qoh >= 0),
  price    number(6,2) check(price >= 0.0),
  olevel   integer);

drop table customers cascade constraints;
create table customers (
  cno      number(5) primary key,
  cname    varchar2(30),
  street   varchar2(30),
  zip      number(5) references zipcodes,
  phone    char(12));

drop table orders cascade constraints;
create table orders (
  ono      number(5) primary key,
  cno      number(5) references customers,
  eno      number(4) references employees,
  received date,
  shipped  date);
```

Figure 2.5 —Continued

```
drop table odetails cascade constraints;
create table odetails (
  ono       number(5) references orders,
  pno       number(5) references parts,
  qty       integer check(qty > 0),
  primary key (ono,pno));
```

Figure 2.6 Creating tables for the investment portfolio database.

```
create table member (
  mid             varchar2 (7),
  password        varchar2 (8) not null,
  fname           varchar2 (15) not null,
  lname           varchar2 (15) not null,
  address         varchar2 (50),
  email           varchar2(30),
  cash_balance    number (10,2) not null,
  primary key (mid)
);

create table security (
  symbol          varchar2 (8),
  cname           varchar2 (30),
  current_price   number (7,3) check (current_price >= 0.0) not null,
  ask_price       number (7,3) check (ask_price >= 0.0),
  bid_price       number (7,3) check (bid_price >= 0.0),
  primary key (symbol)
);

create table transaction (
  mid             varchar2 (7),
  symbol          varchar2 (8),
  trans_date      date,
  trans_type      varchar2 (20) not null,
  quantity        number (7,2) not null,
  price_per_share number (7,3) check (price_per_share >= 0.0)
                  not null,
  commission      number (5,2) check (commission >= 0.0) not null,
  amount          number (8,2) check (amount >= 0.0) not null,
  primary key (mid, symbol, trans_date),
  foreign key (mid) references member,
  foreign key (symbol) references security
);
```

2.2.3 `alter table`

Once a table has been created, it is generally not advisable to change its structure. However, if the need does arise, the **`alter table`** statement can be used. The structure of a table can be altered in two ways: by adding a new column and by changing a column's definition.

Adding a column is straightforward. Suppose you want to add two columns—for fax number and customer type (`I` for individual and `B` for business)—to the **`customers`** table in the mail-order database. This can be done as follows:

```
alter table customers add (
  fax   char(12),
  ctype char check(ctype in ('I','B'))
);
```

Changing the definition of a column in a restricted manner can be accomplished with the **`modify`** keyword. Suppose you want to increase the size of the string column **`street`** in the **`customers`** table to `50` from `30`. This can be accomplished as follows:

```
alter table customers modify (
  street     varchar2(50)
);
```

There are some restrictions on how and when the **`alter table`** statement can be used. For example, it is not possible to add a new column with a **`not null`** constraint imposed on it. This is because the table already exists with data, and by adding a new column, the new column can have only **`null`** values, at least until data are added to the new column. A way around this problem is to define the new column without the **`not null`** constraint; you can then add every row in the table under the new column with some default value and use the **`modify`** option under the **`alter table`** statement to impose the **`not null`** constraint. Other restrictions include decreasing the width of string and number columns, changing the data type, and imposing constraints that do not hold on the current data.

2.3 Inserting Rows

This section introduces a simple form of the SQL **`insert`** statement that adds a row to a table in the database. A more general form is discussed in Section 2.6. The syntax of this simple form of insert is

```
insert into <tablename> [(column {, column})]
  values (expression {, expression});
```

The statement starts with the keywords **insert into**, followed by the name of the table into which the row is to be inserted. This is then followed optionally by a list of columns of the table within parentheses, the keyword **values**, and finally a list of values within parentheses. Here are some examples:

```
insert into components values
  ('f96',1031,'exam1',100,30);
insert into courses values
  ('f96',1031,'csc226',90,80,65,50);
insert into courses(term,lineno,cno) values
  ('f96',1037,'csc326');
insert into enrolls(term,lineno,sid) values
  ('f96',1031,'1111');
```

If the column names are not listed, as is the case in the first two inserts above, the values must be listed in the same order in which the columns were defined while creating the table. The third insert statement lists only three of the seven columns of table **courses** and provides values for each of the three columns. The remaining values are assigned **null** values. In the fourth insert statement, all the columns of the **enrolls** table are listed and their corresponding values are provided. However, note that this is not the order in which the columns were defined while creating the table. An advantage of listing the columns is that you do not have to remember in which order these columns were listed while creating the table. Figures 2.7 and 2.8 list a few of the insert statements needed to load the two sample databases with data.

2.4 Querying the Database

Oracle SQL's **select** statement provides a simple and powerful way of expressing ad hoc queries against the database. The **select** statement, when used in conjunction with the variety of functions Oracle provides for string, number, and date manipulations, is able to extract the specified data from the database and present it to the user in an easy-to-read format. In this section, the **select** statement is discussed.

2.4.1 Simple select Statement

The simplest form of the **select** statement has the following syntax:

```
select [distinct] <expression> {, <expression>}
from <tablename> [<alias>] {, <tablename> [<alias>]}
[where <search_condition>];
```

Figure 2.7 Grade book insert statements.

```
insert into catalog values
  ('csc226','Introduction to Programming I');

insert into students values
  ('1111','Nandita','Rajshekhar','K');
insert into students values
  ('2222','Sydney','Corn','A');

insert into courses values
  ('f96',1031,'csc226',90,80,65,50);

insert into components values
  ('f96',1031,'exam1',100,30);
insert into components values
  ('f96',1031,'quiz',80,20);
insert into components values
  ('f96',1031,'final',100,50);

insert into enrolls values ('1111','f96',1031);
insert into enrolls values ('2222','f96',1031);

insert into scores values ('1111','f96',1031,'exam1',90);
insert into scores values ('1111','f96',1031,'quiz',75);
insert into scores values ('1111','f96',1031,'final',95);
insert into scores values ('2222','f96',1031,'exam1',70);
insert into scores values ('2222','f96',1031,'quiz',40);
insert into scores values ('2222','f96',1031,'final',82);
```

There are three clauses: **`select`** clause, **`from`** clause, and **`where`** clause. The **`where`** clause is optional. The **`select`** clause starts with the **`select`** keyword, followed by the optional keyword **`distinct`** and a list of expressions. The **`distinct`** keyword, if included, would result in duplicates removed from the result of the query. The expression list normally contains columns of tables being queried. However, it could also contain expressions involving operators on the column values. The nature of these expressions will become clear after reading the examples in this section. The **`from`** clause consists of the keyword **`from`** followed by a list of table names. Optionally

Figure 2.8 Mail-order insert statements.

```
insert into  zipcodes values (67226,'Wichita');

insert into employees values
  (1000,'Jones',67226,'12-DEC-95');

insert into parts values
  (10506,'Land Before Time I',200,19.99,20);
insert into parts values
  (10507,'Land Before Time II',156,19.99,20);
insert into parts values
  (10508,'Land Before Time III',190,19.99,20);
insert into parts values
  (10509,'Land Before Time IV',60,19.99,20);

insert into customers values
  (1111,'Charles','123 Main St.',67226,'316-636-5555');

insert into orders values
  (1020,1111,1000,'10-DEC-94','12-DEC-94');

insert into odetails values (1020,10506,1);
insert into odetails values (1020,10507,1);
insert into odetails values (1020,10508,2);
insert into odetails values (1020,10509,3);
```

each table name could be followed by an alias separated by a space. These aliases can serve the purpose of the renaming operator in relational algebra. The **where** clause consists of the keyword **where** followed by a *search condition*, a Boolean expression involving constants, column names, and appropriate operators. The nature of the search condition will also become clear after reading the many examples in this section.

The informal semantics (the result set of tuples) of the simple select statement is computed as follows: The Cartesian product of the tables mentioned in the **from** clause is taken first. Then the selection criteria mentioned in the **where** clause are applied to the product, which results in a subset of the product. Finally, the columns and expressions mentioned in the **select** clause are projected from this subset to form the result of the query.

Here are some examples of simple queries and their corresponding SQL select statements.

Query 2.1 Get pno and pname values of parts that are priced less than $20.00.

```
select pno,pname
from   parts
where  price < 20.00;
```

This is a simple example involving one table with a simple selection condition based on the column price and a projection of two columns, pno and pname.

Query 2.2 Get all the rows of the employees table.

```
select *
from   employees;
```

If all the columns of all the tables mentioned in the **from** clause are to be projected, the * symbol can be used in the **select** clause as shown.

Query 2.3 Get pno values for parts for which orders have been placed.

```
select distinct pno
from   odetails;
```

The **distinct** keyword can be used to eliminate duplicate answers, if present. By default, SQL does not eliminate duplicates. In many situations, it should not matter if duplicates are removed or not; however, there are situations—for example, when using aggregate operations—where the result of the query would depend on whether duplicates are removed.

Query 2.4 Get all the details of customers whose names begin with the letter "A."

```
select *
from   customers
where  cname like 'A%';
```

The **like** operator performs pattern-matching in string data. A percent sign (%) indicates a match with zero or more spaces or characters and the underscore sign (_) indicates a match with exactly one space or character. Additional examples of the usage of the **like** operator are:

```
cname like '_ee%'  -- true if the second and
                      third letters of cname
                      are both 'e'.
cname like '%a%a%' -- true if cname contains
                      at least two a's.
```

Query 2.5 Get the `ono` and `cname` values for customers whose orders have not yet been shipped (i.e., the `shipped` column has a `null` value).

```
select ono,cname
from   orders,customers
where  customers.cno = orders.cno and
       shipped is null;
```

The `is null` predicate tests for `null` values in a particular column. The `is not null` predicate can be used to check to see if a column has a non-`null` value. Using the comparison operators (=, !=, etc.) with the `null` value can give unpredictable results; hence it is always advisable to use the `is null` and `is not null` predicates to check for `null` values.

Query 2.6 Get the `sid` values of students who have scores between 50 and 70 points in any component of any course they have enrolled in.

```
select sid
from   scores
where  points between 50 and 70;
```

The `between` predicate used in this example is a short form for the expression `points >= 50` and `points <= 70`. There is a corresponding `not between` predicate that is the logical opposite of `between`.

Query 2.7 Get `cname` and `ename` pairs such that the customer with name `cname` has placed an order through the employee with name `ename`.

```
select distinct cname,ename
from   customers,orders,employees
where  customers.cno = orders.cno and
       employees.eno = orders.eno;
```

This is a query involving more than one table. The `where` clause consists of two conditions, referred to as *join conditions*, that relate the data present in the three tables being joined.

Query 2.8 For each `odetail` row, get `ono`, `pno`, `pname`, `qty`, and `price` values along with the total price for this item. The total price is simply the product of unit price and quantity.

```
select x.ono, x.pno, p.pname, x.qty,
       p.price, (x.qty * p.price) total
from   odetails x, parts p
where  x.pno = p.pno
```

This query illustrates aliases used in the `from` clause and arithmetic expressions and naming a new column in the `select` clause. If the last expression in the `select` clause did not have the column name `total`, by default the column would be labeled by the text of the expression. The aliases in the `from` clause in this example were not necessary. Since the only common column between the `parts` and `odetails` tables is `pno`, any references to it in the query must be preceded by the table name of the alias, such as `x.pno`. The prefixes on all other references are not necessary even though they are shown in the example.

Query 2.9 Get all pairs of `cno` values for customers based in the same zip code.

```
select c1.cno, c2.cno
from   customers c1, customers c2
where  c1.zip = c2.zip and c1.cno < c2.cno;
```

The aliases used in this query are necessary because there is a reference to two different rows of the same table. The `c1.cno < c2.cno` condition is used to eliminate any redundant answers.

Query 2.10 Get `pno` values for parts that have been ordered by at least two different customers.

```
select distinct y1.pno
from   orders x1, orders x2, odetails y1, odetails y2
where  y1.pno = y2.pno and y1.ono = x1.ono and
       y2.ono = x2.ono and x1.cno < x2.cno
```

Notice the extensive use of aliases in this example. The `x1.cno < x2.cno` condition is used to eliminate any redundant answers.

2.4.2 Sub-Selects

The search criteria in the `where` clause may itself contain a select statement. Such a select statement within the search criteria is referred to as a *sub-select*, and the whole structure is often referred to as a *nested select statement*. SQL supports several built-in predicates that can be used to test the sub-selects for certain conditions. These built-in predicates are `in` and `not in`, the quantified comparisons θ`any` and θ`all`, and `exists` and `not exists`.

Predicates `in` *and* `not in`

The general forms of `in` and `not in` predicates are

```
expr in (sub-select)
expr in (value {, value})
expr not in (sub-select)
expr not in (value {, value})
```

Here are some example queries that use the `in` and `not in` predicates.

Query 2.11 Get `cname` values of customers who place orders with employees living in `Fort Dodge`. The following `select` statement gets the `eno` values of employees from `Fort Dodge`:

```
select eno
from   employees,zipcodes
where  employees.zip = zipcodes.zip and
       city = 'Fort Dodge';
```

The following nested `select` statement, which contains the above `select` statement in its `where` clause using the `in` predicate, returns the answers to the query:

```
select distinct cname
from   orders,customers
where  orders.cno = customers.cno and
       eno in (select eno
               from   employees,zipcodes
               where  employees.zip = zipcodes.zip
                      and city = 'Fort Dodge');
```

Query 2.12 Get **cname** values of customers living in **Fort Dodge** or **Liberal**.

```
select cname
from   customers,zipcodes
where  customers.zip = zipcodes.zip and
       city in ('Fort Dodge','Liberal');
```

In this example, the **in** predicate is used with a fixed set of values.

Query 2.13 Get the **cno** and **cname** values for customers who have placed an order for **Dirty Harry** or **Dr. Zhivago**.

```
select cno,cname
from   customers
where  cno in
        (select cno
         from   orders
         where  ono in
                 (select ono
                  from   odetails
                  where  pno in
                          (select pno
                           from   parts
                           where  pname in
                                ('Dirty Harry',
                                 'Dr. Zhivago'))));
```

This is a deeply nested SQL **select** statement with several occurrences of the **in** predicate.

Query 2.14 Get **cname** values of customers who order a product with **pno = 10506**.

```
select cname
from   customers
where  10506 in
           (select pno
            from   orders,odetails
            where  orders.ono = odetails.pno and
                   orders.cno = customers.cno);
```

This is a nested **select** statement, but with a difference. The inner select (i.e., the sub-select) statement refers to data that are defined in the outer **select** statement. The condition **orders.cno = customers.cno** in the sub-select refers to the cno value in the customers table in the outer select. Inner selects can refer to values in outer selects; however, the outer selects cannot refer to values within the scope of inner select. This scoping rule is analogous to scoping rules for variables in block-structured programming languages. Nested select statements in SQL in which the inner select refers to data in the outer selects are sometimes referred to as *correlated select statements*.

Quantified Comparison Predicates

The general form of the quantified comparison predicates are

```
expr <any  (sub-select)
expr <=any (sub-select)
expr =any  (sub-select)
expr <>any (sub-select)
expr >any  (sub-select)
expr >=any (sub-select)

expr <all  (sub-select)
expr <=all (sub-select)
expr =all  (sub-select)
expr <>all (sub-select)
expr >all  (sub-select)
expr >=all (sub-select)
```

There are two groups of quantified comparisons: all-comparisons, in which the comparisons are made with all the values in the sub-select statement, and any-comparisons, in which the comparison succeeds if it matches any one value in the sub-select. For example, the predicate

```
expr >any (sub-select)
```

is true if the value of the expression is greater than any one value in the sub-select, and the predicate

```
expr >all (sub-select)
```

is true if the value of the expression is greater than all values in the sub-select. The sub-select must result in a set of atomic values (single column); otherwise the comparison will not make sense.

If the sub-select is guaranteed to return exactly one value, the all and any quantification to this comparison may be dropped and the query will check for the one-on-one comparison between the expression and the value returned in the sub-select.

Here are some examples using the quantified comparison predicates.

Query 2.15 Get `pname` values for parts with the lowest price.

```
select pname
from   parts
where  price <=all (select price
                    from   parts);
```

The inner select statement in this example returns a set of values corresponding to the prices of the parts. If the price of the part under consideration in the outer select statement is less than or equal to all the values returned by the inner select, then the part being selected in the outer select statement costs the least.

Query 2.16 Get `cname` values of customers who have ordered parts from any one employee based in `Wichita` or `Liberal`.

```
select cname
from   customers,orders
where  customers.cno = orders.cno and
       eno in
          (select eno
           from   employees,zipcodes
           where  employees.zip = zipcodes.zip and
                  city in ('Wichita','Liberal'));
```

The inner select statement returns the `eno` values of all employees located in `Wichita` or `Liberal`. The outer select then checks to see if the customer under consideration has placed an order with any one of these employees using the `in` predicate. Note that the `=any` predicate has the same meaning as the `in` predicate and hence could be used interchangeably. However, for readability purposes, the `in` predicate is more commonly used.

Query 2.17 Get the `pname` values of parts that cost less than the least expensive `Land Before Time` part.

```
select pname
from   parts
where  price <all
          (select price
           from   parts
           where pname like 'Land Before Time%');
```

Predicates exists *and* not exists

The general form of the **exists** and **not exists** predicates are

```
exists (sub-select)
not exists (sub-select)
```

The **exists** predicate is true if the sub-select results in a nonempty set of values, and it is false otherwise. Similarly, the **not exists** predicate is true if the sub-select results in an empty set of values, and it is false otherwise. Some examples using the **exists** and **not exists** predicates follow.

Query 2.18 Get **cname** values of customers who have placed at least one order through employee with **eno** = 1000.

```
select cname
from   customers
where  exists
         (select 'a'
          from   orders
          where  orders.cno = customers.cno and
                 eno = 1000);
```

This is a correlated query in which the inner select statement returns a list of rows from the **orders** table such that these orders are taken by employee 1000 and are placed by the customer under consideration in the outer select. If this set is nonempty, it means that the customer under consideration in the outer select has indeed placed an order with employee 1000, and the name of the customer is projected in the final result. Note that it does not matter which columns are projected in the inner select statement; the **exists** clause simply checks if any tuple results from the inner select or not. For efficiency purposes, it is best to include some literal such as 'a' in the select list of such expressions.

Query 2.19 Get **cname** values of customers who do not place any orders through employee with **eno** = 1000.

```
select cname
from   customers
where  not exists
         (select 'a'
          from   orders x
          where  orders.cno = customers.cno and
                 eno = 1000);
```

This query is similar to the previous one except that the **not exists** predicate is used.

Query 2.20 Get **cno** values of customers who have placed an order for both parts, pno = 10506 and pno = 10507, within the same order.

```
select cno
from   orders
where  exists (select 'a'
               from   odetails
               where  odetails.ono = orders.ono and
                      odetails.pno = 10506) and
       exists (select 'a'
               from   odetails
               where  odetails.ono = orders.ono and
                      odetails.pno = 10507);
```

This query has two sub-selects. The first returns rows from **odetails** for the order under consideration in the outer select such that the part being ordered is 10506. The second sub-select does the same for part 10507. Since the row under consideration in the outer select is the same for both sub-selects, the query is answered correctly.

It does appear that there are many ways a particular query could be phrased in SQL. Consider the following query: *Get the names of cities of customers who have placed an order through employee with* eno = 1000. Here are five different SQL select statements that answer this query.

```
select distinct city
from   customers,zipcodes
where  customers.zip = zipcodes.zip and
       cno in (select cno
               from   orders
               where  eno = 1000);

select distinct city
from   customers,zipcodes
where  customers.zip = zipcodes.zip and
       cno =any (select cno
                 from   orders
                 where  eno = 1000);
```

```
select distinct city
from   customers,zipcodes
where  customers.zip = zipcodes.zip and
       exists (select *
               from   orders
               where  orders.cno = customers.cno and
                      eno = 1000);

select distinct city
from   customers c, orders o, zipcodes z
where  c.zip = z.zip and
       c.cno = o.cno and
       o.eno = 1000;

select distinct city
from   customers,zipcodes
where  customers.zip = zipcodes.zip and
       1000 in (select eno
                from   orders
                where  orders.cno = customers.cno);
```

There are probably a few more SQL select statements for this query.

2.4.3 Union

Oracle's SQL provides for a **union** operator that computes the union of two subqueries, each of which is expressed as a sub-select. There are two forms:

```
(sub-select) union (sub-select)
(sub-select) union all (sub-select)
```

The **union** operator eliminates duplicates, whereas the **union all** operator keeps duplicates, if there are any. A simple example follows.

Query 2.21 Get cities in which customers or employees are located.

```
select city
from   customers,zipcodes
where  customers.zip = zipcodes.zip
union
select city
from   employees,zipcodes
where  employees.zip = zipcodes.zip
```

The following will not eliminate duplicates:

```
select city
from   customers,zipcodes
where  customers.zip = zipcodes.zip
union  all
select city
from   employees,zipcodes
where  employees.zip = zipcodes.zip
```

2.4.4 Forall Queries

Recall that the division operator of relational algebra was best suited to answer a particular type of query, which we shall refer to as *forall queries*. Unfortunately, SQL does not provide a straightforward equivalent of the division operator. However, such queries can be expressed in SQL using the **not exists** predicate and with a rephrasing of the query into an equivalent form using double negation. This technique is illustrated by the following two examples.

Query 2.22 Get **cno** values of customers who place orders with ALL employees from Wichita.

This query can be rephrased as follows using double negation:

> Get **cno** values of customers such that (the set of employees from **Wichita** with whom the customer has NOT placed an order) is EMPTY.

Notice the double negation used in this rephrased query.[4] Instead of searching for the connections between customers and employees that are present in the **orders** table, this rephrased query would seek the "missing" connections between customers and employees. If missing connections do not exist, it reports the customer in the answer. The SQL version follows:

```
select c.cno
from   customers c
where  not exists
          (select *
           from employees e, zipcodes z
           where e.city = 'Wichita' and
                 e.zip = c.zip and
                 not exists (select *
```

4. Actually, even though the word NOT is used only once, the word EMPTY contains the second negation.

```
                        from orders x
                        where x.cno = c.cno and
                              x.eno = e.eno));
```

Query 2.23 Get the pno values of parts that are ordered by ALL customers from Wichita. The rephrased form is as follows:

> Get the pno values of parts such that (the set of customers from Wichita who have NOT ordered this part) is EMPTY.

The SQL select statement for this query is

```
select pno
from   parts p
where  not exists
         (select cno
          from   customers c, zipcodes z
          where  c.zip = z.zip and
                 z.city = 'Wichita' and
                 not exists
                   (select *
                    from orders o, odetails od
                    where  o.ono = od.ono and
                           od.pno = p.pno and
                           o.cno = c.cno));
```

This query has a structure similar to the previous one with three levels of nesting.

2.4.5 Aggregate Functions

Oracle's SQL supports five aggregate functions: count, sum, avg, max, and min. Figure 2.9 summarizes the characteristics of each. These functions are normally used in the select clause of the select statement, although they could sometimes be used in the conditions in the where clause or the having clause. An important point to note when using aggregate functions is that all null values are discarded before these functions are evaluated. The aggregate functions are illustrated by the following queries.

Query 2.24 Get total quantity of part 10601 that has been ordered.

```
select sum(qty) TOTAL
from   odetails
where  pno = 10601;
```

Figure 2.9 Aggregate functions.

Name	Argument Type	Result Type	Description
`count`	any (can be *)	Numeric	Count of occurrences
`sum`	numeric	Numeric	Sum of arguments
`avg`	numeric	Numeric	Average of arguments
`max`	char or numeric	Same as argument	Maximum value
`min`	char or numeric	Same as argument	Minimum value

This is a straightforward usage of the aggregate function `sum`.

Query 2.25 Get the total sales in dollars on all orders.

```
select sum(price*qty) TOTAL_SALES
from   orders,odetails,parts
where  orders.ono = odetails.ono and
       odetails.pno = parts.pno;
```

The `sum` aggregate function has been applied to the computed column `price*qty`, and the column has been named as `TOTAL_SALES`.

Query 2.26 Get the total number of customers.

```
select count(cno) NUM_CUSTOMERS
from   customers;
```

An alternate solution to this query is

```
select count(*)
from   customers;
```

These two select statements give the same result because `cno` is a key for the `customers` table.

Query 2.27 Get the number of cities in which customers are based.

```
select count(distinct city)
from   customers, zipcodes
where  customers.zip = zipcodes.zip;
```

If the keyword `distinct` is not used, you will get an incorrect result, as there could be more than one customer in the same city.

Query 2.28 Get the `pname` values of parts that cost more than the average cost of all parts.

```
select pname
from   parts
where  price > (select avg(price)
                from   parts);
```

The sub-select statement in this query is guaranteed to return a single value; hence the use of the comparison in the **where** clause is correct.

Query 2.29 Get **pname** values of parts ordered by at least two different customers.

```
select p.pname
from   parts p
where  2 <= (select count(distinct cno)
             from   orders,odetails
             where  orders.ono = odetails.ono and
                    pno = p.pno);
```

This is a correlated nested select statement. Notice the **distinct** keyword used in the sub-select. Without this, an incorrect answer will be generated if a customer orders the same part more than once.

2.4.6 The group by and having Clauses

So far, the aggregate functions have been applied to the whole table or a subset of the table satisfying the **where** clause. But there are many situations where the aggregate functions need to be applied to groups of rows based on certain column values rather than the whole table. SQL's select statement provides the **group by** and **having** clauses to address this situation.

The **group by** clause is used to form groups of rows of a resulting table based on column values. When the **group by** clause is used, all aggregate operations are computed on the individual groups, not on the entire table. The **having** clause is used to eliminate certain groups from further consideration. The syntax of the select statement with these two clauses is

```
select [distinct] <expression> {, <expression>}
from <tablename> [<alias>] {, <tablename> [<alias>]}
[where <search_condition>];
[group by <column> {, <column>}]
[having <condition>]
```

The **group by** clause follows the **where** clause and has a list of column names (at least one) listed after the keywords **group by**. The rows of the resulting table are partitioned into groups of rows, each group having the same value under the columns listed in the `group by` clause. The resulting table would contain a single row of summary information for each group. The **having** clause, if used, follows the **group by** clause, which has a condition that is used to keep some groups and eliminate others from further consideration. If the **having** clause is omitted, Oracle returns summary rows for each group. Some examples follow.

Query 2.30 For each part, get `pno` and `pname` values along with total sales in dollars.

```
select    parts.pno,pname,sum(qty*price) TOTAL_SALES
from      orders,odetails,parts
where     orders.ono = odetails.ono and
          odetails.pno = parts.pno
group by parts.pno,pname;
```

It is important to note that the **where** clause is evaluated first, before any groups are formed. Since only one summary row is returned for each group, any column that may result in more than one value for a group is not allowed in the **select** clause.

Query 2.31 Get employee name, employee number, part name, part number, together with the total quantity each employee supplies of that part to customers with `cno` values `1111` or `2222`.

```
select    e.eno, e.ename, p.pno, p.pname, sum(qty)
from      orders x, parts p, employees a,
          odetails od
where     x.ono = od.ono and x.eno = e.eno and
          od.pno = p.pno and x.cno in (1111, 2222)
group by e.eno, e.ename, p.pno, p.pname;
```

The orders, along with other pertinent information, are grouped according to `eno`, `ename`, `pno`, and `pname` values, and then the sum of the quantities for each group is calculated. The **where** clause condition is applied first in order to consider only the two customers in question before groups are formed and aggregates are calculated.

Query 2.32 For each part, get `pno` and `pname` values along with total sales in dollars, but only when the total sales exceed `1000` dollars.

```
select    parts.pno,pname,sum(qty*price) TOTAL_SALES
from      orders,odetails,parts
where     orders.ono = odetails.ono and
          odetails.pno = parts.pno
```

```
group by parts.pno,pname
having   sum(qty*price) > 1000;
```

This is essentially the same as Query 2.30. The **having** clause eliminates any groups for which the total dollar sales are less than or equal to 1000.

Query 2.33 Get **pno** and **pname** values of parts ordered by at least two different customers.

```
select parts.pno,parts.pname
from   orders,odetails,parts
where  orders.ono = odetails.ono and
       odetails.pno = parts.pno
group by parts.pno,parts.pname
having   count(distinct cno) >= 2;
```

In this query, the parts ordered by customers are grouped by **pno** and **pname**, and any group with two or more distinct **cno** values produces a row in the result.

2.4.7 The Full Select Statement

Oracle SQL's full select statement is summarized in this section. The **order by** clause is introduced, which allows the result of the select statement to be sorted in ascending or descending order based on column values.

The general form of a sub-select statement is

```
select [distinct] <expression> {, <expression>}
from <tablename> [<alias>] {, <tablename> [<alias>]}
[where <search_condition>];
[group by <column> {, <column>}]
[having <condition>]
```

and the general form of SQL's select statement is

```
<sub-select>
{union [all] <sub-select>}
[order by result_column [asc|desc]
        {, result_column [asc|desc]}]
```

The **order by** clause comes at the end and is used to sort the result of a query based on column values. The conceptual order of evaluation of a select statement is as follows:

1. The product of all tables in the **from** clause is formed.

2. The **where** clause is then evaluated to eliminate rows that do not satisfy the **search_condition**.
3. The rows are grouped using the columns in the **group by** clause.
4. Groups that do not satisfy the **condition** in the **having** clause are eliminated.
5. The expressions in the **select** clause target list are evaluated.
6. If the **distinct** keyword is present in the **select** clause, duplicate rows are now eliminated.
7. The **union** is taken after each sub-select is evaluated.
8. The resulting rows are sorted according to the columns specified in the **order by** clause.

Note that this is only the conceptual order; the actual sequence of steps taken by Oracle may be different and may have several additional steps for optimization.

2.4.8 String, Number, and Date Functions

Oracle provides strong support for the **string**, **number**, and **date** data types. A variety of functions are available to manipulate these data types and to convert from one data type to another. Details of these functions along with numerous examples are presented here.

Conversion Functions

Oracle provides functions that can convert data from one data type into another. The three commonly used data conversion functions are **to_char**, **to_number**, and **to_date**.

- The **to_char** function converts a **number** or a **date** into a character string. For example,

  ```
  to_char(1234) equals '1234'
  ```

  The details of converting a **date** into a character string are covered when discussing **date** functions.

- The **to_number** function converts a character string into a number. Of course, for this conversion to be valid, the character string should have only digits and other symbols that make up numbers. For example,

  ```
  to_number('1234') equals 1234
  ```

- The `to_date` function converts a number or a character string into a `date`. The details of this function are presented when discussing `date` functions.

Actually, Oracle performs some of these conversions automatically. Any `number` or `date` value is automatically converted to strings—i.e., you can use string functions on numbers and dates. Any character string data that contain only characters that can be used in numbers are also automatically converted to numbers, and you can use numeric functions on such string data. A character string of the form `'DD-MON-YY'` is automatically converted into a date, and date functions can be used on such string data.

Oracle provides two other functions related to data conversion called `translate` and `decode`. The syntax of the `translate` function is

```
translate(string,from,to)
```

where `string` is the input string to be transformed and `from` and `to` are character strings used in the transformation process. Each character that appears in `string` and also in `from` is transformed into the corresponding character (i.e., in the same position as in `from`) in `to`. If there is no corresponding character in `to`, the character is omitted from the result. For example,

```
translate('abcdef','abcd','1234') equals '1234ef'
translate('abcdef','cde','12') equals 'ab12f'
```

The `decode` function has the following syntax:

```
decode(value,if1,then1,if2,then2,...,ifN,thenN,else)
```

where `value` is the value to be tested, and the rest of the inputs are used to produce the output. The output of the function is `then1` if `value` is equal to `if1`, etc. If the `value` is none of the `if` values, then the `else` value is the output of the function. For example, the select statement

```
select decode(city,'Witchita','Wichita',
                   'Whichita','Wichita',city) CITY
from   zipcodes;
```

could be used to correct the many incorrect spellings of `Wichita`.

String Functions

Oracle's SQL provides a host of string functions that allow the user to manipulate strings and character data. These are summarized here:

- `Concatenation (||)`: Two or more strings can be concatenated using the `||` operator. For example, the concatenation of the `fname` and `lname` with a comma in the middle is denoted as

```
fname || ', ' || lname
```

- `lpad(string,length,['chars'])`: The `lpad` function pads the input `string` to the left with the `chars` until the length of the string reaches `length`. If the `chars` input is not provided, then the padding is done with spaces. For example,

```
lpad('ha',5,'a') equals 'aaaha'
lpad('ha',5,'ab') equals 'abaha'
lpad('ha',5) equals '   ha'
```

- `rpad(string,length,['chars'])`: `rpad` is similar to `lpad` except that the padding occurs to the right of the string. For example,

```
rpad('Jones',10,'.') equals 'Jones.....'
rpad('Jones',10,'xy') equals 'Jonesxyxyx'
rpad('Jones',10) equals 'Jones     '
```

- `ltrim(string,['chars'])`: The `ltrim` function removes from the left of `string` any character that appears in `chars` until it finds one that is not in `chars`. For example,

```
ltrim('abracadabra','abc') equals 'racadabra'
ltrim('    abra') equals 'abra'
```

If `chars` is not provided as input, the space character is trimmed from the left.

- `rtrim(string,['chars'])`: `rtrim` is similar to `ltrim` except that the trimming occurs to the right of the string. For example,

```
rtrim('abracadabra','abc') equals 'abracadabr'
rtrim('abra       ') equals 'abra'
```

- `lower(string)`: Converts all the characters of the `string` input to lowercase. For example,

```
lower('ToNY') equals 'tony'
```

- `upper(string)`: Converts all the characters of the `string` input to uppercase. For example,

```
upper('ToNY') equals 'TONY'
```

- `initcap(string)`: Converts the first character of the `string` input to uppercase. For example,

```
initcap('tony') equals 'Tony'
```

- `length(string)`: Returns the length of the `string` input.

- `substr(string,start,[n])`: Returns the substring of `string` starting at position `start` and of length `n`. If `n` is not provided, the substring ends at the end of `string`. For example,

```
substr('abracadabra',1,5) equals 'abrac'
substr('abracadabra',4) equals 'acadabra'
```

- `instr(string,'chars'[,start [,n]])`: The `instr` function searches the `string` input for `chars` starting from position `start` for the `nth` occurrence and returns the position (returns 0 if not found). If `start` is not provided, the string is searched from the beginning; if `n` is not provided, the string is searched for the first occurrence. For example,

```
instr('Johnny Miller','Mill') equals 8
instr('abracadabra','bra',1,2) equals 9
```

Here are some examples of the usage of the string functions in SQL's `select` statement.

1. The SQL `select` statement

```
select fname || ', ' || lname NAME
from   students;
```

produces the following output:

```
NAME
------------------------------------------
Nandita, Rajshekhar
Sydney, Corn
Susan, Williams
Naveen, Rajshekhar
Elad, Yam
Lincoln, Herring

6 rows selected
```

2. The SQL `select` statement

```
select sid,
       decode(substr(term,1,2),
              'sp','spring'||substr(term,length(term)-1),
              'su','summer'||substr(term,length(term)-1),
              'wi','winter'||substr(term,length(term)-1),
                   'fall'  ||substr(term,length(term)-1))
```

```
         term,
         lineno
from   enrolls;
```

produces the following output

```
SID   TERM                 LINENO
----- ---------------- ----------
1111  fall96                 1031
2222  fall96                 1031
4444  fall96                 1031
1111  fall96                 1032
2222  fall96                 1032
3333  fall96                 1032
5555  spring97               1031
6666  spring97               1031

8 rows selected
```

3. The SQL select statement

```
select rpad(upper(cname),20,'.') CUSTOMER, phone
from   customers;
```

produces the following output:

```
CUSTOMER             PHONE
-------------------- ------------
CHARLES............. 316-636-5555
BERTRAM............. 316-689-5555
BARBARA............. 316-111-1234
```

4. The SQL select statement

```
select pno,pname
from   parts
where  instr(pname,'Time') > 0 or
       instr(pname,'Harry') > 0;
```

produces the following output:

```
       PNO PNAME
---------- ------------------------------
     10506 Land Before Time I
     10507 Land Before Time II
     10508 Land Before Time III
     10509 Land Before Time IV
     10701 When Harry Met Sally
     10800 Dirty Harry

6 rows selected
```

Numeric Functions

Oracle SQL provides numerous functions that manipulate numbers. Among them are addition (+), subtraction (−), multiplication (*), division (/), absolute value (**abs**), ceiling (**ceil**), floor (**floor**), modulus (**mod**), power (**power**), and square root (**sqrt**). These functions could be used in the **select** clause or in the condition of the **where** clause. These are single-valued functions—i.e., the inputs are single values. Numeric functions that operate on a set of values are **min**, **max**, **sum**, and **avg**, which have been discussed in the context of aggregate functions. There are two list-valued functions—i.e., they operate on a list of values. These are **least** and **greatest**. Examples of all these numeric functions are shown in the following select statements.

1. The select statement

```
select qoh,olevel,qoh+olevel PLUS,
       qoh-olevel SUBT, qoh*olevel MULT,
       qoh/olevel DIVD
from   parts;
```

produces the following output:

```
  QOH OLEVEL PLUS SUBT MULT       DIVD
----- ------ ---- ---- ---- ----------
  200     20  220  180 4000         10
  156     20  176  136 3120        7.8
  190     20  210  170 3800        9.5
   60     20   80   40 1200          3
  300     20  320  280 6000         15
  120     30  150   90 3600          4
```

```
  140     30  170   110 4200 4.66666667
  100     30  130    70 3000 3.33333333

8 rows selected
```

2. The select statement

```
select qoh,olevel,qoh/olevel DIVD,
       ceil(qoh/olevel) CEILING,
       floor(qoh/olevel) FLOOR
from   parts;
```

produces the following output:

```
  QOH  OLEVEL       DIVD CEILING FLOOR
----- ------- ---------- ------- -----
  200      20         10      10    10
  156      20        7.8       8     7
  190      20        9.5      10     9
   60      20          3       3     3
  300      20         15      15    15
  120      30          4       4     4
  140      30 4.66666667       5     4
  100      30 3.33333333       4     3

8 rows selected
```

3. The select statement

```
select qoh,olevel,mod(qoh,olevel) MOD,
       power(olevel,3) POWER,sqrt(qoh) SQRT
from   parts;
```

produces the following output:

```
  QOH  OLEVEL  MOD  POWER       SQRT
----- ------- ---- ------ ----------
  200      20    0   8000 14.1421356
  156      20   16   8000  12.489996
  190      20   10   8000 13.7840488
   60      20    0   8000 7.74596669
  300      20    0   8000 17.3205081
  120      30    0  27000 10.9544512
```

```
 140      30   20  27000 11.8321596
 100      30   10  27000         10

8 rows selected
```

4. The select statement

```
select qoh,olevel,least(qoh,8*olevel) LEAST,
       greatest(qoh,8*olevel) GREATEST
from   parts;
```

produces the following output:

```
  QOH OLEVEL LEAST GREATEST
----- ------ ----- --------
  200     20   160      200
  156     20   156      160
  190     20   160      190
   60     20    60      160
  300     20   160      300
  120     30   120      240
  140     30   140      240
  100     30   100      240

8 rows selected
```

Date Functions

Oracle provides the **date** data type to model time and date and a powerful set of operators to format and manipulate such data. Internally, the **date** data are stored in a special format that includes date (day, month, and year) as well as time (hours, minutes, and seconds).[5] However, the user sees the date in an external form, which, as a default, is a string of the form 'DD-MON-YY'.

Some of the commonly used date functions are **sysdate**, **next_day**, **add_months**, **last_day**, **months_between**, **least**, **greatest**, **round**, and **trunc**. In addition to these functions, there are two other conversion functions, which were introduced earlier: to_date and to_char. Moreover, you can overload the addition (+) and subtraction (−) operators with dates. A brief description of these functions follows.

---

5. The **date** value is stored in seven bytes, one each for century, year, month, day, hours, minutes, and seconds.

- `+, -`. You can add (or subtract) a number to (from) a date to get a new date. The number is in days. You can also subtract two dates to find the number of days between them.
- `sysdate`. This function takes no input and returns the current date and time.
- `next_day(d,day)`. This function takes as input a date `d` and a string `day` that represents a day of the week, and returns as output the next date after `d` whose day of the week is the same as `day`.
- `add_months(d,count)`. This function takes a date `d` and a number `count` as inputs and returns a new date that is `count` months after `d`.
- `last_day(d)`. This function takes as input a date `d` and returns the date corresponding to the last day of the month in which `d` belongs.
- `months_between(d2,d1)`. Given two dates `d2` and `d1`, this function returns the number of months between `d1` and `d2` (`d2 - d1`).
- `least(d1,d2,...,dn)`. Given a list of dates, this function returns the earliest date.
- `greatest(d1,d2,...,dn)`. Given a list of dates, this function returns the latest date.
- `trunc(d)`. Given a date `d`, this function returns the same date but with the time reset to `12:00 AM midnight`.
- `round(d)`. Given a date `d`, this function returns the same date with time reset to `12:00 AM midnight` if `d` is before noon and rounds the date up to the next day (again `12:00 AM midnight`) if `d` is after noon.
- `to_char(d,format)`. Given a date `d` and a `format` as a string, this function returns a character string equivalent of the date based on the `format`. The contents of the `format` are summarized in Figure 2.10.
- `to_date(s,format)`. Given a string `s` and a `format`, this function returns a date corresponding to the string `s` based on `format`.

The date functions are illustrated by the following SQL select statements. (Notice the use of a system table called `dual`, which is a dummy table consisting of one column and one row.)

1. The SQL select statement

```
select hdate,sysdate,hdate+2,hdate-2,sysdate-hdate
from   employees;
```

Figure 2.10 Date formats.

Format	Description	Example
MM	Month number	7
MON	3-letter abbreviation of month	JAN
MONTH	Fully spelled-out month	JANUARY
D	Number of days in the week	3
DD	Number of days in the month	16
DDD	Number of days in the year	234
DY	3-letter abbreviation of day of week	WED
DAY	Fully spelled-out day of week	WEDNESDAY
Y	Last digit of year	8
YY	Last two digits of year	98
YYY	Last three digits of year	998
YYYY	Full four-digit year	1998
HH12	Hours of the day (1 to 12)	10
HH24	Hours of the day (0 to 23)	17
MI	Minutes of hour	34
SS	Seconds of minute	35
AM	Displays AM or PM depending on time	AM

produces the following output:

```
HDATE     SYSDATE   HDATE+2   HDATE-2   SYSDATE-HDATE
--------- --------- --------- --------- -------------
12-DEC-95 12-JAN-98 14-DEC-95 10-DEC-95     762.51772
01-JAN-92 12-JAN-98 03-JAN-92 30-DEC-91    2203.51772
01-SEP-94 12-JAN-98 03-SEP-94 30-AUG-94    1229.51772
```

2. The SQL select statement

```
select months_between('02-JAN-96','02-MAY-95')
from   dual;
```

produces the following output:

```
MONTHS_BETWEEN('02-JAN-96','02-MAY-95')
---------------------------------------
                                      8
```

3. The SQL select statement

```
select hdate, to_char(hdate,'DAY') DAY,
       next_day(hdate,'MONDAY'),last_day(hdate),
       add_months(hdate,3)
from   employees;
```

produces the following output:

```
HDATE     DAY       NEXT_DAY( LAST_DAY( ADD_MONTH
--------- --------- --------- --------- ---------
12-DEC-95 TUESDAY   18-DEC-95 31-DEC-95 12-MAR-96
01-JAN-92 WEDNESDAY 06-JAN-92 31-JAN-92 01-APR-92
01-SEP-94 THURSDAY  05-SEP-94 30-SEP-94 01-DEC-94
```

4. The SQL select statement

```
select received,shipped,least(received+4,shipped),
       greatest(received+4,shipped)
from   orders;
```

produces the following output:

```
RECEIVED  SHIPPED   LEAST(REC GREATEST(
--------- --------- --------- ---------
10-DEC-94 12-DEC-94 12-DEC-94 14-DEC-94
12-JAN-95 15-JAN-95 15-JAN-95 16-JAN-95
13-FEB-95 20-FEB-95 17-FEB-95 20-FEB-95
20-JUN-97
```

5. The SQL select statement

```
select to_char(sysdate,'DD-MON-YY, HH:MI:SS')
       SYSDATE, trunc(sysdate),round(sysdate)
from   dual;
```

produces the following output:

```
SYSDATE               TRUNC(SYS ROUND(SYS
-------------------   --------- ---------
12-JAN-98, 12:37:03   12-JAN-98 13-JAN-98
```

6. The SQL select statement

```
select to_date('12 JANUARY 1997','DD MONTH YYYY')+5
from   dual;
```

produces the following output:

```
TO_DATE('
---------
17-JAN-97
```

Here are some queries that involve dates.

Query 2.34 Get `ename` values of employees who placed an order that was received in one month and shipped in a different month.

```
select ename
from   employees
where  eno in
         (select eno
          from   orders
          where  to_char(received,'MM') !=
                 to_char(shipped,'MM'));
```

The dates are converted into numeric months using the `to_char` function and then compared.

Query 2.35 Get `ono` values of orders that were shipped within two days of their receipt.

```
select ono
from   orders
where  (shipped - received) <= 2;
```

Use date subtraction to figure out if the difference in dates is less than or equal to 2.

Query 2.36 Get `ename` values of employees who placed an order within the first week of their hire date.

```
select ename
from   employees
where  eno in
         (select eno
          from   orders
          where  (received - hdate) < 7);
```

Use date subtraction here also.

Query 2.37 Get the name of the employee who was hired on the earliest date.

```
select ename
from   employees
where  hdate = (select min(hdate)
                from   employees);
```

The `min` aggregate function is used on the date column to find the earliest date.

2.5 Views

A *view* is a table that is derived from other views and the base tables that are created using the `create table` statement. Views depend on other tables and views to exist. Views can be used in queries just as if they were ordinary or base tables. However, they are dynamic in nature—i.e., their contents change automatically when the base tables and views, on which their definition is based, change. Views are created in Oracle using the `create view` statement and are dropped from the database using the `drop view` statement.

2.5.1 `create view`

The syntax of the `create view` statement is

```
create view <viewname> as <select-statement>;
```

The statement starts with the keywords `create view`, followed by the name of the view and the keyword `as`, and is terminated by a select statement. The select statement is a query whose result is a table that is assigned to the view. The query results can vary from time to time depending on the database contents, thereby giving the views a dynamic nature. An example of a view definition is

```
create view employee_sales as
  select   employees.eno,ename,sum(price*qty) SALES
  from     employees,orders,odetails,parts
  where    employees.eno = orders.eno and
           orders.ono = odetails.ono and
           odetails.pno = parts.pno
  group by employees.eno,ename;
```

This view creates a derived table that has three columns: `eno`, `ename`, and `SALES`. This table records the number and names of employees along with their total sales.

As another interesting example of views, consider the portfolio of a member in the investment portfolio database. The portfolio can be computed from the

Figure 2.11 Creating views for the investment portfolio database.

```
create view buy_transaction as
  select mid, symbol, sum(quantity) total
  from   transaction
  where  trans_type = 'buy'
  group  by mid, symbol;

create view sell_transaction as
  select mid, symbol, sum(quantity) total
  from   transaction
  where  trans_type = 'sell'
  group  by mid, symbol;

create view portfolio as
  (select b.mid, b.symbol, (b.total - s.total) quantity
   from   buy_transaction b, sell_transaction s
   where  b.mid = s.mid and
          b.symbol = s.symbol and
          (b.total - s.total) > 0)
  union
  (select b.mid, b.symbol, b.total  quantity
   from   buy_transaction b
   where  not exists (
              select *
              from   sell_transaction s
              where  b.mid = s.mid and
                     b.symbol = s.symbol));
```

transaction entries for that member. The shares currently owned by the member are computed by first partitioning the `transaction` table into two parts: `buy_transaction` and `sell_transaction`. Then, the number of shares of a company currently owned by the member is the difference between the number of shares bought and the number of shares sold for that particular company. The current portfolio of members is found in the SQL view `portfolio` shown in Figure 2.11.

2.5.2 drop view

The `drop view` statement has a simple syntax,

```
drop view <viewname>;
```

where the name of the view follows the keywords `drop view`.

2.6 Modifying the Database

Oracle's SQL provides three statements (**insert**, **update**, and **delete**) to modify the contents of the database. The syntax and use of these statements are discussed in this section.

2.6.1 insert

The **insert** statement has one of the following two forms:

```
insert into <tablename> [(column {, column})]
values (expression {, expression})

insert into <tablename> [(column {, column})]
<select-statement>
```

The first form was discussed in an earlier section. The second form allows you to insert rows that are a result of the **<select-statement>**. An example of the second form of the **insert** statement is shown below.

Example 2.6.1 Assume that the **parts** table has grown too large and you have decided to partition it into three smaller tables (horizontal partitions) based on the **price** column. Let the names of these three tables be **cheap_parts**, **soso_parts**, and **expensive_parts**. Assume that these three tables have been created in the database. The following **insert** statements will accomplish the task of loading these tables with data from the **parts** table.

```
insert into cheap_parts
  select *
  from   parts
  where  price <= 20.00;

insert into soso_parts
  select *
  from   parts
  where  price between 20.00 and 50.00;

insert into expensive_parts
  select *
  from   parts
  where  price > 50.00;
```

2.6.2 update

The **update** statement has the following syntax:

```
update <tablename> [alias]
set    <column> = <expression>
       {, <column> = <expression>}
[where <search_condition>]
```

It has three clauses: the **update** clause, which contains the name of the table to be updated along with an optional alias; the **set** clause, which has one or more assignments that assign an expression to a column; and an optional **where** clause, which can restrict the rows to be updated. If the **where** clause is missing, all rows of the table are updated. Some examples of the **update** statement follow.

Example 2.6.2 The **update** statement

```
update parts
set    qoh = qoh + 100
where  qoh < 5*olevel;
```

increases by 100 the **qoh** values of those rows of the **parts** table that have a **qoh** value less than five times the **olevel** value.

The **update** statement

```
update parts
set    qoh = (select max(qoh)
              from   parts)
where  qoh < 100;
```

sets the **qoh** value of those parts whose current **qoh** value is less than 100 to the maximum **qoh** value present in the table. Notice the use of a select statement as an expression in the **set** clause.

The **update** statement

```
update parts
set    qoh = 2*qoh
where  3 <= (select sum(qty)
             from   odetails
             where  odetails.pno = parts.pno);
```

doubles the **qoh** values of those parts that have been ordered in quantities of three or more. Notice the sub-select in the **where** clause.

2.6.3 delete

The **delete** statement has the following syntax:

```
delete from <tablename> [alias]
[where <search_condition>]
```

It has two clauses: the **delete from** clause, which is followed by a table name and an optional alias, and the **where** clause, which is followed by a search condition. The **where** clause, if used, restricts the rows to be deleted. It is important to note that if the **where** clause is missing, all the rows in the table are deleted. Some examples of the **delete** statement follow.

Example 2.6.3 The **delete** statement

```
delete from customers;
```

deletes all rows in the **customers** table.

The **delete** statement

```
delete from customers
where  zip in (select zip
               from   zipcodes
               where city = 'Fort Hays');
```

deletes all customers who live in Fort Hays.

The **delete** statement

```
delete from employees
where  eno in (select   eno
               from     orders,odetails,parts
               where    orders.ono = odetails.ono and
                        odetails.pno = parts.pno
               group by eno
               having   sum(price*qty) < 200);
```

deletes all employees who have orders totaling less than $200. Notice the sub-select statement in the **where** clause.

2.6.4 commit and rollback

The changes made to the database using the **insert**, **delete**, and **update** statements can be reversed if necessary. Oracle SQL provides two statements: **commit** and **rollback**. The changes made to the database can be made permanent by using the `commit` statement. The changes made to the database since the last commit can be reversed by using the `rollback` statement. There are some actions that force a commit even without the user issuing the `commit` statement. When the user exits an SQL session, the system automatically commits all the changes. Other statements that result in an automatic commit include `create table`, `drop table`, and `alter table`.

2.7 Sequences

A *sequence* is an object that consists of an integer value initialized to a particular value at its definition time. Oracle creates the next value in the sequence each time a request is made for the next value. This mechanism is particularly useful when assigning unique key values to columns. The syntax of the `create sequence` statement is

```
create sequence <seq-name>
  [increment by integer]
  [start with integer]
  [maxvalue integer | nomaxvalue]
  [minvalue integer | nominvalue]
  [cycle|nocycle]
```

where `<seq-name>` is the name given to the sequence. The default increment value is 1. However, by providing a positive integer in the `increment by` clause, the sequence can be defined as an increasing sequence with an increment value other than 1. In a similar manner, a decreasing sequence can be obtained by providing a negative integer in the `increment by` clause. By using the `start with` clause, the sequence can start at any integer. The default start value for an increasing sequence is `minvalue` and that for a decreasing sequence is `maxvalue`. `Minvalue`, the lowest value the sequence will generate, has a default of 1. `Maxvalue` is the highest integer the sequence will generate. By specifying the `cycle` clause, the integers will be recycled if the `minvalue` or `maxvalue` is specified. An example of a sequence definition is

```
create sequence custseq start with 1000;
```

which creates a sequence that starts with the value `1000` and is incremented by 1 each time a new value is requested.

The sequences are accessed by the two functions `nextval` and `currval`. The `nextval` function is basically a request to the system to generate the next value in the sequence. The `currval` function returns the current value of the sequence. This function cannot be invoked before the first **nextval** function is called. A sample usage of the **nextval** function is

```
insert into customers
  values(custseq.nextval,'Jones','123 Main St.',
         67226,'111-111-1111');
```

2.8 Oracle Data Dictionary

The Oracle data dictionary stores all information about the objects of the database. This includes the names and structures of all tables, constraints, indices, views, synonyms, sequences, triggers, procedures, functions, and packages. The data dictionary is stored in specially created system tables. This section will focus on the most commonly used data dictionary tables. The tables that constitute the data dictionary are all accessible via the system view **dictionary** or its synonym **dict**. This is the starting point for any exploration of the data dictionary.

2.8.1 The user_catalog Table

The **user_catalog** table contains information about the tables and views defined by a particular user. The schema for this table is

```
user_catalog(table_name,table_type);
```

This table can also be referred to by its public synonym, **cat**. The following SQL select statement lists all the tables and views defined by the current user.

```
select *
from   cat;
```

2.8.2 The user_objects Table

The **user_objects** table contains information about all objects defined by the current user. In addition to the information available under **user_cat**, you can find out views, functions and procedures, indices, synonyms, triggers, etc., defined by the current user. The schema for this table is

```
user_objects(object_name,object_id, object_type,
             created, last_ddl_time, timestamp,
             status)
```

Here, `created` is a date column indicating the time that the object was created; `last_ddl_time` is a date column indicating the time that the object was affected by a Data Definition Language statement; `timestamp` is the same as `created` except in character string form; and the `status` column indicates a `valid` or `invalid` object.

2.8.3 The `user_tables` Table

If you want more information about the user tables than just its name, the dictionary table `user_tables` can be used. In addition to the name of the table, you can obtain here space-related information and statistical information about the table. To get the names of all of its columns, use the `describe user_tables` command on the `SQL>` prompt. This table can also be accessed via its public synonym `tabs`.

2.8.4 The `user_tab_columns` Table

Information specific to the columns of tables is listed in the dictionary table `user_tab_columns`. In addition to the table name to which the column belongs and the column name, definition-related information as well as statistical information is kept in this table. The detailed column names of this table can be obtained by using the `describe` command. This table can also be accessed via its public synonym `cols`.

2.8.5 The `user_views` Table

Information about user views are kept in the table `user_views`. The schema of this table is

```
user_views(view_name,text_length,text)
```

where `text_length` is the length in characters of the base query on which the view is based and `text` is the actual text of the base query.

2.9 Oracle8 Object Features

A gentle introduction to Oracle8's object-oriented features is presented in this section. Oracle8 is referred to as an Object-Relational Database Management System as it supports the purely relational view (as in Oracle 7), the object-relational view in which the user designs the database using the relational model but incorporates several object-oriented features and concepts into the design, and the purely object-oriented view in which the user designs the database based solely on an object-oriented approach. Topics introduced in this section are: abstract data types, collection objects such as varying arrays and nested relations, and querying and updating object-relational tables. The mail-order database is used to illustrate the various concepts. The design of the mail-order database, of course, is modified to show one possible object-relational design.

2.9.1 The `create type` Statement

The **create type** statement in Oracle8 is versatile and can be used to create an object type, named varying array (**VARRAY**), or a nested table type.

The simplest form[6] of the **create type** statement to create an object type has the following syntax:

```
create type [schema.]type_name as object (
  attribute_name  datatype
  [, attribute_name  datatype]...
  | [ member {procedure_specification | function_specification}
    [, member {procedure_specification |
              function_specification}]... ]
  | [ pragma restrict_references (method_name, constraints)
    [, pragma restrict_references (method_name,
       constraints)]... ]  );
```

After naming the object type, one or more attributes must be included in the type definition. The data types of these attributes could be any Oracle data type including another object type. After the attributes are defined, member functions or procedures can be specified. Note that only the specification of the member functions or procedures are included in the type definition. The implementations of these functions or procedures are done separately in the **create type body** statement to be discussed in Section 4.11. Finally, one or more **pragma**s or compiler directives may be included. These impose certain restrictions on the functions or procedures such as restricting the function or procedure from updating the database state (**WNDS: Write No Database State**), restricting the function or procedure from querying the database (**RNDS: Read No Database State**), etc.

---

6. For the detailed syntax, please consult the Oracle8 SQL Reference.

An object type is essentially an abstract datatype which is capable of storing both variables and methods that operate on the variables. As an example, consider the address attribute used in the mail-order database. Assume that this attribute is present in both the **customers** and **employees** tables. A good way to model this situation is to create an object type, called **address_type** and include attributes of this type in the **customers** and **employees** tables. The **create type** statement necessary to accomplish this is shown below:

```
create type address_type as object (
  street varchar2(30),
  city   varchar2(30),
  state  varchar2(20),
  zip    number(5)
);
```

This creates a new object type called **address_type**, and also creates default methods to construct objects of this type and to access data members of objects of this type. User-defined methods can also be included and will be discussed later.

2.9.2 The varying array Collection Type

Oracle8 supports two kinds of collection object types: varying arrays and nested tables. Varying arrays allow the possibility of storing multiple values for an attribute within a row. While defining the type, the maximum number of values that will be allowed must be specified.

The general syntax of the **create type** statement to create a varying array is:

```
CREATE TYPE type_name AS VARRAY (limit) OF datatype;
```

where **type_name** is the name given to the type, **limit** is the maximum number of values allowed in the varying array, and **datatype** can be any Oracle8 basic type or an object type.

For example, consider the fact that customers and employees may have more than one phone number. A varying array type can be created for phone numbers and attributes of the varying array type can then be included in the **customers** and **employees** tables. The **create type** statement to define the varying array for phone numbers is shown below:

```
create type phones_varray_type as varray(3) of char(12);
```

In this case, a varying array type, called **phones_varray_type** is created with a maximum of three phone numbers. Each phone number is defined to be of type char(12). In general, varying arrays of any basic Oracle datatype or even other abstract types can be created.

Proceeding further with the design of the mail-order database, a **person_type** object type is created as follows:

```
create type person_type as object (
  name      varchar2(30),
  address   address_type,
  phones    phones_varray_type
);
```

This type includes the name, address, and phone numbers of the person. Notice the use of the object type, **address_type**, defined earlier.

Now the **employees** and **customers** tables can be defined using the **create table** statement as usual. However, this time, the newly created object types are used to define various attributes of these tables. The **create table** statements are shown below:

```
create table o_employees (
  eno       number(4) not null primary key,
  person    person_type,
  hdate     date
);

create table o_customers (
  cno       number(5) not null primary key,
  person    person_type
);
```

Notice that the tables have been renamed with the **o_** prefix so as not to cause confusion with the tables defined in the mail-order database. Both these tables include an attribute called **person**, which is of type **person_type**. The **person_type** object type includes an address object type and a varying array of phone numbers. The **parts** table is left unchanged from the earlier version. The **create table** statement to create it is shown below:

```
create table o_parts(
  pno       number(5) not null primary key,
  pname     varchar2(30),
  qoh       integer check(qoh >= 0),
  price     number(6,2) check(price >= 0.0),
  olevel    integer;
);
```

2.9.3 Inserting Rows

Once the object-relational tables have been created, rows can be inserted with the **insert into** SQL statement. The syntax for inserting values into columns associated with object types uses the object type constructors that go by the same name as the object type itself. The following insert statements illustrate the syntax for inserting values into the `o_employees` table.

```
insert into o_employees values
  (1000,
   person_type(
     'Jones',
     address_type('123 Main St','Wichita','KS',67226),
     phones_varray_type('316-555-1212',null,null)),
   '12-DEC-95');

insert into o_employees values
  (1001,
   person_type(
     'Smith',
     address_type('101 Elm St','Fort Dodge','KS',60606),
     phones_varray_type('316-555-2121','316-555-2323',null)),
   '01-JAN-92');

insert into o_employees values
  (1002,
   person_type(
     'Brown',
     address_type('100 Elm St','Kansas City','KS',50302),
     phones_varray_type('780-555-1111',null,null)),
   '01-SEP-94');

insert into o_employees values
  (1003,
   person_type(
     'Green',
     null,
     phones_varray_type('316-666-1212',null,null)),
   '12-OCT-95');
```

Notice the nested syntax for the `insert` statement. Also notice how the constructor methods for the various object types at the different levels of the nesting are employed with appropriate arguments to create the object instances for column values. The `null` specification for the missing phone numbers in the varying arrays is not necessary. If it is not specified, the values are undefined. Also note that the last employee has a `null` value for the `address_type` attribute.

A similar set of `insert into` statements for the `o_customers` table is shown below:

```
insert into o_customers values
  (1111,
   person_type(
     'Charles',
     address_type('123 Main St','Wichita','KS',67226),
     phones_varray_type('316-636-5555',null,null)));

insert into o_customers values
  (2222,
   person_type(
     'Bertram',
     address_type('237 Ash Avenue','Wichita','KS',67226),
     phones_varray_type('316-689-5555','316-689-5556',null)));

insert into o_customers values
  (3333,
   person_type(
     'Barbara',
     address_type('111 Inwood St','Fort Dodge','KS',60606),
     phones_varray_type('316-111-1234','316-111-1235',null)));
```

2.9.4 User-Defined Methods

An object type typically includes several attributes or variables and methods that operate on the variables. When an object type is created, Oracle automatically creates methods to construct and access objects of that type. In addition to these methods, the user may specify other methods for an object type. The user-defined methods are created by specifying the method prototype in the `create type` statement and by completing the method implementation in the `create type body` statement.

Consider the order details information in the mail order database containing the line item details for a particular order. The following **create type** statement creates an object type called **odetails_type** containing two attributes, **pno** and **qty**, along with a method, called **cost**, which computes the cost of this line item in the order.

```
create type odetails_type as object (
  pno      number(5),
  qty      integer,
  member function cost return number,
  pragma restrict_references(cost,WNDS)
);
```

The two lines that define the method **cost** for this object type are:

```
member function cost return number,
pragma restrict_references(cost,WNDS)
```

The first line specifies the member function prototype. In this case, the method has no parameters, but in general, one could specify certain parameters. The body of this method, which should be specified in the **create type body** statement, is presented in Section 4.11. The method could potentially modify the database state if it wishes, which is neither desirable nor allowed if this method is to be used in an SQL query. Therefore, a **pragma** statement must be specified which restricts the method from updating the database state (**WNDS: Write No Database State**). Other available restrictions are: **RNDS: Read No Database State** (no queries allowed), **WNPS: Write No Package State** (no values of package variables are modified), and **RNPS: Read No Package State** (no package variables are referenced).

2.9.5 Nested Tables

The second type of collection object supported by Oracle8 is the nested table. In contrast to varying arrays which have a fixed maximum number of entries, nested tables can support an unlimited number of entries per row. As the name suggests, nested tables are tables within tables. The general syntax of the **create type** statement to create a nested table is:

```
CREATE TYPE type_name AS TABLE OF datatype;
```

where **type_name** is the name given to the nested table and **datatype** is any valid Oracle8 basic data type or an object type.

In the mail order database example, a table object type consisting of many **odetails_type** objects can be defined as follows:

```
create type odetails_ntable_type as
  table of odetails_type;
```

An attribute of this type can then be included in another object type, called `o_order_type`, which corresponds to the orders in the mail order database. This way, the order details for a particular order are logically associated with the order information itself rather than in a separate table as was the case in the relational design of the mail order database. The `o_order_type` object type includes all the information that was included in the `orders` table in the earlier design of the mail order database. It also includes a nested table for order details and a user-defined method, called `total_cost`, which computes and returns the total cost for the entire order. The object type definition is shown below:

```
create type o_order_type as object (
  ono      number(5),
  odetails odetails_ntable_type,
  cno      number(5),
  eno      number(4),
  received date,
  shipped  date,
  member function total_cost return number,
  pragma restrict_references(total_cost,WNDS)
);
```

The method implementation for `total_cost` is presented in Section 4.11.

2.9.6 Object Tables

In Oracle8, it is possible to create tables made up of objects instead of rows. Once an object type has been defined, a table of that object type can be created using a variation of the `create table` statement that is illustrated in the following example. Consider the `o_order_type` object type. A table, called `o_orders`, can be created using the following statement:

```
create table o_orders of o_order_type (
  primary key (ono)
)
nested table odetails store as odetails_tab;
```

This table consists of objects of type `o_order_type`. The primary key constraint is included here. Notice the `of` keyword used in this statement. Object tables offer considerable flexibility in that one can define a single object type and then create as many tables as required from that object type template. Constraints such as primary keys are applicable at the table level. The syntax for accessing attributes of object rows in an object table is the same as if the attributes were defined at the table level. Examples of queries that access the object rows are presented later. The clause

```
nested table odetails store as odetails_tab;
```

that appears at the end of the `create table` statement above specifies that the nested table attribute `odetails` is to be stored externally under the user-chosen name `odetails_tab`. Unlike varying arrays, which are stored in-line by Oracle8, nested tables are stored externally and the clause naming the external table is required for any table that includes a nested table.

2.9.7 Inserting Rows into Nested Tables

Inserting rows into a table containing a nested table is done in a similar manner as varying arrays. The object type constructors are invoked and individual rows of the nested table are specified in a comma-separated manner. The following `insert into` statements insert four orders into the `o_orders` table.

```
insert into o_orders values
  (1020,
   odetails_ntable_type(odetails_type(10506,1),
                        odetails_type(10507,1),
                        odetails_type(10508,2),
                        odetails_type(10509,3)),
   1111,1000,'10-DEC-94','12-DEC-94');

insert into o_orders values
  (1021,
   odetails_ntable_type(odetails_type(10601,4)),
   1111,1000,'12-JAN-95','15-JAN-95');

insert into o_orders values
  (1022,
   odetails_ntable_type(odetails_type(10601,1),
                        odetails_type(10701,1)),
   2222,1001,'13-FEB-95','20-FEB-95');

insert into o_orders values
  (1023,
```

```
odetails_ntable_type(odetails_type(10800,1),
                     odetails_type(10900,1)),
3333,1000,'20-JUN-97',null);
```

Since the `o_orders` table is a table of objects, the above inserts should have technically invoked the object constructor for `o_order_type` as follows:

```
insert into o_orders values
  (o_order_type(1025,
      odetails_ntable_type(odetails_type(10601,1),
                           odetails_type(10701,1)),
      2222,1001,'13-FEB-95','20-FEB-95'));
```

However, Oracle8 allows the object tables to be viewed as relational tables and allows both types of insert statements (with and without invoking the object constructor). This feature makes it easy to migrate from the purely relational approach to the object-relational approach.

2.9.8 Querying and Accessing Data

Querying object-relational tables is accomplished using the SQL `select` statement. To access the nested attributes, the dot notation is used. For example, consider the following query:

```
-- Get the names and street addresses for employees
-- hired after 01-JAN-93
select e.person.name, e.person.address.street
from   o_employees e
where  e.hdate > '01-JAN-93';
```

Here, the query refers to the innermost basic attributes in the complex object structure using the dot notation. The expression

```
e.person.address.street
```

refers to the `street` attribute defined within the `address` attribute which is defined within the `person attribute` of the `o_employees` table. Notice the use of table aliases in this query. Table aliases are required when table definitions are based on object types.

The next query performs a join of the two tables `o_employees` and `o_customers` based on the `zip` attribute which lies deep in the object structure.

```
-- Get the names of employees and customers who
-- live in the same zip code
select e.person.name EMPLOYEE, c.person.name CUSTOMER
from   o_employees e, o_customers c
where  e.person.address.zip = c.person.address.zip;
```

Querying Collection Objects

It is not possible to query a varying array in SQL; however, one can access the varying array in PL/SQL using procedural notation. This will be covered in Section 4.11. However, querying nested tables is possible with the SQL **select** statement. Consider the query: **Get pno and qty values for parts ordered in order with ono = 1020 with qty > 1**. Our first attempt might be to write something like this:

```
select nt.pno, nt.qty
from   (select o.odetails   -- WRONG!!
        from   o_orders o
        where  o.ono = 1020)
where  nt.qty > 1;
```

The conceptual problem with this is that the result of any select operation on a table is a table. Hence, the result of the nested select above is a table within a table! For logical consistency, Oracle provides the THE operator which essentially *flattens* the nested table. It is also necessary to give an alias to the flattened table a name so that it can be referenced in the outer select statement. So, the correct SQL query is:

```
select nt.pno, nt.qty
from   THE(select o.odetails
           from   o_orders o
           where  o.ono = 1020) nt
where  nt.qty > 1;
```

This query accesses the nested table column **odetails** in the **o_orders** table. The nested table can be placed in the **from clause** of the SQL **select** query provided it appears in the select-list of a nested **select** statement and the nested **select** statement is enclosed as an argument to the special THE operator which *flattens* the nested table. Notice the use of the **where** clause both in the nested table and in the main table implying that it is possible to restrict rows within the nested table object as well as within the main table in the same query. The aliasing of the tables in the query is also required.

Another point to note with respect to the above query is that it is incorrect to specify a nested select statement which may result in more than one nested table such as the following variant of the above query:

```
select nt.pno, nt.qty
from   THE(select o.odetails    -- WRONG!!
           from   o_orders o
           where  o.ono > 1020) nt
where  nt.qty > 1;
```

Here, the nested **select** may result in more than one nested table, hence an error message will be generated.

The next query invokes the user-defined method, **cost**, to compute the line item cost of each item in a particular order.

```
-- Get pno, qty, and line item cost values for parts
-- ordered in order number 1020 with qty > 1
select nt.pno, nt.qty, nt.cost()
from   THE(select o.odetails
           from   o_orders o
           where  o.ono = 1020) nt
where  nt.qty > 1;
```

To obtain the total cost for a particular order, the following query sums the line item costs.

```
-- Get the total cost of items in order number 1020
select sum(nt.cost())
from THE(select o.odetails
         from   o_orders o
         where  o.ono = 1020) nt;
```

The previous query can also be solved by invoking the method called **total_cost** on the row objects of the o_orders table as follows:

```
-- Get the total cost of items in order number 1020
select o.total_cost()
from   o_orders o
where  o.ono = 1020;
```

The THE operator can also be used to perform inserts into a nested table directly. For example, the following statement inserts a new line item in the nested table for the order number 1020.

```
insert into THE(select o.odetails
                from   o_orders o
                where ono = 1020)
values  (10800,5);
```

Updates and Deletes

Updates and deletes to object-relational tables are done in a similar manner to purely relational tables using the **update** and **delete** statements. Attributes are accessed in a similar manner as in the queries.

The following **update** statement changes the street address for a particular customer:

```
update o_customers c
set    c.person.address.street = '111 New Street'
where  c.cno = 1111;
```

and the following **delete** statement deletes a particular customer row:

```
delete from o_customers c
where  c.person.address.street like '111%';
```

Exercises

2.1 To get interesting answers to queries in subsequent exercises, populate the mail-order database, using SQL **insert** statements, with at least 30 customers, 10 employees, 5 zip codes, and 50 parts. Also insert around 100 orders (an average of about 3 per customer), with each order containing an average of 2 parts.

2.2 Populate the grade book database, using SQL **insert** statements, with at least 50 rows in the **students** table, 10 rows in the **catalog** table, 12 rows in the **courses** table, 40 rows in the **components** table (resulting in an average of between 3 and 4 components per course), 120 rows in the **enrolls** table (resulting in an average of about 10 students in each course), and the appropriate number of rows in the **scores** table to complete the database.

2.3 Consider the following relations of the mail-order database:

```
EMPLOYEES(ENO,ENAME,ZIP,HDATE)
PARTS(PNO,PNAME,QOH,PRICE,LEVEL)
CUSTOMERS(CNO,CNAME,STREET,ZIP,PHONE)
ORDERS(ONO,CNO,ENO,RECEIVED,SHIPPED)
```

```
ODETAILS(ONO,PNO,QTY)
ZIPCODES(ZIP,CITY)
```

Write SQL expressions that answer the following queries:

(a) Get the names of parts that cost less than `20.00`.

(b) Get the names and cities of employees who have taken orders for parts costing more than `50.00`.

(c) Get the pairs of customer number values of customers having the same zip code.

(d) Get the names of customers who have ordered parts from employees living in `Wichita`.

(e) Get the names of customers who have ordered parts ONLY from employees living in `Wichita`.

(f) Get the names of customers who have ordered ALL parts costing less than `20.00`.

(g) Get the names of employees along with their total sales for the year `1995`.

(h) Get the numbers and names of employees who have never made a sale to a customer living in the same zip code as the employee.

(i) Get the names of customers who have placed the highest number of orders.

(j) Get the names of customers who have placed the most expensive orders.

(k) Get the names of parts that have been ordered the most (in terms of quantity ordered, not number of orders).

(l) Get the names of parts along with the number of orders they appear in, sorted in decreasing order of the number of orders.

(m) Get the average waiting time for all orders in number of days. The waiting time for an order is defined as the difference between the shipped date and the received date. *Note:* The dates should be truncated to `12:00 AM` so that the difference is always a whole number of days.

(n) Get the names of customers who had to wait the longest for their orders to be shipped.

(o) For all orders greater than `100.00`, get the order number and the waiting time for the order.

2.4 Consider the following relations of the grade book database:

```
CATALOG(CNO,CTITLE)
STUDENTS(SID,FNAME,LNAME,MINIT)
COURSES(TERM,LINENO,CNO,A,B,C,D)
COMPONENTS(TERM,LINENO,COMPNAME,MAXPOINTS,WEIGHT)
```

```
ENROLLS(SID,TERM,LINENO)
SCORES(SID,TERM,LINENO,COMPNAME,POINTS)
```

Write SQL expressions that answer the following queries:

(a) Get the names of students enrolled in the `Automata` class in the `f96` term.

(b) Get the course numbers and titles of courses in which `Timothy Thomas` has enrolled.

(c) Get the `SID` values of students who did not enroll in any class during the `f96` term.

(d) Get the `SID` values of students who have enrolled in `csc226` and `csc227`.

(e) Get the `SID` values of students who have enrolled in `csc226` or `csc227`.

(f) Get the `SID` values of students who have enrolled in ALL the courses in the catalog.

(g) Get the names of students who have enrolled in the highest number of courses.

(h) Get the names of students who have enrolled in the lowest number of courses (the student must have enrolled in at least one course).

(i) Get the names of students who have not enrolled in any course.

(j) Get the titles of courses that have had enrollments of five or fewer students.

(k) Get the terms, line numbers, course numbers, and course titles of courses along with their total enrollments.

(l) Get the terms, line numbers, and course titles of courses with the highest enrollments.

(m) Get the terms, line numbers, and course titles of courses that have enrollments greater than or equal to the average enrollment in all courses.

(n) Get the student IDs of students, the terms and line numbers of courses they have enrolled in, the component names of the courses, the student scores in the components of the courses, and the weighted average of the component scores.

(o) Given a term and line number of a course (for example, `w98` and `1585`), get the student IDs, last names, and first names of students enrolled in the class along with each student's course average rounded off to the nearest integer. The course average is the sum of the weighted averages of the individual component scores.

2.5 Consider the following relations of the investment portfolio database.

```
MEMBER(MID,PASSWORD,FNAME,LNAME,ADDRESS,EMAIL,CASH_BALANCE)
SECURITY(SYMBOL,CNAME,CURRENT_PRICE,ASK_PRICE,BID_PRICE)
TRANSACTION(MID,SYMBOL,TRANS_DATE,TRANS_TYPE,QUANTITY,
            PRICE_PER_SHARE,COMMISSION,AMOUNT)
```

(a) Get company names of securities whose current price is greater than 100.00.
(b) Get names of members who have purchased `ORCL` shares.
(c) Get names of members who have purchased `ORCL` shares but NOT `SYBS` shares.
(d) Get names of members who purchase ONLY `ORCL` shares.
(e) Get company names of securities whose shares are purchased by ALL members.
(f) Get the names of members who have purchased shares from ALL of the companies that the member with `mid = 11000` has purchased shares from.
(g) Get the names of members who have purchased shares ONLY from a subset of the companies that the member with `mid = 11000` has purchased shares from.
(h) Get the names of members who have purchased shares from EXACTLY the same companies that the member with `mid = 11000` has purchased shares from.

2.6 For the mail-order database, write SQL expressions to perform the following updates to the database:

(a) Decrease by 15 percent the prices of all parts that cost less than `20.00`.
(b) Update all the `null`-valued shipped dates of orders to the current date.
(c) Decrease by `10.00` the prices of parts that cost more than the average price of all parts.
(d) Transfer all the orders belonging to the employee with `eno = 1000` to the employee with `eno = 1001`.
(e) Delete all the orders for customers living in `Wichita`.
(f) Delete all the orders for employees with the minimum sales.

2.7 For the grade book database write SQL expressions to perform the following updates to the database:

(a) Update all the `null`-valued scores to zeros.
(b) Delete the component `QUIZ2` from the `components` table.
(c) Drop the student with `sid = 1234` from the `f97` course with `lineno = 1111`.
(d) Enroll all students in the `f97` course with `lineno = 1111` into the `f97` course with `lineno = 1112`.
(e) Give all students in the `f97` course with `lineno = 1111` 10 extra points in the `EXAM1` component.
(f) Delete all the courses from the `courses` table that have enrollments of fewer than five students.

2.8 For the investment portfolio database write SQL expressions to perform the following updates to the database:

(a) Delete the member with `mid = 11000` from the database. Make sure that all the transactions for this member are archived in a back up table with the same structure as the `transaction` table. These transactions then must be deleted from the `transaction` table.

(b) Insert a *buy* transaction for the member with `mid = 10000` for `100` shares of `ORCL` at the present bid price. Assume a commission of 1 percent and that the transaction takes place at the same time as the insert. The member's cash balance should be updated appropriately.

(c) Insert a *sell* transaction for the member with `mid = 10000` for `250` shares of `SYBS` at the present ask price. Assume a commission of 1 percent and that the transaction takes place at the same time as the insert. The member's cash balance should be updated appropriately.

(d) Make necessary updates to reflect a stock split of `2:1` for `ORCL`. The stock split implies the doubling of the number of shares currently owned by each member and halving the current price of the security. The ask and bid prices should be reset to `null`.

(e) Make necessary updates to the database to reflect the merger of two companies: Mindspring Enterprises Inc. (symbol: `MSPG`) and EarthLink Network Inc. (symbol: `ELNK`). The merger agreement indicates that the new company will trade under the `ELNK` symbol and be called `EarthSpring Enterprises Inc.` Also, each shareholder of `MSPG` will receive one share of the new company's for each `MSPG` share they own and each shareholder of `ELNK` will receive 1.5 shares for each `ELNK` share they own. The current price for the new company should be the current price of `MSPG`. The ask and bid prices should be set to `null`.

CHAPTER

3

Embedded SQL

Oracle SQL, introduced in the previous chapter, is not a language that can be used to build sophisticated database applications, but it is a very good language for defining the structure of the database and generating ad hoc queries. However, to build applications, the power of a full-fledged high-level programming language is needed. Embedded SQL provides such an environment to develop application programs. The basic idea behind embedded SQL is to allow SQL statements in a program written in a high-level programming language such as C or C++. By embedding SQL statements in a C/C++ program, one can now write application programs in C/C++ that interact (read and write) with the database. Oracle provides a tool, called Pro*C/C++, which allows for applications to be developed in the C or C++ language with embedded SQL statements. The Pro*C/C++ preprocessor parses the embedded program and converts all SQL statements to system calls in C/C++ and produces a C/C++ program as its output. This C/C++ program can be compiled in the usual manner to produce the executable version of the application program. This chapter introduces concepts and techniques needed to write successful embedded SQL programs in Oracle using the C or C++ language. Most of the concepts are introduced using the C language. A separate section is devoted to C++ programs.

3.1 Host Variables

Since SQL statements are to be embedded within the C program, there is a need for a mechanism to pass values between the C program environment and the SQL statements that communicate with the Oracle database server. Special variables, called *host variables*, are defined in the embedded program for this purpose. These host variables are defined between the **begin declare section** and **end declare section** directives of the preprocessor as follows:

```
EXEC SQL begin declare section;
  int     cno;
  varchar cname[31];
  varchar street[31];
  int     zip;
  char    phone[13];
EXEC SQL end declare section;
```

The data types of the host variables must be compatible with the data types of the columns of the tables in the database. Figure 3.1 shows data types in C that are compatible with commonly used data types in Oracle. The **char** data type in Oracle is mapped to the **char** data type in C. The **char(N)** data type in Oracle is mapped to an array of characters in C. Notice that the size of the C array is one more than the size of the character string in Oracle. This is due to the fact that C character strings require an additional character to store the end-of-string character (\0). Oracle's Pro*C preprocessor provides a **varchar** array data type in C that corresponds to the **varchar(N)** Oracle data type. Again, the size of the C **varchar** array is one more than the maximum size of the **varchar** string of Oracle. The **varchar** array in C is declared as

```
varchar cname[31];
```

and the Pro*C preprocessor produces the following C code corresponding to the above declaration:

```
/* varchar cname[31]; */
struct {
  unsigned short len;
  unsigned char arr[31];
} cname;
```

Note that the **varchar** array variable **cname** has been transformed into a structure (with the same name) containing two fields: **arr** and **len**. The **arr** field will store the actual string and the **len** field will store the length of the character string. When sending a **varchar** value to the database, it is the responsibility of the programmer to make sure that both fields, **arr** and **len**, are assigned proper values. When receiving such a value from the database, both fields are assigned appropriate values by the system. The **date** data type is mapped to a fixed-length (10 characters, corresponding to the default **date** format in Oracle) character string in C. The

Figure 3.1 Compatible Oracle and C data types.

Oracle Data Type	C Data Type
`char`	`char`
`char(N)`	`char array[N+1]`
`varchar(N)`	`varchar array[N+1]`
`date`	`char array[10]`
`number(6)`	`int`
`number(10)`	`long int`
`number(6,2)`	`float`

numeric data types are appropriately mapped to **`small int`**, **`int`**, **`long int`**, **`float`**, or **`double`**, depending on their precisions in Oracle.

The host variables are used in the usual manner within C language constructs; however, when they are used in the embedded SQL statements, they must be preceded by a colon (`:`). Some examples of their usage are shown in the following code fragment.

```
scanf("%d",&cno);
EXEC SQL select cname
         into   :cname
         from   customers
         where  cno = :cno;

scanf("%d%s%s%d%s",&cno,cname.arr,street.arr,&zip,phone);
cname.len  = strlen(cname.arr);
street.len = strlen(street.arr);
EXEC SQL insert into customers
         values (:cno,:cname,:street,:zip,:phone);
```

The select statement in the above example has an additional clause, the **`into`** clause, which is required in embedded SQL since the results of the SQL statements must be stored someplace. The **`select into`** statement can be used only if it is guaranteed that the query returns exactly one or zero rows. A different technique is used to process queries that return more than one row. This technique, which uses the concept of a *cursor*, is discussed in Section 3.5. Note that all occurrences of the host variables within the embedded SQL statements are preceded by a colon. Also, the **`len`** fields of all **`varchar`** arrays in C are set to the correct lengths before sending the host variables to the database.

3.2 Indicator Variables

A `null` value in the database does not have a counterpart in the C language environment. To solve the problem of communicating `null` values between the C program and Oracle, embedded SQL provides *indicator variables*, which are special integer variables used to indicate if a `null` value is retrieved from the database or stored in the database. Consider the **orders** table of the mail-order database. The following is the declaration of the relevant host and indicator variables to access the **orders** table.

```
EXEC SQL begin declare section;
struct {
    int     ono;
    int     cno;
    int     eno;
    char    received[12];
    char    shipped[12];
  } order_rec;
  struct {
    short     ono_ind;
    short     cno_ind;
    short     eno_ind;
    short     received_ind;
    short     shipped_ind;
  } order_rec_ind;
  int  onum;
EXEC SQL end declare section;
```

The code below reads the details of a particular row from the **orders** table into the host variables declared above and checks to see whether the **shipped** column value is `null`. A `null` value is indicated by a value of -1 for the indicator variable. The database server returns a value of 0 for the indicator variable if the column value retrieved is not `null`.[1]

```
scanf("%d",&onum);
EXEC SQL select *
         into   :order_rec indicator :order_rec_ind
```

1. The indicator variable is also used for other purposes—for example, it is used to indicate the length of a string value that was retrieved from the database and that was truncated to fit the host variable into which it was retrieved.

```
          from   orders
          where  ono = :onum;
if (order_rec_ind.shipped_ind == -1)
  printf("SHIPPED is Null\n");
else
  printf("SHIPPED is not Null\n");
```

To store a **null** value into the database, a value of -1 should be assigned to the indicator variable and the indicator variable should be used in an update or insert statement. For example, the following code sets the **shipped** value for the order with order number **1021** to **null**.

```
onum = 1021;
order_rec_ind.shipped_ind  = -1;
EXEC SQL update orders
         set shipped = :order_rec.shipped indicator
                       :order_rec_ind.shipped_ind
         where ono = :onum;
```

Notice that the **order_rec.shipped** value is undefined, because it will be ignored by the database server.

3.3 SQL Communications Area (sqlca)

Immediately after the Oracle database server executes an embedded SQL statement, it reports the status of the execution in a variable called **sqlca**, the SQL communications area. This variable is a structure with several fields, the most commonly used one being **sqlcode**. Typical values returned in this field are shown below.

sqlca.sqlcode	Interpretation
0	SQL statement executed successfully
> 0	No more data present or values not found
< 0	Error occurred while executing SQL statement

To include the **sqlca** definition, the following statement must appear early in the program:

```
EXEC SQL include sqlca;
```

Here are two code fragments that illustrate the use of **sqlca.sqlcode**.

Error check: Consider the following code fragment, which attempts to add a new row into the **customers** table.

```
EXEC SQL set transaction read write;
EXEC SQL insert into customers values
         (custseq.nextval,:customer_rec.cname,
          :customer_rec.street,:customer_rec.zip,
          :customer_rec.phone);
if (sqlca.sqlcode < 0) {
  printf("\n\nCUSTOMER (%s) DID NOT GET ADDED\n",
         customer_rec.cname.arr);
  EXEC SQL rollback work;
  return;
}
EXEC SQL commit;
```

After starting a transaction to read and write to the database,[2] this program fragment attempts to insert a new row into the `customers` table using the `EXEC SQL insert into` statement. There could be several reasons why this statement may not execute successfully, among them primary key constraint violation, data type mismatches, and wrong number of columns in the insert statement. The value of `sqlca.sqlcode` is checked to see if it is less than 0. If an error is indicated, a message is sent to the user and the transaction is rolled back. Otherwise, the transaction is committed and the row is successfully inserted.

`Not found` check: Consider the following code fragment:

```
EXEC SQL select zip, city
         into   :zipcode_rec
         from   zipcodes
         where  zip = :customer_rec.zip;
if (sqlca.sqlcode > 0) {
  zipcode_rec.zip = customer_rec.zip;
  printf("Zip Code does not exist; Enter City: ");
  scanf("%s",zipcode_rec.city.arr);
  zipcode_rec.city.len = strlen(zipcode_rec.city.arr);
  EXEC SQL set transaction read write;
  EXEC SQL insert into zipcodes (zip, city)
           values (:zipcode_rec);
  EXEC SQL commit;
}
```

2. Transactions will be covered in Section 3.9.

In this code fragment, a particular zip code value is checked to see if it is already present in the **zipcodes** table using the **EXEC SQL select into** statement. If the zip code (indicated by the host variable **:customer_rec.zip**) is not found in the **zipcodes** table, Oracle returns a positive integer in **sqlca.sqlcode**. This is checked for in the program fragment, and the user is prompted for the **City** value for this zip code and a new row is added to the **zipcodes** table.

3.4 Connecting to Oracle

The SQL **connect** statement is used to establish a connection with Oracle. Such a connection must be established before any embedded SQL statements can be executed. The following code fragment illustrates the use of the **connect** statement. The fragment, when executed, will prompt the user for the Oracle user name and password. If the connection is not established in three tries, the program exits.

```
EXEC SQL begin declare section;
  varchar userid[10], password[15];
EXEC SQL end declare section;
int     loginok=FALSE,logintries=0;

do {
  printf("Enter your USERID: ");
  scanf("%s", userid.arr);
  userid.len = strlen(userid.arr);
  printf("Enter your PASSWORD: ");
  system("stty -echo");
  scanf("%s", password.arr);
  password.len = strlen(password.arr);
  system("stty echo");
  printf("\n");
  EXEC SQL connect :userid identified by :password;
  if (sqlca.sqlcode == 0)
    loginok = TRUE;
  else
    printf("Connect Failed\n");
  logintries++;
} while ((!loginok) && (logintries <3));
if ((logintries == 3) && (!loginok)) {
```

```
    printf("Too many tries at signing on!\n");
    exit(0);
  }
```

The `userid` and `password` values cannot be provided as literal strings in the `connect` statement. They must be provided in host variables, as is shown in the above program fragment. Here, these variables are assigned values entered by the user; however, if the values were already known, these variables could be initialized as follows:

```
strcpy(userid.arr,"UUUU");
userid.len = strlen(userid.arr);
strcpy(password.arr,"PPPP");
password.len = strlen(password.arr);
```

where `UUUU` is the user name and `PPPP` is the associated password.

To disconnect from the database, which should be done at the end of the program, the following statement is used:

```
EXEC SQL commit release;
```

This commits any changes that were made to the database and releases any locks that were placed during the course of the execution of the program.

3.5 Cursors

When an embedded SQL select statement returns more than one row in its result, the simple form of the `select into` statement cannot be used anymore. To process such queries in embedded SQL, the concept of a *cursor*—a mechanism that allows the C program to access the rows of a query one at a time—is introduced. The cursor declaration associates a cursor variable with an SQL select statement. To start processing the query, the cursor must first be *opened*. It is at this time that the query is evaluated. It is important to note this fact, since the query may contain host variables that could change while the program is executing. Also, the database tables may be changing (other users are possibly updating the tables) while the program is executing. Once the cursor is opened, the `fetch` statement can be used several times to retrieve the rows of the query result, one at a time. Once the query results are all retrieved, the cursor should be `closed`.

The syntax for cursor declaration is

```
EXEC SQL declare ⟨cur-name⟩ cursor for
  ⟨select-statement⟩
  [for {read only | update [of ⟨column-list⟩]}];
```

where ⟨*cur-name*⟩ is the name of the cursor and ⟨*select-statement*⟩ is any SQL select statement associated with the cursor. The select statement, which may involve host variables, is followed by one of the following two optional clauses:

```
for read only
```

or

```
for update [of ⟨column-list⟩]
```

The `for update` clause is used in cases of *positioned* deletes or updates, discussed later in this section. The `for read only` clause is used to prohibit deletes or updates based on the cursor. If the optional `for` clause is left out, the default is `for read only`.

A cursor is opened using the following syntax:

```
EXEC SQL open ⟨cur-name⟩;
```

When the `open` statement is executed, the query associated with the cursor is evaluated, and an imaginary pointer points to the position before the first row of the query result. Any subsequent changes to the host variables used in the cursor declaration or changes to the database tables will not affect the current cursor contents.

The syntax for the `fetch` statement is

```
EXEC SQL fetch ⟨cur-name⟩ into
         ⟨host-var⟩, ..., ⟨host-var⟩;
```

where ⟨*host-var*⟩ is a host variable possibly including an indicator variable.

The syntax of the `close` cursor statement is

```
EXEC SQL close ⟨cur-name⟩;
```

The following procedure illustrates the use of a cursor to print all the rows in the `customers` table.

```
void print_customers() {
EXEC SQL declare customer_cur cursor for
         select cno, cname, street, zip, phone
         from   customers;
```

```
EXEC SQL set transaction read only;
EXEC SQL open customer_cur;
EXEC SQL fetch customer_cur into
        :customer_rec indicator :customer_rec_ind;
while (sqlca.sqlcode == 0) {
 customer_rec.cname.arr[customer_rec.cname.len] = '\0';
 customer_rec.street.arr[customer_rec.street.len] = '\0';
 printf("%6d  %10s  %20s  %6d  %15s\n",
        customer_rec.cno,customer_rec.cname.arr,
        customer_rec.street.arr,customer_rec.zip,
        customer_rec.phone);
EXEC SQL fetch customer_cur into
        :customer_rec indicator :customer_rec_ind;
}
EXEC SQL close customer_cur;
EXEC SQL commit;
}
```

Positioned Deletes and Updates

Cursors can also be used with the **delete** and **update** statements, which are referred to as positioned deletes or updates. When cursors are used for positioned deletes or updates, they must have exactly one table (the table from which the rows are to be deleted or updated) in the **from** clause of the main select statement defining the cursor. When used in this manner, the cursor declaration will have a **for update** clause, which is optionally followed by a list of columns. If such a list is provided, then only those columns that are listed there can be updated using the **update** statement. To do a positioned delete, the **for update** clause should not be followed by any list of columns. The following example illustrates a positioned delete.

```
EXEC SQL declare del_cur cursor for
    select *
    from   employees
    where  not exists
             (select 'a'
              from   orders
              where  orders.eno = employees.eno)
    for update;

  EXEC SQL set transaction read write;
  EXEC SQL open del_cur;
```

```
EXEC SQL fetch del_cur into :employee_rec;
while (sqlca.sqlcode == 0) {
  EXEC SQL delete from employees
           where current of del_cur;
  EXEC SQL fetch del_cur into :employee_rec;
}
EXEC SQL commit release;
```

This program fragment deletes all employees who do not have any orders. The cursor is defined using the `for update` clause and involves only the `employees` table in its `from` clause. Positioned updates are done in a similar manner.

3.6 Mail-Order Database Application

An application program, written and compiled using Oracle's Pro*C, is presented in this section. This program allows the user to interact with the mail-order database and provides the following functionality:

- *Add customer:* The user is prompted for the name, street address, phone, and zip code for the new customer. The customer number is generated internally using the sequence `custseq`. To maintain the referential integrity constraint (zip must also exist in the `zipcodes` table), the zip code is checked against the `zipcodes` table. If not present, the user is prompted for the city corresponding to the zip code and an entry is made in the `zipcodes` table before the new customer is added. The `insert` statement is used in this function.
- *Print customers:* This function simply prints all the customers present in the database. A simple cursor is used to accomplish this task.
- *Update customer:* The user is given the opportunity to update the street address, zip code, and phone number for a given customer. If the user updates the zip code, a similar check as in the *Add Customer* function is made to maintain the referential integrity constraint. The `update` statement is used to make the update in the database.
- *Process order:* The function keeps prompting for a valid employee number until it receives one from the user. If the customer is new, the *Add Customer* function is invoked; otherwise the customer number is requested from the user. An order number is then generated internally, using the sequence `orderseq`, and the parts and quantities are requested from the user. Finally, one row corresponding to this order is made in the `orders` table and several entries that correspond to this

order are made in the **odetails** table. Notice how carefully this function was designed so that none of the primary and foreign key constraints are violated.

- *Remove customer:* Given a customer number, this function tries to remove the customer from the database. If **orders** exists for this customer, the customer is not removed. One possibility that existed in this case was to cascade this delete, by deleting all the rows in the **orders** table and the **odetails** table that correspond to this customer, and then to delete the customer. This cascading of deletes could be done by providing explicit **delete** statements in the program; it could also be done automatically by providing the **cascade delete** property when the foreign keys were defined. However, this option was not chosen here.
- *Delete old orders:* All orders having a shipped date that is five or more years before the current date are deleted. The corresponding rows in the **odetails** table are also deleted to maintain the referential integrity.
- *Print invoice:* Given an order number, this function prints the invoice for this order, which includes the customer details, employee details, and parts in the order, including their quantities and total price. This is a typical reporting function that uses cursors to get the information from several tables.

To compile this or any other embedded SQL program for Oracle under UNIX, use the following command, where **prog.pc** is the name of the file containing the embedded SQL program.

```
make -f proc.mk EXE=prog OBJS="prog.o" build
```

The file **proc.mk** comes with the Oracle distribution and can be found under the **ORACLE_HOME** directory.

The main program is included here.

```
#include <stdio.h>
#include <string.h>
#define TRUE 1
#define FALSE 0

typedef struct {
  int cno; varchar cname[31]; varchar street[31];
  int zip; char phone[13];
} customer_record;
typedef struct {
  short cno_ind,cname_ind,street_ind,zip_ind,phone_ind;
} customer_indicator_record;
```

```
typedef struct {
  int zip; varchar city[31];
} zipcode_record;
typedef struct {
  int eno; varchar ename[31]; int zip; char hdate[12];
} employee_record;
typedef struct {
  short eno_ind,ename_ind,zip_ind,hdate_ind;
} employee_indicator_record;
typedef struct {
  int ono,cno,eno; char received[12],shipped[12];
} order_record;
typedef struct {
  short ono_ind,cno_ind,eno_ind,received_ind,shipped_ind;
} order_indicator_record;

EXEC SQL include sqlca;

void print_menu();
void add_customer();
void print_customers();
void update_customer();
void process_order();
void remove_customer();
void delete_old_orders();
void print_invoice();
void prompt(char [],char []);

void main() {
  EXEC SQL begin declare section;
    varchar userid[10], password[15];
  EXEC SQL end declare section;
  char ch;
  int  done=FALSE,loginok=FALSE,logintries=0;

  do {
    prompt("Enter your USERID: ",userid.arr);
    userid.len = strlen(userid.arr);
    printf("Enter your PASSWORD: ");
```

```
    system("stty -echo");
    scanf("%s", password.arr);getchar();
    password.len = strlen(password.arr);
    system("stty echo");
    printf("\n");
    EXEC SQL connect :userid identified by :password;
    if (sqlca.sqlcode == 0)
      loginok = TRUE;
    else
      printf("Connect Failed\n");
    logintries++;
  } while ((!loginok) && (logintries <3));
  if ((logintries == 3) && (!loginok)) {
    printf("Too many tries at signing on!\n");
    exit(0);
  }

  while (done == FALSE) {
    print_menu();
    printf("Type in your option: ");
    scanf("%s",&ch); getchar();
    switch (ch) {
      case '1': add_customer(); printf("\n"); break;
      case '2': print_customers(); printf("\n"); break;
      case '3': update_customer(); printf("\n"); break;
      case '4': process_order(); printf("\n"); break;
      case '5': remove_customer(); printf("\n"); break;
      case '6': delete_old_orders(); printf("\n"); break;
      case '7': print_invoice();
                printf("\nPress RETURN to continue");
                getchar(); printf("\n"); break;
      case 'q': case 'Q': done = TRUE; break;
      default:  printf("Type in option again\n"); break;
    }
  };
  EXEC SQL commit release;
  exit(0);
}
void print_menu() {
```

```
    printf("****************************************\n");
    printf("<1> Add a new customer\n");
    printf("<2> Print all customers\n");
    printf("<3> Update customer information\n");
    printf("<4> Process a new order\n");
    printf("<5> Remove a customer\n");
    printf("<6> Delete old orders \n");
    printf("<7> Print invoice for a given order\n");
    printf("<q> Quit\n");
    printf("****************************************\n");
  }
  void prompt(char s[], char t[]) {
    char c;
    int i = 0;

    printf("%s",s);
    while ((c = getchar()) != '\n') {
      t[i] = c;
      i++;
    }
    t[i] = '\0';
  }
```

After declaring the various record structures and indicator record structures for database access, including the `sqlca` structure, and declaring the function prototypes, the `main` function is defined. The `main` function first connects to the database and then presents a menu of choices for the user to select from. It then processes the user option by calling the appropriate function. The `prompt` function is a utility function that displays a prompt and reads a string variable. It is used throughout the application program.

3.6.1 Customer Functions

The customer-related functions are presented here. These functions allow the user to add a new customer, update the information for an existing customer, and delete an existing customer from the database. The function to print the list of customers was presented in Section 3.5.

The following is the `add_customer` function.

```
void add_customer() {
  EXEC SQL begin declare section;
    customer_record crec;
    zipcode_record  zrec;
  EXEC SQL end declare section;

  prompt("Customer Name: ",crec.cname.arr);
  crec.cname.len = strlen(crec.cname.arr);
  prompt("Street        : ",crec.street.arr);
  crec.street.len = strlen(crec.street.arr);
  printf("Zip Code      : ");
  scanf("%d",&crec.zip); getchar();
  prompt("Phone Number : ",crec.phone);

  EXEC SQL select zip, city
           into   :zrec
           from   zipcodes
           where  zip = :crec.zip;
  if (sqlca.sqlcode > 0) {
     zrec.zip = crec.zip;
     prompt("Zip not present; Enter City: ",zrec.city.arr);
     zrec.city.len = strlen(zrec.city.arr);
     EXEC SQL set transaction read write;
     EXEC SQL insert into zipcodes (zip, city)
              values (:zrec);
     EXEC SQL commit;
  }

  EXEC SQL set transaction read write;
  EXEC SQL insert into customers values
    (custseq.nextval,:crec.cname,:crec.street,
     :crec.zip,:crec.phone);
  if (sqlca.sqlcode < 0) {
    printf("\n\nCUSTOMER (%s) DID NOT GET ADDED\n",
           crec.cname.arr);
    EXEC SQL rollback work;
    return;
  }
  EXEC SQL commit;
}
```

This function requests information for a new customer and inserts the customer into the database. If the zip code value is not present in the database, this function also requests the city information and makes an entry into the **zipcodes** table.

The **update_customer** function is shown below:

```
void update_customer() {
  EXEC SQL begin declare section;
    customer_record crec;
    zipcode_record zrec;
    int cnum;
    varchar st[31];
    char ph[13], zzip[6];
  EXEC SQL end declare section;

  printf("Customer Number to be Updated: ");
  scanf("%d",&cnum);getchar();

  EXEC SQL select *
           into   :crec
           from   customers
           where  cno = :cnum;
  if (sqlca.sqlcode > 0) {
    printf("Customer (%d) does not exist\n",cnum);
    return;
  }
  crec.street.arr[crec.street.len] = '\0';
  printf("Current Street Value           : %s\n",crec.street.arr);
  prompt("New Street (n<ENTER> for same): ",st.arr);
  if (strlen(st.arr) > 1) {
    strcpy(crec.street.arr,st.arr);
    crec.street.len = strlen(crec.street.arr);
  }
  printf("Current ZIP Value      : %d\n",crec.zip);
  prompt("New ZIP (n<ENTER> for same): ",zzip);
  if (strlen(zzip) > 1) {
    crec.zip = atoi(zzip);
    EXEC SQL select zip, city
             into   :zrec
             from   zipcodes
             where  zip = :crec.zip;
```

```
      if (sqlca.sqlcode > 0) {
        zrec.zip = crec.zip;
        prompt("Zip not present; Enter City: ",zrec.city.arr);
        zrec.city.len = strlen(zrec.city.arr);
        EXEC SQL set transaction read write;
        EXEC SQL insert into zipcodes (zip, city)
           values (:zrec);
        EXEC SQL commit;
      }
    }
    printf("Current Phone Value: %s\n",crec.phone);
    prompt("New Phone (n<ENTER> for same): ",ph);
    if (strlen(ph) > 1) {
      strcpy(crec.phone,ph);
    }

    EXEC SQL set transaction read write;
    EXEC SQL update customers
             set street = :crec.street,
                 zip    = :crec.zip,
                 phone  = :crec.phone
             where cno = :crec.cno;
    if (sqlca.sqlcode < 0) {
       printf("\n\nError on Update\n");
       EXEC SQL rollback work;
       return;
    }
    EXEC SQL commit;
    printf("\nCustomer (%d) updated.\n",crec.cno);
  }
```

This function first prompts the user for the customer number. After checking if the customer exists in the database, it displays the street address, zip, and phone, and it then prompts the user for new values. The user may enter `n` followed by the `enter` key if no change is needed for a particular value. If a new zip value is entered, the city value is prompted in case the new zip is not present in the database, to ensure the integrity of the database. Finally, an update is made to the customer row in the `customers` table.

The `remove_customer` function is presented below:

```
void remove_customer() {
  EXEC SQL begin declare section;
    customer_record crec;
    int cnum,onum;
  EXEC SQL end declare section;

  printf("Customer Number to be deleted: ");
  scanf("%d",&cnum); getchar();

  EXEC SQL select *
           into :crec
           from customers
           where cno = :cnum;
  if (sqlca.sqlcode > 0) {
    printf("Customer (%d) does not exist\n",cnum);
    return;
  }

  EXEC SQL declare del_cur cursor for
      select ono from orders where cno = :cnum;

  EXEC SQL set transaction read only;
  EXEC SQL open del_cur;
  EXEC SQL fetch del_cur into :onum;
  if (sqlca.sqlcode == 0) {
      printf("Orders exist - cannot delete\n");
      EXEC SQL commit;
      return;
  }
  EXEC SQL commit;

  EXEC SQL set transaction read write;
  EXEC SQL delete from customers
           where cno = :cnum;
  printf("\nCustomer (%d) DELETED\n",cnum);
  EXEC SQL commit;
}
```

This function first prompts for the customer number. After checking to see if the customer exists in the database, it checks to see if any orders exist for this customer.

If orders exist, the delete is aborted; otherwise the customer is deleted from the database.

3.6.2 Process Orders

The `process_order` function is shown below:

```
void process_order() {
  EXEC SQL begin declare section;
    customer_record crec;
    int eenum,cnum,pnum,qqty,ord_lev,qqoh;
  EXEC SQL end declare section;
  FILE *f1; char ch; int nparts;

  EXEC SQL set transaction read only;
  do {
    printf("Employee Number: ");
    scanf("%d",&eenum); getchar();
    EXEC SQL select eno
             into   :eenum
             from   employees
             where  eno = :eenum;
    if (sqlca.sqlcode > 0)
      printf("Employee (%d) does not exist\n",eenum);
  } while (sqlca.sqlcode!=0);
  EXEC SQL commit;

  do {
    printf("New Customer (y or n)? ");
    scanf("%s",&ch); getchar();
  } while ((ch != 'y') && (ch != 'Y') &&
           (ch != 'n') && (ch != 'N'));
  if ((ch == 'y') || (ch == 'Y')) {
    add_customer();
    EXEC SQL set transaction read only;
    EXEC SQL select custseq.currval
             into   :cnum
             from   dual;
    EXEC SQL commit;
  }
```

```
else {
  printf("Customer Number: ");
  scanf("%d",&cnum); getchar();
}

EXEC SQL set transaction read only;
EXEC SQL select *
         into  :crec
         from  customers
         where cno = :cnum;
if (sqlca.sqlcode > 0){
  printf("Customer (%d) does not exist\n",cnum);
  EXEC SQL commit;
  return;
}
EXEC SQL commit;

EXEC SQL set transaction read write;
EXEC SQL insert into orders (ono,cno,eno,received)
         values (ordseq.nextval,:cnum,:eenum,sysdate);
if (sqlca.sqlcode != 0) {
  printf("Error while entering order\n");
  EXEC SQL rollback work;
  return;
}
nparts = 0;
do {
  printf("Enter pno and quantity,(0,0)to quit:  ");
  scanf("%d%d",&pnum,&qqty); getchar();
  if (pnum != 0) {
    EXEC SQL select qoh,olevel
             into   :qqoh,:ord_lev
             from   parts
             where  pno=:pnum;
    if (qqoh > qqty) {
      EXEC SQL insert into odetails
               values (ordseq.currval,:pnum,:qqty);
      if (sqlca.sqlcode == 0) {
        nparts++;
        EXEC SQL update parts
```

```
                    set qoh = (qoh - :qqty)
                    where pno=:pnum;
             if (qqoh < ord_lev){
               EXEC SQL update parts
                      set qoh = 5*olevel
                      where pno=:pnum;
               f1 = fopen("restock.dat","a");
               fprintf(f1,"Replenish part (%d) by (%d)\n",
                        pnum, 5*ord_lev - qqoh);
               fclose(f1);
             }
          }
          else  printf("Cannot add part (%d) to order\n",pnum);
        }
        else
          printf("Not enough quantity in stock for (%d)\n",pnum);
      }
    } while(pnum > 0);
    if (nparts > 0)
      EXEC SQL commit;
    else
      EXEC SQL rollback work;
    printf("NEW ORDER PROCESSING COMPLETE\n");
  }
```

This function first requests that the user enter a valid employee number, and then it asks if the customer is new or old. If the customer is new, the function invokes the routine to add a new customer; otherwise it requests the customer number. After verifying that the customer is valid, it makes an entry into the **orders** table and then repeatedly requests for the part number and quantity of each part being ordered. Each of these parts is then entered into the **odetails** table. The function terminates when the user enters 0 for the part number. If the number of parts added to the order is more than 0, the transaction is committed; otherwise the transaction is rolled back and the order entry is erased from the **orders** table. Although this function does take user input while a transaction is alive, it is not a good idea in general, as the database tables may be locked for an indefinite time and other users would not get access to these tables. One way to fix this problem is to read the parts to be ordered into an array and perform the database inserts after the user is done with the input.

3.6.3 Delete Old Orders

The `delete_old_orders` function is shown below:

```
void delete_old_orders() {
  EXEC SQL set transaction read write;
  EXEC SQL delete from ospecs
           where ono in
                  (select ono
                   from orders
                   where shipped <  (sysdate - 5*365));
  EXEC SQL delete from orders
           where shipped < (sysdate - 5*365);
  EXEC SQL commit;
  printf("ORDERS SHIPPED 5 YEARS or EARLIER DELETED!\n");
}
```

This function deletes orders that have been shipped more than five years ago. To maintain referential integrity, it also deletes the corresponding rows in the `odetails` table.

3.6.4 Print Order Invoice

The `print_invoice` function is shown below:

```
void print_invoice() {
  EXEC SQL begin declare section;
    int zzip,cnum,eenum,onum,pnum,qqty;
    varchar st[31],eename[31],ccname[31],
            ccity[31],ppname[31];
    char ph[13];
    float sum,pprice;
    order_record orec;
    order_indicator_record orecind;
  EXEC SQL end declare section;

  EXEC SQL declare od_cur cursor for
    select parts.pno, pname, qty, price
    from   odetails, parts
    where  odetails.ono = :onum and
           odetails.pno = parts.pno;
```

```
printf("Order Number: ");
scanf("%d",&onum); getchar();

EXEC SQL set transaction read only;
EXEC SQL select *
        into   :orec indicator :orecind
        from   orders
        where  ono = :onum;
if (sqlca.sqlcode == 0) {
  EXEC SQL select cno,cname,street,city,
                  customers.zip, phone
           into   :cnum,:ccname,:st,:ccity,:zzip,:ph
           from   customers, zipcodes
           where  cno = :orec.cno and
                  customers.zip = zipcodes.zip;
  ccname.arr[ccname.len] = '\0';
  st.arr[st.len] = '\0';
  ccity.arr[ccity.len] = '\0';
  printf("***************************************");
  printf("***********************\n");
  printf("Customer: %s \t Customer Number: %d \n",
         ccname.arr, cnum);
  printf("Street  : %s \n", st.arr);
  printf("City    : %s \n", ccity.arr);
  printf("ZIP     : %d \n",zzip);
  printf("Phone   : %s \n", ph);
  printf("----------------------------------------");
  printf("----------------------\n");

  EXEC SQL select eno, ename
           into   :eenum, :eename
           from   employees
           where  eno = :orec.eno;
  eename.arr[eename.len] = '\0';
  printf("Order No: %d \n",orec.ono);
  printf("Taken By: %s (%d)\n",eename.arr, eenum);
  printf("Received On: %s\n",orec.received);
  printf("Shipped  On: %s\n\n",orec.shipped);
```

```
    EXEC SQL open od_cur;
    EXEC SQL fetch od_cur
             into :pnum, :ppname, :qqty, :pprice;
    printf("Part No.              ");
    printf("Part Name    Quan.   Price     Ext\n");
    printf("------------------------------------");
    printf("----------------------\n");
    sum = 0.0;
    while (sqlca.sqlcode == 0) {
      ppname.arr[ppname.len] = '\0';
      printf("%8d%25s%7d%10.2f%10.2f\n",pnum,
        ppname.arr, qqty, pprice, qqty*pprice);
      sum = sum + (qqty*pprice);
      EXEC SQL fetch od_cur
               into :pnum, :ppname, :qqty, :pprice;
     }
     EXEC SQL close od_cur;
     printf("------------------------------------");
     printf("------------------------\n");
     printf("                                 ");
     printf("TOTAL:          %10.2f\n",sum);
     printf("************************************");
     printf("*************************\n");
     EXEC SQL commit;
  }
}
```

Given an order number, this function prints an invoice for the order. The invoice includes information about the customer, employee who took the order, details of the order, prices, and total due.

3.7 Recursive Queries

SQL is a powerful language to express ad hoc queries. But it has its limitations. It is impossible to express arbitrary recursive queries in SQL. However, the power of embedded SQL, which gives access to all the features of a high-level programming

Figure 3.2 emps table.

emps

EID	MGRID
Smith	Jones
Blake	Jones
Brown	Smith
Green	Smith
White	Brown
Adams	White

language, can be used to solve recursive queries. Consider a simple relational table **emps** defined as follows:

```
create table emps (
  eid   integer,
  mgrid integer);
```

This table has two columns: (1) **eid**, the employee ID, and (2) **mgrid**, the ID of the employee's manager. A possible instance is shown in Figure 3.2. Consider the following deductive rules that define a recursive query on the **emps** table:

```
query(X) :- emps(X,'Jones');
query(X) :- emps(X,Y), query(Y).
```

The query gets all the employees who work under **Jones** at all levels. The first deductive rule gets the employees who work directly under **Jones**. The second deductive rule is a recursive rule stating that if **X** works under **Y** and **Y** is already in the answer to the query, then **X** must also be in the answer to the query.

To solve this query using embedded SQL, the following algorithm is used:

```
insert into query
  select eid from emps where mgrid = 'Jones';
repeat
  insert into query
    select eid from query,emps where mgrid = a;
until (no more changes to query);
```

where **query** is a table with one column named **a**. Basically, the algorithm first computes the answers from the first deductive rule. It then repeatedly computes the answers from the second recursive rule until no more answers are generated. The program is as follows:

```
#include <stdio.h>
EXEC SQL begin declare section;
  int  eid, a;
EXEC SQL end declare section;
EXEC SQL include sqlca;
main()
{ int newrowadded;
/* Cursor for emps at next level (Initial answers) */
  EXEC SQL declare c1 cursor for
    select eid from emps where mgrid = :eid;
/* query(X) if emps(X,Y) and query(Y) */
  EXEC SQL declare c2 cursor for
    select eid from emps,query where mgrid = a;
/* Cursor to print the answers */
  EXEC SQL declare c3 cursor for select a from query;

  EXEC SQL create table query(
           a integer not null, primary key (a));

/*Get initial answers using Cursor c1*/

  printf("Type in employee id:");
  scanf("%d",&eid);

  EXEC SQL open c1;
  EXEC SQL fetch c1 into :a;
  while (sqlca.sqlcode == 0) {
    EXEC SQL insert into query values (:a);
    EXEC SQL fetch c1 into :a;
  }
  EXEC SQL close c1;
  EXEC SQL commit work;
/* repeat loop of algorithm */
   do {
     newrowadded = FALSE;
     EXEC SQL open c2;
     EXEC SQL fetch c2 into :a;
     while (sqlca.sqlcode == 0) {
       EXEC SQL insert into query values (:a);
       if (sqlca.sqlcode == 0)
```

```
          newrowadded = TRUE;
        EXEC SQL fetch c2 into :a;
      }
      EXEC SQL close c2;
    } while (newrowadded);
  EXEC SQL commit work;
/*Print results from query table*/

  printf("Answer is\n");
  EXEC SQL open c3;
  EXEC SQL fetch c3 into :a;
  while (sqlca.sqlcode == 0) {
    printf("%d\n",a);
    EXEC SQL fetch c3 into :a;
  }
  EXEC SQL close c3;
  EXEC SQL commit work;

  EXEC SQL drop table query;
  EXEC SQL commit work;
}/*end of main*/
```

Note the use of the `primary key` clause in the `query` table definition. Checking to see if any new row was added in the `do-while` loop in the program is based on the fact that the only column of `query` is defined as the primary key, and if a new row was indeed added, the value of `sqlca.sqlcode` would be 0.

3.8 Error Handling

Oracle reports any errors or warnings caused by the embedded SQL statements in the SQL communications area introduced in Section 3.3. There are at least two methods of handling these errors and warnings in the embedded program: *explicit handling* by writing code that inspects the `sqlca` structure and takes appropriate action, and *implicit handling* by using the `whenever` statement. Both methods are discussed in this section.

Figure 3.3 The `sqlca` structure in Oracle.

```
struct sqlca {
  char    sqlcaid[8];
  long    sqlabc;
  long    sqlcode;
  struct {
    unsigned short sqlerrml;
    char           sqlerrmc[70];
  } sqlerrm;
  char    sqlerrp[8];
  long    sqlerrd[6];
  char    sqlwarn[8];
  char    sqlext[8];
};
```

3.8.1 Explicit Handling

After each database call, errors or warnings are checked and, if necessary, are processed at that point by the application program. The SQL communications area is used for this purpose. Earlier in this chapter the **sqlcode** field of the **sqlca** structure was introduced. Now other important fields of the **sqlca** structure will be discussed. The **sqlca** structure as defined in Oracle is shown in Figure 3.3. The individual fields of the **sqlca** structure are as follows:

- `sqlcaid`: A character string that identifies the SQL communications area. It is equal to `'SQLCA   '`.
- `sqlabc`: The size of the **sqlca** structure; it is initialized to

  ```
  sizeof(struct sqlca).
  ```

- `sqlcode`: The status of the most recent SQL statement execution. A 0 value indicates successful execution of the most recent embedded SQL statement; a negative value indicates an error in the execution of the most recent embedded SQL statement; a positive value indicates a warning situation encountered while executing the most recent embedded SQL statement. A warning occurs when no data are found as a result of a **select** or **fetch** statement or when no rows are inserted as a result of an **insert** statement.
- `sqlerrm`: A substructure that contains the error message. This field should be accessed only if **sqlcode** is negative. This substructure contains two fields:

`sqlerrml`, the length of the error message, and `sqlerrmc`, the error message itself. This error message is limited to 70 characters and is not `null` terminated. Therefore, it should be `null` terminated as follows before it is used in the C program:

```
sqlca.sqlerrm.sqlerrmc[sqlca.sqlerrm.sqlerrml] = '\0';
```

If the error message is longer than 70 characters, a call to the `sqlglm` function can be made to print the entire error message as follows:

```
char error_message[512];
long buffer_length, message_length;

buffer_length = sizeof (error_message);
sqlglm(error_message,&buffer_length,&message_length);
printf("%.*s\n", message_length, error_message);
```

Note that `error_message` is the buffer in which Oracle would store the entire error message, `buffer_length` is the maximum size of the buffer (usually set to 512), and `message_length` is the actual length of the error message.

- `sqlerrp`: A character string field unused at this time.
- `sqlerrd`: An array of six integers used to record error diagnostic information. Only `sqlerrd[2]` and `sqlerrd[4]` are in use at this time. `sqlerrd[2]` records the number of rows processed successfully by a `select`, `insert`, `update`, or `delete` statement. For cursors, `sqlerrd[2]` is assigned 0 when the cursor is opened and incremented after each fetch. `sqlerrd[4]` contains the parse error offset, the position in a dynamic SQL statement that is syntactically incorrect. `sqlerrd[4]` is useful only in the context of dynamic SQL statements, which are discussed in Section 3.10.
- `sqlwarn`: An array of eight characters used as warning flags having the following meanings:
  - `sqlca.sqlwarn[0]` is set to `W` if one of the other flags is set.
  - `sqlca.sqlwarn[1]` is assigned a nonzero value if a character data value is truncated when assigned to a host variable.
  - `sqlca.sqlwarn[3]` is assigned a nonzero value if in a `fetch` or a `select into` statement the number of columns is not equal to the number of host variables in the `into` clause. The value assigned is the smaller of these two numbers.

- `sqlca.sqlwarn[4]` is assigned a nonzero value if all the rows of a table are affected by a **delete** or an **update** statement.
- `sqlca.sqlwarn[5]` is assigned a nonzero value when the compilation of a PL/SQL statement fails.

The remaining entries in this array are unused at this time and are initialized to 0.

- **sqlext**: A character string field not in use at this time.

Based on the information provided in the **sqlca** structure, the programmer can inspect these values and take appropriate action in the embedded SQL program to handle errors. The **sqlca** structure can be initialized by using the following **define** statement:

```
#define SQLCA_INIT
```

3.8.2 Implicit Handling

One of the disadvantages of explicit handling of errors is that the code becomes cluttered with error-handling statements. To avoid this, the errors can be handled implicitly using the **whenever** statement, which is actually a directive to the Pro*C preprocessor to insert certain statements after each database call in the program under the scope of the **whenever** statement. The syntax of the **whenever** statement is

```
EXEC SQL whenever ⟨condition⟩ ⟨action⟩;
```

where ⟨*condition*⟩ is one of the following:

```
sqlerror    : an error situation  (sqlcode < 0)
sqlwarning  : a warning situation (sqlcode > 0)
not found   : data not found      (sqlcode = 1403)
```

and ⟨*action*⟩ is one of the following:

```
continue     : ignore condition and continue
do function  : call a function
do break     : perform a break out of a control
               structure
do return    : perform a return statement
goto label   : branch to a label
stop         : stop program and roll back uncommitted
               changes
```

The `whenever` statement can be used any number of times in the program. However, you must be careful, since the scope of the statement is positional, not logical. The positional nature of the scope of the `whenever` statement means that it is applicable to the statements that physically follow it until another `whenever` statement for the same ⟨*condition*⟩ is encountered. A typical use of the `whenever` statement is

```
EXEC SQL whenever sqlerror do
  sql_error("ORACLE error--\n");
```

This is placed at the beginning of the source file, and an error-handling procedure called `sql_error` is defined as follows:

```
void sql_error(char msg[]) {
  char error_message[512];
  long buffer_length, message_length;

  EXEC SQL whenever sqlerror continue;
  buffer_length = sizeof (error_message);
  sqlglm(error_message,&buffer_length,&message_length);
  printf("%.*s\n", message_length, error_message);
  EXEC SQL rollback release;
  exit(1);
}
```

This is a procedure that prints the error message using the `sqlglm` procedure call and exits the program. Notice the use of the

```
EXEC SQL whenever sqlerror continue;
```

statement in this procedure. This ensures that an infinite loop is not created if the `rollback` statement or any other database call in this procedure encounters an error.

3.9 Transaction Control

A transaction is a sequence of database statements that must execute as a whole to maintain consistency. If for some reason one of the statements fails in the transaction, all the changes caused by the statements in the transaction should be undone to maintain a consistent database state. Oracle provides the following statements to create transactions within the embedded SQL program.

- `EXEC SQL set transaction read only`. This is typically used before a sequence of `select` or `fetch` statements that do only a read from the database.

The statement begins a read-only transaction. At the end of the sequence of statements, the `commit` statement is executed to end the transaction.

- `EXEC SQL set transaction read write`. This is typically used before a sequence of statements that performs some updates to the database. This statement begins a read-write transaction. The transaction is terminated by either a `commit` statement that makes the changes permanent in the database or a `rollback` statement that undoes all the changes made by all the statements within the transaction.
- `EXEC SQL commit`. This statement commits all the changes made in the transaction and releases any locks placed on tables so that other processes may access them.
- `EXEC SQL rollback`. This statement undoes all the changes made in the course of the transaction and releases all locks placed on the tables.

Notice the use of these statements in the mail-order database application program discussed earlier. An important point to note while creating transactions in the embedded SQL program is that while a transaction is active, user input should be avoided, if at all possible. This is because the tables are locked by the system during the transaction, and other processes may not get access to the database tables if these locks are not released soon. By waiting for user input during a transaction, there is the danger of a long delay before the input is received by the program, which means that the transaction could be kept active for long durations.

3.10 Dynamic SQL

The embedded SQL statements seen so far have been static in nature—i.e., they are fixed at compile time. However, there are situations when the SQL statements to be executed in an application program are not known at compile time. These statements are built spontaneously as the program is executing. These are referred to as *dynamic* SQL statements, which can be executed through several mechanisms, discussed in this section.

3.10.1 The `execute immediate` Statement

The simplest form of executing a dynamic SQL statement is to use the **`execute immediate`** statement. The syntax of the **`execute immediate`** statement is

```
EXEC SQL execute immediate ⟨host-var⟩;
```

where ⟨*host-var*⟩ is a host variable defined as a character string and has as its value a valid SQL statement, which cannot have any built-in host variables. It must be a complete SQL statement ready to be executed. Furthermore, it is restricted to be one of the following: **`create table`**, **`alter table`**, **`drop table`**, **`insert`**, **`delete`**, or **`update`**. Dynamic select statements are not allowed. Another approach is necessary to perform dynamic selects and is discussed later in this section. An example of the **`execute immediate`** statement is shown below:

```
#include <stdio.h>
EXEC SQL begin declare section;
  char sql_stmt[256];
  varchar userid[10], password[15];
EXEC SQL end declare section;
EXEC SQL include sqlca;

void main() {
 strcpy(username.arr,"book");
 username.len = strlen(username.arr);
 strcpy(password.arr,"book");
 password.len = strlen(password.arr);
 EXEC SQL connect :username identified by :password;

 strcpy(sql_stmt,
   "update employees set hdate=sysdate where eno = 1001");

 EXEC SQL set transaction read write;
 EXEC SQL execute immediate :sql_stmt;
 EXEC SQL commit release;
 exit(0);
}
```

In the above program, **`sql_stmt`** is the host variable that has as its value a valid SQL **`update`** statement. When executed successfully, it sets the **`hired date`** value for employee `1001` to the current date.

3.10.2 The `prepare` and `execute using` Statements

One of the drawbacks of the **`execute immediate`** statement is that the SQL statement that it executes has to be compiled each time the **`execute immediate`** statement is executed. This can cause a lot of overhead if the SQL statement has to be executed many times in the program. Another problem is that the SQL statement cannot have host variables, which reduces the flexibility of dynamic statements. To address these problems, the **prepare** and **execute using** statements are introduced. The dynamic SQL statement that needs to be executed is compiled once using the **prepare** statement and then executed any number of times using the **execute using** statement. This approach also allows host variables to be present in the dynamic SQL statement. The syntax of the **prepare** statement is

```
EXEC SQL prepare s from :sql_stmt;
```

where **sql_stmt** is a host variable defined as a character string and has as its value a valid SQL statement, which may include host variables. The **prepare** statement basically compiles the dynamic SQL statement and stores the compiled form in the variable s, which need not be declared. The syntax of the **execute using** statement is

```
EXEC SQL execute s using :var1, ..., :varn;
```

where **s** is a previously prepared compiled form of an SQL statement, and **var1, ..., varn** are host variables that will substitute the corresponding host variables in the dynamic SQL statement (assuming there are **n** host variables used in the dynamic SQL statement). An example of this approach is shown below:

```
#include <stdio.h>
EXEC SQL begin declare section;
  char sql_stmt[256];
  int num;
  varchar userid[10], password[15];
EXEC SQL end declare section;
EXEC SQL include sqlca;

void main() {

  strcpy(username.arr,"book");
  username.len = strlen(username.arr);
  strcpy(password.arr,"book");
  password.len = strlen(password.arr);
  EXEC SQL connect :username identified by :password;

  strcpy(sql_stmt,
   "update employees set hdate=sysdate where eno = :n");

  EXEC SQL set transaction read write;
```

```
    EXEC SQL prepare s from :sql_stmt;

    do {
      printf("Enter eno to update (0 to stop):>");
      scanf("%d",&num);
      if (num > 0) {
        EXEC SQL execute s using :num;
        EXEC SQL commit;
      }
    } while (num > 0);

    EXEC SQL commit release;
    exit(0);
}
```

In the above program, the user is prompted for the employee number several times, and the particular employee's hired date is updated using the employee number entered by the user. Notice that the **prepare** statement is used once and the **execute using** statement is used in a loop several times.

3.10.3 Dynamic Select

The previous approaches discussed cannot be used to do dynamic selects because the number of columns in the **select** clause of the select statement and their data types are unknown at compile time. It is not possible to use the **into** clause in the **select** or the **fetch** statements, as the number of host variables to be used is unknown. To solve this problem, a new data structure is introduced, called the **SQL Descriptor Area**, or **sqlda**. This data structure will store the results of the current **fetch**, and the embedded program can obtain the current row from the **sqlda**.

The **sqlda** structure is shown in Figure 3.4. The individual fields of the **sqlda** structure are explained with comments next to their definition. Some of these fields (such as `N`, `M`, and `Y`) of the **sqlda** structure are initialized when initial space for the structure is allocated using the **sqlald** function. Other fields (such as `T`, `F`, `S`, `C`, `X`, and `Z`) are assigned values when the **describe** statement is executed. The actual values (fields `V`, `L`, and `I`) of the columns being retrieved are assigned values when the **fetch** statement is executed.

The **describe** statement returns the names, data types, lengths (including precision and scale), and **null/not null** statuses of all the columns in a compiled form of a dynamic SQL select statement. It must be used after the dynamic SQL

Figure 3.4 The `sqlda` structure in Oracle.

```
struct sqlda {
  long      N; /* Maximum number of columns
                  handled by this sqlda       */

  char    **V; /* Pointer to array of pointers
                  to column values            */
  long     *L; /* Pointer to array of lengths
                  of column values            */
  short    *T; /* Pointer to array of data
                  types of columns            */
  short   **I; /* Pointer to array of pointers
                  to indicator values      */

  long      F; /* Actual Number of columns found
                  by describe                 */

  char    **S; /* Pointer to array of pointers
                  to column names             */
  short    *M; /* Pointer to array of max lengths
                  of column names             */
  short    *C; /* Pointer to array of actual
                  lengths of column names     */

  char    **X; /* Pointer to array of pointers
                  to indicator variable names */
  short    *Y; /* Pointer to array of max lengths
                  of indicator variable names  */
  short    *Z; /* Pointer to array of actual lengths
                  of indicator variable names */
};
```

statement has been compiled using the **prepare** statement. The syntax of the **describe** statement is

```
EXEC SQL describe select list for s into da;
```

where **s** is the compiled form of the dynamic SQL statement and **da** is the **sqlda** structure.

The cursor manipulation for dynamic selects using the **sqlda** is done as follows:

```
EXEC SQL declare c cursor for s;

EXEC SQL open  c using descriptor da;
EXEC SQL fetch c using descriptor da;
.
.
.
EXEC SQL fetch c using descriptor da;
EXEC SQL close c;
```

Notice the `USING DESCRIPTOR` phrase used in the `open` and `fetch` statements. Also notice the cursor declaration that specifies the compiled form `s` of the dynamic select. These statements should follow the `prepare` statement.

An embedded SQL program that involves a dynamic `select` is shown below. The program has a string variable assigned to the following select statement:

```
select eno,ename,hdate
from   employees
where  eno>=1;

/* Dynamic Select Program */

#include <stdio.h>
#include <string.h>

#define MAX_ITEMS          40/* max number of columns*/
#define MAX_VNAME_LEN      30/* max length for column names*/
#define MAX_INAME_LEN      30/* max length of indicator names*/

EXEC SQL begin declare section;
  varchar username[20];
  varchar password[20];
  char    stmt[256];
EXEC SQL end declare section;

EXEC SQL include sqlca;
EXEC SQL include sqlda;

SQLDA *da;

extern SQLDA *sqlald();
```

```
extern void sqlnul();
int process_select_list();

main() {
  int i;

  /* Connect to the database. */
  strcpy(username.arr,"book");
  username.len = strlen(username.arr);
  strcpy(password.arr,"book");
  password.len = strlen(password.arr);
  EXEC SQL connect :username identified by :password;

  /* Allocate memory for the SQLDA da and pointers
     to indicator variables and data. */
  da = sqlald (MAX_ITEMS, MAX_VNAME_LEN, MAX_INAME_LEN);
  for (i = 0; i < MAX_ITEMS; i++) {
      da->I[i] = (short *) malloc(sizeof(short));
      da->V[i] = (char *) malloc(1);
  }

  strcpy(stmt,
  "select eno,ename,hdate from employees where eno>=1");

  EXEC SQL prepare s from :stmt;

  process_select();

  /* Free space */
  for (i = 0; i < MAX_ITEMS; i++) {
      if (da->V[i] != (char *) 0)
         free(da->V[i]);
      free(da->I[i]);
  }
  sqlclu(da);

  EXEC SQL commit work release;
  exit(0);
}
```

```
void process_select(void) {
  int i, null_ok, precision, scale;
  EXEC SQL declare c cursor for s;


  EXEC SQL open c using descriptor da;

  /* The describe function returns their names, datatypes,
     lengths (including precision and scale), and
     null/not null statuses. */
  EXEC SQL describe select list for s into da;

  /* Set the maximum number of array elements in the
     descriptor to the number found. */
  da->N = da->F;

  /* Allocate storage for each column.  */
  for (i = 0; i < da->F; i++) {
    /* Turn off high-order bit of datatype */
    sqlnul (&(da->T[i]), &(da->T[i]), &null_ok);
    switch (da->T[i]) {
      case  1 : break; /* Char data type */
      case  2 : /* Number data type */
        sqlprc (&(da->L[i]), &precision, &scale);
        if (precision == 0) precision = 40;
        if (scale > 0) da->L[i] = sizeof(float);
        else da->L[i] = sizeof(int);
        break;
      case 12 : /* DATE datatype */
        da->L[i] = 9;
        break;
    }
    /* Allocate space for the column values.
       sqlald() reserves a pointer location for
       V[i] but does not allocate the full space for
       the pointer.  */
     if (da->T[i] != 2)
       da->V[i] = (char *) realloc(da->V[i],da->L[i] + 1);
     else
       da->V[i] = (char *) realloc(da->V[i],da->L[i]);
```

```
  /* Print column headings, right-justifying number
        column headings. */
  if (da->T[i] == 2)
     if (scale > 0)
       printf ("%.*s ", da->L[i]+3, da->S[i]);
     else
       printf ("%.*s ", da->L[i], da->S[i]);
  else
      printf ("%-.*s ", da->L[i], da->S[i]);

  /* Coerce ALL datatypes except NUMBER to
     character. */
  if (da->T[i] != 2) da->T[i] = 1;

  /* Coerce the datatypes of NUMBERs to float or
     int depending on the scale. */
  if (da->T[i] == 2)
   if (scale > 0) da->T[i] = 4;  /* float */
    else da->T[i] = 3;  /* int */
}
printf ("\n\n");

/* FETCH each row selected and print the
   column values. */
EXEC SQL whenever not found goto end_select_loop;
for (;;) {
  EXEC SQL fetch c using descriptor da;
  for (i = 0; i < da->F; i++) {
    if (*da->I[i] < 0)
        if (da->T[i] == 4)
          printf ("%-*c ",(int)da->L[i]+3, ' ');
        else
          printf ("%-*c ",(int)da->L[i], ' ');
    else
        if (da->T[i] == 3)     /* int datatype */
          printf ("%*d ", (int)da->L[i],*(int *)da->V[i]);
        else if (da->T[i] == 4)     /* float datatype */
          printf ("%*.2f ", (int)da->L[i],*(float *)da->V[i]);
        else                         /* character string */
          printf ("%-*.*s ", (int)da->L[i],
```

```
                              (int)da->L[i], da->V[i]);
      }
      printf ("\n");
    }
    end_select_loop:
    EXEC SQL close c;
    return;
  }
```

The following characteristics should be noted about the program:

- The `sqlda` structure needs to be initialized by the function call

  ```
  da = sqlald (MAX_ITEMS, MAX_VNAME_LEN,
               MAX_INAME_LEN);
  ```

  At this point, `N`, the maximum number of columns; `M`, the maximum size of column names; and `Y`, the maximum size of indicator variable names, are initialized.

- Immediately after the `sqlda` structure is initialized, the space for the indicator and column value pointers (`I` and `V` fields) must be allocated as follows.

  ```
  for (i = 0; i < MAX_ITEMS; i++) {
      da->I[i] = (short *) malloc(sizeof(short));
      da->V[i] = (char *) malloc(1);
  }
  ```

- Before the dynamic statement can be used, it should be compiled using the following statement:

  ```
  EXEC SQL prepare s from :stmt;
  ```

- The `T` field has encoded in it the `null/not null` status of the column in its high-order bit. To turn it off, use the following procedure call:

  ```
  /* Turn off high-order bit of datatype */
  sqlnul (&(da->T[i]), &(da->T[i]), &null_ok);
  ```

- After determining the data types (`T` field) of each column, the `L` field must be set to indicate the maximum lengths of each column value. After this is done, the actual space to store the column values must be allocated, which is based on the `L` field.

- The three data types, `Character String (T = 1)`, `Number (T = 2)`, and `Date (T = 12)`, are handled in this program.

- The `sqlprc()` function call is used to extract precision and scale from the length (`da->L[i]`) of the `NUMBER` columns.
- The column names are obtained from the `S` field and are available after the **`describe`** statement has executed.
- The column values are obtained from the `V` field after the **`fetch`** takes place.
- At the end, it is good practice to free the space occupied by the `sqlda` structure. This is done by the following:

```
/* Free space */
for (i = 0; i < MAX_ITEMS; i++) {
    if (da->V[i] != (char *) 0)
       free(da->V[i]);
    free(da->I[i]);
}
sqlclu(da);
```

3.11 Pro*C++

Oracle's Pro*C/C++ allows the programmer to embed SQL statements in a C++ program. In this section, three sample programs written in C++ are presented. These sample programs illustrate various aspects of embedded-SQL programming in C++ such as single answer querying using the **`select into`** statement, multiple answer querying using cursors, and dynamic querying using cursors and the **`prepare`** statement.

3.11.1 Compiling Pro*C++ programs

To compile Pro*C++ programs, use the following command:

```
make -f proc.mk EXE=prog OBJS="prog.o" cppbuild
```

where `prog.pc` is the name of the Pro*C++ program and `proc.mk` is the Oracle-supplied makefile.

3.11.2 A Simple Query Example

The following program prompts the user for a member id, then queries the member table for the member's last name, address, and email, and prints the information.

```
#include <iostream.h>
#include <stdio.h>
#include <string.h>
#include <stdlib.h>

EXEC SQL begin declare section;
  varchar user[20];
  varchar pass[20];

  struct memberRecord {
      varchar   lname[16];
      varchar   address[50];
      varchar   email[31];
  } mrec;

  struct memberindRecord {
      short     lname_ind;
      short     addr_ind;
      short     email_ind;
  } mrec_ind;

  char mmid[8];
EXEC SQL end declare section;

class member {
  char    lname[16];
  char    address[50];
  char    email[31];
public:
  member(const memberRecord&, const memberindRecord&);
  friend ostream& operator<<(ostream&, member&);
};

member::member(const memberRecord& m, const memberindRecord& i) {
  strncpy(lname, (char *)m.lname.arr, m.lname.len);
  lname[m.lname.len] = '\0';
```

```
  if (i.addr_ind < 0)
    strncpy(address,"NULL",4);
  else
    strncpy(address, (char *)m.address.arr, m.address.len);
  address[m.address.len] = '\0';
  if (i.email_ind < 0)
    strncpy(email,"NULL",4);
  else
    strncpy(email, (char *)m.email.arr, m.email.len);
  email[m.email.len] = '\0';
}

ostream& operator<<(ostream& s, member& m) {
  return s << m.lname << " " << m.address
           << " " << m.email << endl;
}

#include <sqlca.h>

int main() {

  user.len = strlen(strcpy((char *)user.arr, "book"));
  pass.len = strlen(strcpy((char *)pass.arr, "book"));

  EXEC SQL connect :user identified by :pass;

  cout << "\nConnected to ORACLE as user: "
       << (char *)user.arr << endl << endl;

  while (1) {
    cout << "Enter member number (0 to quit): ";
    gets(mmid);
    if (strcmp(mmid,"0") == 0)
      break;
    EXEC SQL select member.lname, member.address,
                    member.email
             into   :mrec indicator :mrec_ind
             from   member
             where  member.mid = :mmid;
```

```
        if (sqlca.sqlcode == 0) {
          member m(mrec, mrec_ind);
          cout << m;
        }
        else {
          cout << "Not a valid member number." << endl;
          cout << sqlca.sqlerrm.sqlerrmc << endl;
        }
      }

      EXEC SQL commit work release;
      exit(0);
    }
```

A class called `member` is declared that has three instance variables `lname`, `address`, and `email`. The information retrieved from the database is used to create a `member` object using the constructor method defined for this class. A method to print the `member` object to the output stream is defined.

The main program first connects to the database. It then repeatedly asks the user for a member id and performs the query to retrieve the necessary information from the database. This information is sent to the constructor method to create a `member` object, which is then sent to the output stream. The address and email information retrieved from the database is checked for `null` values in the constructor method using indicator variables.

An important point to note is that the database-related statements in this program are exactly the same as would have been written in a Pro*C program. This is indeed true for any Pro*C++ program.

3.11.3 Multiple Answer Query using Cursors

Consider the following two additional tables in the investment portfolio database.

```
create table analyst (
  aid       varchar2 (4),
  name      varchar2 (15)  not null,
  password  varchar2 (8),
  primary key (aid)
);
```

```
create table rating (
  aid     varchar2(4),
  symbol  varchar2(8),
  rating  number  check (rating in (1,2,3,4,5)),
  primary key (aid, symbol),
  foreign key (aid) references analyst,
  foreign key (symbol) references security
);
```

The **analyst** table records information about various analysts who rate the securities on a scale of 1–5. The ratings of securities themselves are recorded in the **ratings** table.

The following Pro*C++ program reads rows from the **analyst** and **security** tables and creates the rating table by assigning a random number between 1 and 5 for each analyst-security combination. The net effect of running this program is that every security gets a rating from each of the analysts.

```
#include <fstream.h>
#include <iostream.h>
#include <iomanip.h>
#include <string.h>
#include <stdlib.h>
#include <time.h>

#define UNAME_LEN 20
#define PWD_LEN   40

exec sql begin declare section;
  varchar username[UNAME_LEN];
  varchar password[PWD_LEN];

  // Host variables for input
  int totalRatIns, totalAnalysts, totalSecurities;

  // Host variables for analyst id, security symbol, and rating
  varchar analystId[5];
  varchar symbol[9];
  int rating;
```

```
  // indicator variables for analyst id and security symbol
  short analystIdInd, symbolInd;
exec sql end declare section;

#include <sqlca.h>

// Error handler
void sql_error (char *msg);

void main() {
  // Register sql_error as the error handler
  exec sql whenever sqlerror
      do sql_error("ORACLE ERROR: ");

  cout << "Enter userid : ";
  cin  >> username.arr;
  cout << "Enter your password : ";
  cin  >> password.arr;

  username.len = strlen((char *) username.arr);
  password.len = strlen((char *) password.arr);

  exec sql connect :username identified BY :password;
  cout << "\nConnected to ORACLE as user: "
       << (char *)username.arr << endl;

  srand(time(NULL));
  totalRatIns = 0;
  totalAnalysts = 0;
  totalSecurities = 0;

  exec sql declare analyst_cur cursor for
           select aid
           from   analyst;

  exec sql declare security_cur cursor for
           select symbol
           from   security;
```

```
exec sql open analyst_cur;
exec sql fetch analyst_cur
         into :analystId indicator :analystIdInd;

while (sqlca.sqlcode == 0) {
  totalAnalysts++;
  exec sql open security_cur;
  exec sql fetch security_cur
           into :symbol indicator :symbolInd;
  while (sqlca.sqlcode == 0) {
    totalSecurities++;
    exec sql set transaction read write;
    rating = 1 + rand()%5;
    exec sql insert into rating values
       (:analystId,:symbol,:rating);
    if (sqlca.sqlcode != 0) {
      cout << " Error while inserting rating for "
           << analystId.arr  << " symbol "
           << symbol.arr << endl;
      exec sql rollback release;
    }
    else {
      cout << " Analyst " << analystId.arr
           << " rated " << symbol.arr
           << " as " << rating << endl;
      totalRatIns++;
      exec sql commit work;
    }
   exec sql fetch security_cur
            into :symbol INDICATOR :symbolInd;
 }
 exec sql fetch analyst_cur
          into :analystId indicator :analystIdInd;
}
exec sql close analyst_cur;
exec sql close security_cur;
cout << endl << "Total analysts = " << totalAnalysts << endl;
cout << endl << "Total securities = "
     << totalSecurities << endl;
```

```
  cout << endl << "Total ratings inserted = "
       << totalRatIns << endl << endl;

  // Disconnect from ORACLE
  exec sql commit work release;
  exit(0);
}

void sql_error(char *msg) {
  exec sql whenever sqlerror continue;
  cout << msg << sqlca.sqlerrm.sqlerrmc << endl;
  exec sql rollback release;
  exit(1);
}
```

The program begins by connecting to the database. It then uses two cursors to query the **analyst** and **security** tables. A nested loop is set up to go through every analyst-security pair. For each such pair, a random number between 1 and 5 is generated and the values are inserted into the **rating** table. Appropriate error checks are made and finally the total number of analysts, securities, and ratings is printed. Once again, notice how the database-related statements in this program are exactly the same as in a Pro*C program.

3.11.4 Dynamic SQL Query

The following program uses dynamic SQL to retrieve all the analyst ratings for a given security symbol.

```
#include <iostream.h>
#include <stdio.h>
#include <string.h>
#include <stdlib.h>

#define UNAME_LEN 20
#define PWD_LEN   40

exec sql begin declare section;
  varchar username[UNAME_LEN];
  varchar password[PWD_LEN];
```

```
  varchar sqlstmt[80];
  varchar aname[16];
  varchar symbol[9];
  int     rating;
exec sql end declare section;

#include <sqlca.h>

// Error handler
void sql_error(char *msg);

main() {
  // Register sql_error as the error handler
  exec sql whenever sqlerror
       do sql_error("ORACLE ERROR: ");

  cout << "Enter userid : ";
  cin  >> username.arr;
  cout << "Enter your password : ";
  cin  >> password.arr;

  username.len = strlen((char *) username.arr);
  password.len = strlen((char *) password.arr);

  exec sql connect :username identified BY :password;
  cout << "\nConnected to ORACLE as user: "
       << (char *)username.arr << endl;

  strcpy((char *)sqlstmt.arr,
         "select a.name, r.rating ");
  strcat((char *)sqlstmt.arr,
         "from rating r, analyst a ");
  strcat((char *)sqlstmt.arr,
         "where r.aid = a.aid and r.symbol = :v1");
  sqlstmt.len = strlen((char *)sqlstmt.arr);

  cout << "Enter Symbol: ";
  cin >> symbol.arr;
  symbol.len = strlen((char *)symbol.arr);
```

```
  cout << (char *)sqlstmt.arr << endl;
  cout << "   v1 = " << symbol.arr << endl;

  exec sql prepare S from :sqlstmt;
  exec sql declare c cursor for S;
  exec sql open c using :symbol;
  exec sql whenever not found do break;
  while (1) {
    exec sql fetch c into :aname,:rating;
    aname.arr[aname.len] = '\0';
    cout << (char *)aname.arr << "   "
         << rating << endl;
  }

  printf("\nQuery returned %d row%s.\n\n",
         sqlca.sqlerrd[2],
         (sqlca.sqlerrd[2] == 1) ? "" : "s");

  exec sql close c;
  exec sql commit release;
  exit(0);
}

void sql_error(char *msg) {
  cout << endl << msg << endl;
  sqlca.sqlerrm.sqlerrmc[sqlca.sqlerrm.sqlerrml] = '\0';
  cout << sqlca.sqlerrm.sqlerrmc << endl;
  exec sql whenever sqlerror continue;
  exec sql close c;
  exec sql rollback release;
  exit(1);
}
```

After connecting to the database, the program assigns the SQL query to a string variable. The SQL query has a place holder for the security symbol. The user is prompted for the security symbol for which the ratings are to be retrieved. The **prepare** statement is used to create a compiled form of the SQL statement. A cursor is then declared for this prepared statement. The cursor is opened by providing the actual value for the place holder in the query. The rows of the cursor are retrieved one at a time and the ratings are sent to the output stream.

Exercises

Grade Book Database Problems

3.1 Write an embedded SQL program that prompts the user for the student ID and prints a report for the student containing information about all the courses taken by the student and the average and grade obtained by the student in these courses. The format of the report is shown below:

```
Student ID:   1111
Student NAME: Nandita Rajshekhar

TERM LINENO CNO     TITLE     AVERAGE GRADE
---- ------ ------  --------  ------- -----
F96  1031   CSc481  Automata   98.50    A
.
.
.
-------------------------------------------
```

3.2 Write an embedded SQL program that prompts the user for the term and line number for a course and prints a course report containing information about the students enrolled in the course, their scores in each of the components, and their average and grade for the course. At the end of the report, the total number of A, B, C, D, and F grades awarded in the course should be listed along with the course average (the average of the individual student averages). The report should be sorted based on the student name. The format of the report is shown below:

```
      CSc 481 Automata (LineNo 1585) W98

SID  LNAME FNAME EXAM1 EXAM2 HW  QUIZ AVG   GRADE
-------------------------------------------------
2243 Green Tony  76    78    225 100  89.10   A
0213 Jones Pat   60    67    166  94  74.12   C
.
.
.
-------------------------------------------------
Total As: 5
Total Bs: 3
Total Cs: 3
Total Ds: 2
Total Fs: 1
Course Average: 78.66
```

3.3 Write an embedded SQL program that prints a report containing all courses taught along with total number of students in each course. The report should also contain the number of students enrolled in courses per calendar year and must end with a grand total of all students in all courses. The courses must be sorted according to the term and calendar year—i.e., the courses for earlier calendar years must appear before the courses for later calendar years. Within a year, the courses must be listed according to the term order: **winter**, **spring**, **summer**, **fall**. You may assume that the last two characters of the term column contains a two-digit year, and the possible values of the term column are **wXX**, **spXX**, **suXX**, and **fXX**, where **XX** is the two-digit year. The format of the report is shown below:

```
Term CNO    Course-Title   #Students Year-Total
---- ------ -------------  --------- ----------
w97  CSc226 Programming I      24
sp97 CSc227 Programming II     32
f97  CSc343 Assembly Prog      27
                                         83
sp98 CSc226 Programming I      39
f98  CSc343 Assembly Prog      22
                                         61
.
.
.
--------------------------------------------------
Total number of students:               697
```

3.4 Write an embedded SQL program that will perform the task of entering student scores for a given component in a course. The program should first prompt for the term and line number for the course. It should then list all the components of the course, request the user to select the component for which the scores are to be entered, prompt the user for the names of the students enrolled in the course, one at a time, and read in the scores for each of the students for the selected component. The program should process these scores by inserting the appropriate row in the **scores** table. The program should be robust and should handle all possible error situations, such as invalid term, invalid line number, invalid component selection, and invalid scores.

To verify that this program indeed worked, write another embedded SQL program that prompts the user for the term, line number, and component name and prints the scores for all the students for this component.

3.5 Write an embedded SQL program that will perform the task of updating student scores and dropping students from a course. The program should begin by prompting the user for the term and line number of the course. It should then display the following menu:

```
(1) Display Students
(2) Display Student Score
(3) Update Student Score
(4) Drop Student from Course
(5) Quit
```

The `Display Students` option, when selected by the user, should display the names of all the students enrolled in the course. The `Display Student Score` option, when selected by the user, should prompt the user for the student ID and component name and then display the student's score in the component. The `Update Student Score` option, when selected, should prompt the user for the student ID and component name, display the current score, and request the user to enter the new score. It should then update the database with the new score. The `Drop Student from course` option, when selected, will prompt the user for the student ID and then drop the student from the course (delete the row in the `enrolls` table). Since the `scores` table has a foreign key referring to the `enrolls` table, the corresponding rows must first be deleted from the `scores` table before the student row is deleted from the `enrolls` table. The program should be robust and should handle all possible error situations.

Mail-Order Database Problems

3.6 Write an embedded SQL program that will produce a report containing the ten most ordered parts during a calendar year. The program should prompt for a year and then produce a report with the following format:

```
                 YEAR: 1997

Rank PNO   Part-Name             Quantity-Ordered
---------------------------------------------
1.   10506 Land Before Time I        98
2.   10507 Land Before Time II       87
.
.
.
10.  10900 Dr. Zhivago               24
---------------------------------------------
```

3.7 Write an embedded SQL program that will produce a performance report for all employees. The report should contain the number and name of the employee along with the total sales generated by the employee. The report should also contain the hire date of the employee and the number of months from the hire date to the current date. In addition, the report should list the average sales per 12 months (called `RATING`) for each employee. This average can be used to compare the sales performances of the employees. The report should be sorted in decreasing order of this average performance rating and should have the following format:

```
                 PERFORMANCE REPORT
                Dated: 12 April 1998

RANK ENO   ENAME  HIRED-ON  MONTHS TOTAL-SALES RATING
-----------------------------------------------------
1.   1000  Jones  12-DEC-95  29      2,900       1200
2.   3000  Smith  01-JAN-92  76      6,500       1027
3.   2000  Brown  01-SEP-92  68      4,000        706
-----------------------------------------------------
```

3.8 Write an embedded SQL program that will produce a mailing list of customers living in a given city. The program should prompt the user for a city and then produce the report. The format of the report is a simple listing of customers and their mailing addresses, similar to a mailing label program output.

3.9 Write an embedded SQL program that will update an incorrect zip code in the database. The program should prompt the user for the incorrect and then the correct zip code. It should then replace all the occurrences of the incorrect zip code by the correct zip code in all the tables.

To verify that the program did work, write another embedded SQL program that reads in a zip code and prints all the customers and employees living at that zip code. This program should be run before and after the previous program is executed in order to verify the execution of the previous program.

3.10 Write an embedded SQL program that reads data from a text file and updates the `qoh` column in the `parts` table. The text file consists of several lines of data, with each line containing a part number followed by a positive quantity. The `qoh` value in the `parts` table for the part should be increased by the quantity mentioned next to the part number. Assume that the last line of the text file ends with a part number of 0 and a quantity of 0. The dynamic SQL statements `PREPARE` and `EXECUTE USING` should be used to accomplish this task.

Investment Portfolio Database Problems

3.11 Write an embedded SQL program that will print the current portfolio for a member. The program should prompt the user for the member id and then print the current portfolio in the following format:

```
                         MY PORTFOLIO

Symbol Shares   Current  Market    Purchase    Gain    %Gain
                  PPS    Value      Price
-------------------------------------------------------------
ORCL    100.00   23.25   2325.00   2708.06   -383.06   -14.14
SEG     100.00   30.00   3000.00   3244.62   -244.62    -7.53
-------------------------------------------------------------
  Security Value:        5325.00   5952.68   -627.68   -10.54
  Cash Balance:         94047.33
  Account Value:        99372.33
-------------------------------------------------------------
```

3.12 Write an embedded SQL program to view the ratings of a particular security. The program should prompt the user for the security symbol and produce the ratings list as follows:

```
Symbol: ORCL
Company: Oracle Corporation
Ratings:  Strong Buy  (rating = 1) : *****
          Buy         (rating = 2) : **
          Hold        (rating = 3) : **
          Sell        (rating = 4) :
          Strong Sell (rating = 5) :
          Consensus:        1.67
```

The number of stars after each rating is the number of analysts rating the start with that particular rating. The **Consensus** is the weighted mean of the ratings.

3.13 Write an embedded SQL program that prompts the user for the month and year and produces a monthly transaction log with the following format:

```
                MONTHLY TRANSACTION REPORT
                         05/1999
-------------------------------------------------------
  Date        Type Symbol Shares PPS   Commission  Amount
-------------------------------------------------------
20-MAY-1999  buy  ORCL   100.00 26.81   26.80    2708.05
20-MAY-1999  buy  SEG    100.00 32.12   32.11    3244.61
-------------------------------------------------------
```

3.14 Write an embedded SQL program that prompts the user for a substring of a company name and prints the price quotes for all securities whose company name has the substring. For example, if the user provided `Qu` as the substring, the following quotes (in the format specified) must be generated:

```
Symbol  Company               Last Sale    Ask      Bid
-------------------------------------------------------
QNTM  Quantum Corp            19.93      20.00    19.93
EAGL  Quotes                   0.00      37.87    37.75
BMY   Bristol-Myers Squibb    66.00       null     null
-------------------------------------------------------
```

Recursive Query Problems

3.15 Recursive queries are easily expressed in rule-based languages such as Datalog or Prolog. Rules are generally of the form

```
P :- Q1, Q2, ..., Qn
```

and are interpreted as follows:

```
if Q1 and Q2 and ... and Qn then P
```

Consider the database table

```
parent(child,childs_parent)
```

that records information about persons and their parents. The following set of recursive rules describes certain family relationships based on the `parent` relation:

```
sibling(X,Y) :- parent(X,Z), parent(Y,Z), X <> Y.

cousin(X,Y)  :- parent(X,Xp), parent(Y,Yp),
                sibling(Xp,Yp).
cousin(X,Y)  :- parent(X,Xp), parent(Y,Yp),
                cousin(Xp,Yp).

related(X,Y) :- sibling(X,Y).
related(X,Y) :- related(X,Z), parent(Y,Z).
related(X,Y) :- related(Z,Y), parent(X,Z).
```

The rule for `sibling` says that if two different persons `X` and `Y` have the same parent `Z`, then `X` and `Y` are siblings. The other rules are interpreted in a similar manner. Write an embedded SQL program that implements the following menu-based application that queries the family relationship database.

```
     MENU
(1) Given person, find all siblings
(2) Given person, find all cousins
(3) Given person, find all related persons
(4) Given two persons, test to see if they are
    siblings, cousins or related
(5) Quit
```

3.16 Consider a database describing a network of train connections in a large metropolitan train system. Assume that there are several lines and that trains operate between stations on particular lines. A relation, called `leg`, contains data indicating which two stations are directly connected without any intermediate stops. This relation has 3 columns: `line`, `depart`, and `arrive`. A row in this table indicates a direct connection starting at `depart` station and arriving at `arrive` station without stops on the line named `line`. A second relation, called `interchange`, records information about stations where it is possible to transfer from one line to another. This table has 3 columns: `station`, `line1`, and `line2`. A row in this table indicates that it is possible to transfer from `line1` to `line2` in the station named `station`. Now, consider the following rules that define a `trip`:

```
trip(L,S,E) :- leg(L,S,E).
trip(L,S,E) :- leg(L,S,I), trip(L,I,E).
trip(L,S,E) :- interchange(I,L,M), trip(L,S,I), trip(M,I,E).
```

The first rule states that if there is a direct connection between two stations then a trip can be made between those two stations. The second rule is a recursive rule which allows trips to be made on the same line and the third rule allows trips to be made with a possible change of lines. Write an embedded SQL program which will prompt the user for a starting station and a starting line and print all stations on the train network to which a trip can be made from the starting station and line.

CHAPTER

4

PL/SQL

This chapter introduces PL/SQL, its syntax and semantics, through several illustrative examples. Topics covered include data types and variables, program control statements, program structure constructs such as blocks, procedures, functions, and packages, database access using cursors, exception handling, triggers, stored procedures and functions, and two built-in packages: **dbms_output**, useful for debugging purposes, and **dbms_sql**, useful for dynamic SQL. PL/SQL access to Oracle8 objects is introduced at the end.

4.1 What Is PL/SQL?

PL/SQL is Oracle's procedural extension to SQL. It supplements SQL with several high-level programming language features such as block structure, variables, constants and types, assignment statement, conditional statements, loops, customized error handling, and structured data. Since PL/SQL is seamlessly integrated with Oracle's SQL implementation, many of the data types in PL/SQL are compatible with those of the database columns. In addition, almost any SQL statement can be used in a PL/SQL program without any special preprocessing, unlike embedded SQL. In this sense, PL/SQL can be considered a superset of SQL. The one exception is SQL's data definition statements such as **create table**. These are not allowed in PL/SQL, because PL/SQL code is compiled and it cannot refer to objects that do not yet exist at compile time. You can work around this restriction by using the dynamic SQL package **dbms_sql**, which allows for the data definition statements to be created dynamically at run time and have them executed.

Figure 4.1 PL/SQL scalar data types.

CATEGORY	DATA TYPE	DESCRIPTION
Numeric	`binary_integer`	Integer in the range $-2^{31}-1$ to $2^{31}-1$.
	`natural`	Integer in the range 0 to 2^{31}
	`positive`	Integer in the range 1 to 2^{31}
	`number(p,s)`	Same as Oracle SQL's `number`, where `p` is the precision and `s` is the scale
Character	`char(n)`	Fixed-length character string of length `n`.
	`varchar2(n)`	Variable-length character string of maximum length `n`
Boolean	`boolean`	Boolean data type `(true, false)`
Date-Time	`date`	Same as Oracle SQL's `date`

An interesting feature of PL/SQL is that it allows the user to store compiled code in the database, thereby allowing any number of applications to access and share the same functions and procedures. These applications can be running as a Web application, under the Web Application Server, or in a form application under the Developer/2000 environment. PL/SQL can also be used to implement program logic embedded within a client-side application such as those found in Oracle Forms triggers. Oracle's SQL*Plus environment also allows the execution of PL/SQL code, which makes it more than an SQL interpreter.

4.2 Data Types and Variables

PL/SQL supports a variety of data types. Since it is closely tied to Oracle SQL, many of these data types are compatible with Oracle SQL's data types, which can be classified into two categories: *scalar* and *composite*. The scalar data types include all of the Oracle SQL data types and a few new ones, such as `binary_integer` and `boolean`. The scalar data types are summarized in Figure 4.1.

Variables[1] are declared in PL/SQL using the syntax

⟨*variable-name*⟩ ⟨*datatype*⟩ `[not null][:=` ⟨*initial-value*⟩`];`

and constants are declared as follows:

1. PL/SQL identifiers are formed in the usual manner, by starting with a letter and containing letters, digits, and underscore characters. They are not case sensitive.

Figure 4.2 Variable and constant declaration.

```
i binary_integer;
cno number(5) not null := 1111;
cname varchar2(30);
commission real(5,2) := 12.5;
maxcolumns constant integer(2) := 30;
hired_date date;
done boolean;
```

Figure 4.3 Anchored variable declarations.

```
cnum customers.cno%type;
cname customers.cname%type;
commission real(5,2) := 12.5;
x commission%type;
```

⟨*constant-name*⟩ `constant` ⟨*datatype*⟩ `:=` ⟨*value*⟩`;`

Example 4.2.1 Some examples of variable and constant declarations are shown in Figure 4.2.

Any variable that is declared to be `not null` must be initialized in its declaration. All variables that are not defined to be `not null` are initialized to have the value `null`.

An important point to note here is that PL/SQL allows only one variable to be declared at a time. For example, the following would be invalid in PL/SQL:

```
a, b, c number;
```

Variables can also be declared to have *anchored* data types—i.e., their data types are determined by looking up another object's data type. This other object could be a column in the database, thereby providing the ability to match the data types of PL/SQL variables with the data types of columns defined in the database. The anchored declarations have the syntax

⟨*variable-name*⟩ ⟨*object*⟩`%type [not null][:=` ⟨*initial-value*⟩`];`

where `<object>` is another previously declared PL/SQL variable or a database column.

Example 4.2.2 Some examples of anchored declarations are shown in Figure 4.3.

There are at least two advantages to variables with anchored data types. First, these variables are synchronized with the database columns. The database columns may change their data types, and the PL/SQL program will remain compatible. Second, variables declared within the PL/SQL program are normalized—i.e., changing one data type does not affect how the corresponding anchored variables will be used. Of course, in both cases, the changes in data types have to be minor—i.e., changes in widths, precisions, or scales only. An important point to note is that anchored data types are evaluated at compile time. Therefore, if any changes are made to the data types of variables that affect other types, the program must be recompiled before these changes are reflected in their anchored variables.

PL/SQL provides two composite data types: *tables* and *records*, which are discussed in separate sections later in this chapter.

Comments in PL/SQL are expressed using one of two notations:

- *Single-line comments*. Any characters that follow two dashes (`--`) in a line are treated as comments by PL/SQL.
- *Block comments*. Any characters that follow the sequence of two-characters `/*` until the two-character sequence `*/` are treated as comments by PL/SQL.

4.3 Program Control Statements

Similar to any other high-level programming language, PL/SQL provides for the `null` statement, assignment statement, conditional statements, and loops. These statements are introduced in this section.

4.3.1 `null` Statement

The syntax of the `null` statement is

```
null;
```

and it performs no action. This statement is sometimes useful to improve readability of the program.

4.3.2 Assignment Statement

The assignment statement has the syntax

⟨*variable*⟩ `:=` ⟨*expression*⟩`;`

Figure 4.4 Assignment statements.

```
i := i + 1;
cname := 'Jones';
sales := price * qty;
```

where the expression on the right side is compatible with the data type of the variable on the left side of the assignment.

Example 4.3.1 Some examples of the assignment statement are given in Figure 4.4.

4.3.3 Conditional Statements

There are three varieties of the conditional statement in PL/SQL:

```
if-then
if-then-else
if-then-elsif
```

These are discussed next.

`if-then`

The syntax of the `if-then` statement in PL/SQL is

```
if <condition> then
  <statement-list>;
end if;
```

where `<condition>` is any Boolean expression. This statement ends with the keywords `end if`. Note the space character between the `end` and `if` keywords. The statements between these keywords are executed if the `condition` evaluates to `true`. Otherwise, these statements are skipped. In either case, control passes to the statement following the `if-then` statement.

Example 4.3.2 An example of the use of the `if-then` statement is shown in Figure 4.5.[2] The `put_line` procedure within the `dbms_output` package takes as input a `number`, `string`, or `date` value and sends it to the standard output. In this

2. This, and many subsequent examples, use the built-in package `dbms_output` and several of its procedures. Some of the built-in packages, including `dbms_output`, are discussed in Section 4.9.

Figure 4.5 `if-then` statement.

```
if (cnum > 1000) and (cnum < 9000) then
  i := i + 1;
  dbms_output.put_line('Customer ' || cnum);
end if;
```

Figure 4.6 `if-then-else` statement.

```
if (cnum > 1000) and (cnum < 9000) then
  i := i + 1;
  dbms_output.put_line('Valid Customer ' || cnum);
else
  j := j + 1;
  dbms_output.put_line('Invalid Customer ' || cnum);
end if;
```

example, a `string` value is sent in to the `put_line` procedure. The `||` operator is the PL/SQL concatenation operation, the same operator used in Oracle SQL.

if-then-else

The syntax of the `if-then-else` statement in PL/SQL is

```
if <condition> then
  <statement-list-1>;
else
  <statement-list-2>;
end if;
```

where `<condition>` is any Boolean expression. This statement also ends with the keywords `end if`. The statements between the `then` and `else` keywords are executed if the `condition` evaluates to `true`; the statements between the `else` and `end if` keywords are executed if the `condition` evaluates to `false` or `null`. In either case, control passes to the statement following the `if-then-else` statement.

Example 4.3.3 An example of the use of the `if-then-else` statement is shown in Figure 4.6.

Figure 4.7 `if-then-elsif` statement.

```
if (score > 90) then
    na := na + 1;
  elsif (score > 80) then
    nb := nb + 1;
  elsif (score > 70) then
    nc := nc + 1;
  elsif (score > 60) then
    nd := nd + 1;
  else
    nf := nf + 1;
end if;
```

if-then-elsif

The `if-then-elsif` variety of the conditional statement is used when one has to deal with multiple and mutually exclusive conditions. The syntax is as follows:

```
if <condition-1> then
    <statement-list-1>;
  elsif <condition-2> then
    <statement-list-2>;
  .
  .
  .
  elsif <condition-n> then
    <statement-list-n>;
  else
    <statement-list-n+1>
end if;
```

The conditions are evaluated from the beginning. The group of statements associated with the first condition that evaluates to **`true`** is executed, and control passes to the statement following this statement. If all the conditions evaluate to **`false`** or **`null`**, then the statements associated with the **`else`** keyword are executed. The final **`else`** clause is optional.

Example 4.3.4 An example of the **`if-then-elsif`** statement is given in Figure 4.7.

Figure 4.8 `loop` statement.

```
loop
  i := i + 1;
  if i > 10 then
    exit;
  end if;
  sum := sum + i;
end loop;
```

4.3.4 Loops

There are three kinds of loop control structures available in PL/SQL: `loop`, `for loop`, and `while loop`. These loops are discussed here.

loop

The basic `loop` statement has the following syntax:

```
loop
  <statement-list>;
end loop;
```

This loop repeatedly executes the statement list until it finds an `exit` statement.

Example 4.3.5 An example of the `loop` statement is given in Figure 4.8.

By placing the `exit` statement in a conditional statement within the loop body, the statements in the body of the loop are executed a certain number of times and control is transferred to the next statement following the loop when the condition is met. The `if-then` statement in the above example could have been replaced by the following equivalent `exit-when` statement:

```
exit when i > 10;
```

The basic loop has the potential for not terminating at all. If the `exit` statement is never encountered within the body of the loop, the loop will never terminate.

for loop

If the number of times the loop body is to be executed is known, the `for loop` statement can be used. The syntax of the `for loop` is

Figure 4.9 `for loop`.

```
for i in 1..10 loop
  dbms_output.put_line('i = ' || i);
  sum := sum + i;
end loop;

for i in reverse 1..5 loop
  dbms_output.put_line('i = ' || i);
  sum := sum + 2*i;
end loop;
```

```
for <loop-counter> in [reverse] <lower>..<upper> loop
  <statements>;
end loop;
```

where `<loop-counter>` is the loop control variable that is implicitly declared by PL/SQL. It should not be declared in the program. The lower and upper bounds for the loop control variable are specified in `<lower>` and `<upper>` respectively. These must be integer expressions. The **`reverse`** keyword is optional; if it is not used, the loop starts with the loop control variable set at the lower bound, each time incrementing (by 1) the loop counter variable until it reaches the upper bound. If the **`reverse`** keyword is used, the loop control variable starts at the upper bound and each time is decremented (by 1) until it reaches the lower bound. In either case, if the lower bound is greater than the upper bound, the loop body is skipped. PL/SQL does not provide the **`steps`** feature in its `for loop`, which would allow the increment or decrement of the loop control variable to be done by a number other than 1.

Example 4.3.6 A couple of examples of the `for loop` statement are shown in Figure 4.9. The first `for loop` executes 10 times, with `i` starting at 1 and terminating at `10`. Since the loop control variable is automatically declared by PL/SQL in the `for loop`, its scope is the `for loop` and is not available outside of the loop. Therefore, it would be incorrect to use the value of the loop control variable after the loop has terminated. The second `for loop` executes five times, with `i` starting at `5` and terminating at `1`.

`while loop`

The `while loop` statement has the syntax

Figure 4.10 `while loop`.

```
i := 1;
sum := 0;
while (i < 1000) loop
  sum := sum + i;
  i := 2 * i;
end loop;
```

```
while <condition> loop
  <statement-list>
end loop;
```

and it continues to execute the statements in its body as long as the condition remains **`true`**. The loop terminates when the condition evaluates to **`false`** or **`null`**. The **`exit`** statement may also be used to exit the loop.

Example 4.3.7 An example of the **`while loop`** statement is given in Figure 4.10. This program fragment that involves the **`while loop`** computes the sum of the powers of 2 that do not exceed 1000.

4.4 Program Structure

PL/SQL, like many high-level languages, groups its statements into units called *blocks*. Blocks can be unnamed (*anonymous blocks*) or named (*sub-programs*). The sub-programs can be either functions or procedures, just as in any high-level programming language. PL/SQL further allows the possibility of grouping related functions, procedures, and data types into *packages*. These features of PL/SQL are discussed in this section.

4.4.1 Anonymous Blocks

An anonymous block has the following structure:

```
declare
  -- Declaration Section
  -- Data, sub-program declarations
```

```
begin
  -- Executable Section
  null; -- Program statements

exception
  -- Exception Section
  -- Exception handlers
  when others then
     null; -- default Handler

end;
```

There are three parts to an anonymous block: (1) the declaration section, (2) the executable section, and (3) the exception section. The declaration section begins with the keyword **declare** and ends with the keyword **begin**. The declaration section consists of type, constant, variable, exception, and cursor declarations. At the end, sub-programs, if there are any, are declared.

Example 4.4.1 An example of an anonymous block is shown in Figure 4.11. This block gets all the rows from the **customers** table and prints the names of the customers on the screen. It does use several features of PL/SQL, such as PL/SQL tables and cursors, that will be covered later in this chapter.

Anonymous blocks can be executed within the SQL*Plus environment similar to SQL statements. Normally, the anonymous block is placed in a file, and the file is executed within SQL*Plus.

Example 4.4.2 A sample run of the anonymous block is shown in Figure 4.12. It is assumed that the anonymous block is placed in a file `p2.sql`.

4.4.2 Procedures and Functions

Procedures are declared using the following syntax:

```
procedure <proc-name>
     [(<parameter>, ... , <parameter>)] is
  [<declarations>]
begin
  executable section;
[exception
  exception handlers;]
end;
```

Figure 4.11 Anonymous block.

```
declare
  type customers_table is table  of customers%rowtype
       index by binary_integer;

  c_table customers_table;
  cursor c is select cno,cname,street,zip,phone
              from   customers;
  c_rec c%rowtype;
  i binary_integer;
begin
  i := 1;
  for c_rec in c loop
    exit when c%notfound;
    c_table(i) := c_rec;
    i := i + 1;
  end loop;
  for i in 1..c_table.count loop
    dbms_output.put_line(
      'c_table(' || i || ').cname = ' || c_table(i).cname);
  end loop;
end;
/
```

Figure 4.12 Execution script for an anonymous block.

```
SQL> start p2
c_table(1).cname = Charles
c_table(2).cname = Bertram
c_table(3).cname = Barbara

PL/SQL procedure successfully completed.

SQL> exit
```

where

- `<proc-name>` is the name given to the procedure.
- `<parameter>` is a parameter with the following syntax:[3]

  ```
  <variable-name> [in | out | in out] <datatype>
  ```

  The `in`, `out`, and `in out` parameter types are for input, output, and input/output parameters respectively.
- `<declarations>` is the declaration of local variables, constants, etc.
- After the executable section, the procedure may end with an optional exception section, similar to anonymous blocks.

Example 4.4.3 The anonymous block shown below contains a procedure that accepts as input a customer number and returns the name, phone, and city values for that customer. If such a customer is not found, `status` is returned as `false`; otherwise `status` is returned as `true`.

```
DECLARE
  cnum customers.cno%type;
  ccname customers.cname%type;
  cphone customers.phone%type;
  ccity zipcodes.city%type;
  status boolean;

  procedure get_cust_details(
      cust_no    in  customers.cno%type,
      cust_name  out customers.cname%type,
      cust_phone out customers.phone%type,
      cust_city  out zipcodes.city%type,
      status     out boolean) is
  begin
    select cname,phone,city
    into   cust_name,cust_phone,cust_city
    from   customers,zipcodes
    where  customers.zip = zipcodes.zip and
           customers.cno = cust_no;
    status := true;
```

3. The data type of the parameter cannot be constrained—i.e., it is illegal to specify the data type as `char(20)` or `varchar2(40)`; these must be specified simply as `char` or `varchar2`.

```
    exception
      when no_data_found then
        status := false;
  end;
begin
  cnum := 1111;
  get_cust_details(cnum,ccname,cphone,ccity,status);
  if (status) then
    dbms_output.put_line(cnum   || '  ' || ccname || '  ' ||
                         cphone || '  ' || ccity);
  else
    dbms_output.put_line('Customer ' || cnum       ||
                         ' not found');
  end if;
  cnum := 5555;
  get_cust_details(cnum,ccname,cphone,ccity,status);
  if (status) then
    dbms_output.put_line(cnum   || '  ' || ccname || '  ' ||
                         cphone || '  ' || ccity);
  else
    dbms_output.put_line('Customer ' || cnum       ||
                         ' not found');
  end if;
end;
/
```

The following is a session capture of the run under SQL*Plus (assuming that the above block is stored in a file called `p3.sql`).

```
SQL> start p3
1111  Charles  316-636-5555  Wichita
Customer 5555 not found

PL/SQL procedure successfully completed.

SQL>
```

Functions are declared using the following syntax:

```
function <function-name>
     [(<parameter>, ... , <parameter>)]
   return <datatype> is
```

```
  [<declarations>]
begin
  executable section;
[exception
  exception handlers;]
end;
```

The syntax is almost identical to that of a procedure declaration except that the function declaration requires the **return** keyword followed by a data type.

Example 4.4.4 The anonymous block shown below contains a function declaration. Given an employee number, the function computes and returns the total sales for that employee.

```
declare
  enum customers.cno%type;
  total number(10,2);
  status boolean;

  function total_emp_sales(emp_no in  employees.eno%type)
    return number is
  sales number;
  begin
    select sum(price*qty)
    into   sales
    from   orders,odetails,parts
    where  orders.eno = emp_no and
           orders.ono = odetails.ono and
           odetails.pno = parts.pno;
    return (sales);
  end;

begin
  enum := 1000;
  total := total_emp_sales(enum);
  dbms_output.put_line('Total sales for employee ' ||
                         enum   || ' is ' || total);
end;
/
```

The following is a screen capture of the run under SQL*Plus (assuming that the above block is stored in a file `p4.sql`).

```
SQL> start p4
Total sales for employee 1000 is 279.87

PL/SQL procedure successfully completed.

SQL>
```

4.4.3 Stored Procedures and Functions

Until now, the procedures and functions discussed were part of an anonymous block and were called from within the executable section of the anonymous block. However, it is possible to store the procedure or function definition in the database and have it invoked from various environments that have access to the database. This feature in PL/SQL is very attractive, as it allows for sharing of PL/SQL code by different applications running at different places. The `create procedure` and `create function` statements are used to create the stored procedures and functions. Their syntax is shown below:

```
create [or replace] procedure <proc-name>
  [(<parameter-list>)] as
  <declarations>
begin
  <executable-section>
  [exception
    <exception-section>]
end;

create [or replace] function <func-name>
  [(<parameter-list>)] return <datatype> as
  <declarations>
begin
  <executable-section>
  [exception
    <exception-section>]
end;
```

The syntax is almost identical to declaring procedures or functions within anonymous blocks, except for the `create` keyword at the beginning and the `as` keyword instead of the `is` keyword.

Example 4.4.5 The stored function shown below takes as input a customer number and returns the city in which the customer lives.

```
create or replace function get_city(cnum in customers.cno%type)
      return zipcodes.city%type as
  ccity zipcodes.city%type;
begin
  select city
  into   ccity
  from   customers,zipcodes
  where  cno = cnum and
         customers.zip = zipcodes.zip;
  return (ccity);
end;
/
```

A stored procedure or a function can be invoked from various environments, including an SQL statement, another stored procedure or function, an anonymous block or a procedure or function defined within it, an embedded SQL program, a database trigger, and Oracle tools such as Developer/2000 Forms. There are some restrictions when a stored function is invoked from within an SQL statement—for example, that there should be no `out` parameters, the function should be applicable to a row in the table, and the return data type should be compatible with an SQL data type.

Example 4.4.6 The following is a call made to the stored function `get_city` in an SQL query:

```
    SQL> select cno,cname,get_city(cno)
      2  from customers;

          CNO CNAME    GET_CITY(CNO)
        ----- -------- -------------
         1111 Charles  Wichita

         2222 Bertram  Wichita

         3333 Barbara  Fort Dodge
  SQL>
```

4.4.4 Packages

A *package* is a group of related PL/SQL objects (variables, constants, types, and cursors), procedures, and functions that is stored in the database. A package definition consists of two parts: the package *specification* and the package *body*. The package specification is the interface that is used by other programs to make a call to the functions and procedures stored in the database as part of the package or to use certain types or cursors defined in the package. The package body contains the actual code and any other implementation-dependent details for the functions and procedures of the package. It may also contain some private objects not visible to the user of the package. The concept of a package is similar to that of an object in an object-oriented language. An advantage of creating packages in this manner is that the package body can change without affecting any programs that are accessing the package.

The syntax for creating a package specification is

```
create [or replace] package <package-name> as
  <PL/SQL declarations>;
end;
```

where `<PL/SQL declarations>` is any set of variable, type, constant, procedure, or function declarations. The procedure and function declarations consist only of the name, parameter list, and function return type. They do not contain the actual code, since this has to be specified in the package body. The syntax to create a package body is

```
create [or replace] package body <package-name> as
  <PL/SQL declarations>;
[begin
  <initialization-code>
 end;]
end;
```

where the `<PL/SQL declarations>` now contain the code for the functions and procedures defined in the specification. At the end of the body, you can specify an initialization code fragment that initializes variables and other features of the package.

Example 4.4.7 The code fragment below defines a package called `process_orders`, containing three procedures:

- `add_order`: This procedure takes as input an order number, customer number, employee number, and received date and tries to insert a new row in the `orders` table. If the received date is `null`, the current date is used. The shipped date is left as `null`. In case of any errors, an entry is made in the `orders_errors` table, which is assumed to have three columns: (1) transaction date, (2) order number, and (3) message column.

- `add_order_details`: This procedure receives as input an order number, part number, and quantity, and attempts to add a row corresponding to the input in the `odetails` table. If the quantity on hand for the part is less than what is ordered, an error message is sent to the `odetails_errors` table, which consists of four columns: (1) transaction date, (2) order number, (3) part number, and (4) message column. Otherwise, the part is sold by subtracting the quantity ordered from the quantity on hand for this part. A check is also made for the reorder level. If the updated quantity for the part is below the reorder level, a message is sent to the `restock` table, which consists of two columns: the transaction date and the part number of the part to be reordered.
- `ship_order`: This procedure takes as input an order number and a shipped date and tries to update the `shipped` value for the order. If the shipped date is `null`, the current date is used. In case of any errors, a message is left in the `orders_errors` table.

```
-- PACKAGE PROCESS_ORDERS SPECS ---

create or replace package process_orders as
  procedure add_order_details
    (onum      in odetails.ono%type,
     pnum      in odetails.pno%type,
     quantity  in odetails.qty%type);
  procedure add_order
    (onum in orders.ono%type,
     cnum in orders.cno%type,
     enum in orders.eno%type,
     receive in date);
  procedure ship_order
    (onum in orders.ono%type,
     ship in date);
end;
/
show errors
```

```
-- PACKAGE PROCESS_ORDERS BODY ---

create or replace package body process_orders as

  procedure add_order_details
    (onum      in odetails.ono%type,
     pnum      in odetails.pno%type,
     quantity  in odetails.qty%type) is
  cur_q parts.qoh%type;
  lev parts.olevel%type;
  begin
    select qoh,olevel
    into   cur_q,lev
    from   parts
    where  pno = pnum;
    if (cur_q > quantity) then
      update parts
      set qoh = qoh - quantity
      where pno = pnum;
      if (cur_q - quantity) < lev then
        insert into restock
          values (sysdate,pnum);
      end if;
      insert into odetails
        values (onum,pnum,quantity);
    else
      insert into odetails_errors
        values(sysdate,onum,pnum,'Do not have enough to sell');
    end if;
  exception
    when others then
      rollback work;
      insert into odetails_errors
        values(sysdate,onum,pnum,'error inserting order detail');
  end;

  procedure add_order
    (onum in orders.ono%type,
     cnum in orders.cno%type,
```

```
     enum in orders.eno%type,
     receive in date) is
  begin
    if (receive is null) then
      insert into orders
        values (onum,cnum,enum,sysdate,null);
    else
      insert into orders
        values (onum,cnum,enum,receive,null);
    end if;
  exception
    when others then
      rollback work;
      insert into orders_errors
        values(sysdate,onum,'error inserting order');
  end;

  procedure ship_order
    (onum in orders.ono%type,
     ship in date) is
  begin
    if (ship is null) then
      update orders
      set    shipped = sysdate
      where  ono = onum;
    else
      update orders
      set    shipped = ship
      where  ono = onum;
    end if;
  exception
    when others then
      rollback work;
      insert into orders_errors
        values(sysdate,onum,'error updating shipped date');
  end;
end;
/
show errors
```

The user is encouraged to execute the following commands against the mail-order database in SQL*Plus.

```
SQL> execute process_orders.add_order
        (2000,1111,1000,null);
SQL> execute process_orders.add_order_details
        (2000,10509,50);
SQL> execute process_orders.add_order_details
        (2000,10701,200);
SQL> execute process_orders.ship_order
        (2000,'29-JAN-98');
SQL> execute process_orders.add_order
        (2001,1234,1000,null)
SQL> execute process_orders.add_order_details
        (2000,10999,5);
```

After these commands are executed in SQL*Plus, it would be interesting to examine the three tables **restock**, **orders_errors**, and **odetails_errors**.

4.5 Triggers

An SQL *trigger* is a mechanism that automatically executes a specified PL/SQL block (referred to as the *triggered action*) when a *triggering event* occurs on a table. The triggering event may be one of **insert**, **delete**, or **update**. The trigger is associated with a database table and is *fired* when the triggering event takes place on the table.

Triggers are created in Oracle using the **create trigger** statement, whose syntax is

```
create [or replace] trigger trigger-name
{before | after}
{delete | insert | update [of column [, column] ...]}
[or
{delete | insert | update [of column [, column] ...]}
] ...
ON table-name
[ [referencing { old [as] <old> [new [as] <new>]
              | new [as] <new> [old [as] <old>] } ]
 for each row
 [when (condition)] ]
pl/sql_block
```

where the following assumptions can be made:

- The optional **or replace** is used to change the definition of an existing trigger without first dropping it.
- **trigger-name** is the name of the trigger to be created.
- **before** indicates that Oracle fires the trigger before executing the triggering statement, and **after** indicates that Oracle fires the trigger after executing the triggering statement.
- **delete** indicates that the triggering event is a **delete** statement.
- **insert** indicates that the triggering event is an **insert** statement.
- **update...of** indicates that the triggering event is an **update** statement involving the columns mentioned.
- **table-name** is the name of the table on which the trigger is defined.
- **referencing** specifies correlation names that can be used to refer to the old and new values of the row components that are being affected by the trigger.
- **for each row** designates the trigger to be a row trigger—i.e., the trigger is fired once for each row that is affected by the triggering event and meets the optional trigger constraint defined in the **when** clause. If this clause is omitted, the trigger is a statement trigger—i.e., the trigger is fired only once when the triggering event is met if the optional trigger constraint is met.
- **when** specifies the trigger restriction. The trigger restriction contains an SQL condition that must be satisfied for the trigger to be fired.
- **pl/sql_block** is the PL/SQL block that Oracle executes as the trigger action.

Example 4.5.1 The trigger that follows is executed when a row is inserted into the **odetails** table. The trigger checks to see if the quantity ordered is more than the quantity on hand. If it is, an error message is generated, and the row is not inserted. Otherwise, the trigger updates the quantity on hand for the part and checks to see if it has fallen below the reorder level. If it has, it sends a row to the **restock** table indicating that the part needs to be reordered.

```
create or replace trigger insert_odetails
before insert on odetails
for each row
declare my_qoh parts.qoh%type;
        my_olevel parts.olevel%type;
        out_of_stock exception;
begin
```

```
  select qoh, olevel
  into   my_qoh, my_olevel
  from   parts
  where  parts.pno = :new.pno;

  if (:new.qty < my_qoh) then
    update parts
    set    qoh = qoh - :new.qty
    where  parts.pno = :new.pno;
    if ((my_qoh - :new.qty) < my_olevel) then
       update parts
       set    qoh = olevel * 5
       where  parts.pno = :new.pno;
       insert into restock values (sysdate,:new.pno);
    end if;
  else
    raise out_of_stock;
 end if;
exception
  when out_of_stock then
-- error number between -20000 and -20999
    raise_application_error(-20001,'CANNOT ADD THIS ODETAILS ROW');
end;
/
```

Assume that the following anonymous block (stored in file `trig2test.sql`) is executed to create a new order.

```
declare
  quantity_ordered_too_big exception;
  pragma exception_init(quantity_ordered_too_big,-20001);
begin
  process_orders.add_order(2000,1111,1000,null);
  insert into odetails values(2000,10900,10);
  dbms_output.put_line('Added row to odetails table');
  insert into odetails values(2000,10506,1500);
exception
  when quantity_ordered_too_big then
    dbms_output.put_line('Could not add part to order');
    dbms_output.put_line(sqlerrm);
end;
/
```

The following SQL*Plus session illustrates the use of the trigger. The part numbers, quantity on hand, and reorder levels before the block executes are shown below:

```
SQL> select pno,qoh,olevel
  2  from parts
  3  where pno in (10900,10506);

       PNO        QOH     OLEVEL
---------- ---------- ----------
     10506        200         20
     10900         90         30
```

The execution of the **trig2test** block is shown next:

```
SQL> start trig2test
Added row to odetails table
Could not add part to order
ORA-20001: CANNOT ADD THIS ODETAILS ROW
ORA-06512: at "BOOK.INSERT_ODETAILS",
line 27
ORA-04088: error during execution of trigger
'BOOK.INSERT_ODETAILS'

PL/SQL procedure successfully completed.
```

Notice that the first **odetails** row was added successfully, but did result in an entry being added to the **restock** table as the **qoh** value went below the reorder level. The second row is not added to the **odetails** table since the quantity ordered is greater than the quantity on hand. The trigger raises an **application error** and sends it back to the anonymous block that caused the trigger to fire. The anonymous block then processes this exception and exits gracefully. The **restock** table and the relevant columns of the **parts** table, after the trigger is executed, are shown below:

```
SQL> select * from restock;

TDATE            PNO
--------- ----------
14-APR-98      10900

SQL> select pno,qoh,olevel
  2  from parts
  3  where pno in (10900,10506);
```

```
       PNO        QOH     OLEVEL
---------- ---------- ----------
     10506        200         20
     10900        150         30
```

Notice that the quantity on hand value for the `10900` part has been reset to five times the `olevel` value by the trigger.

The **`raise_application_error`** procedure is a useful way to communicate application-specific errors from the server side (usually a database trigger) to the client-side application (in this case it is the anonymous block). The anonymous block in this example is executed in the server side itself, but the block running on the client side can be easily envisioned.

Example 4.5.2 The trigger that follows is defined on the **`parts`** table and is triggered when the **`price`** column is updated. Each time someone updates the price of a particular part, the trigger makes an entry in a log file of this update along with the **`userid`** of the person performing the update and the date of update. The log file is created using

```
create table parts_log (
  pno            number(5),
  username       char(8),
  update_date    date,
  old_price      number(6,2),
  new_price      number(6,2));
```

The trigger is defined as

```
create or replace trigger update_price_of_parts
after update of price on parts
for each row
begin
 insert into parts_log
 values (:old.pno,user,sysdate,:old.price,:new.price);
end;
/
show errors
```

The following SQL*Plus session illustrates the use of this trigger.

```
SQL> update parts set price = 55.00 where pno = 10900;

1 row updated.
```

```
SQL> select * from parts_log;

       PNO USERNAME UPDATE_DA  OLD_PRICE  NEW_PRICE
---------- -------- --------- ---------- ----------
     10900 BOOK     26-JAN-98      24.99         55

SQL>
```

4.6 Database Access Using Cursors

As was mentioned earlier, almost any SQL statement can be used in a PL/SQL program. However, as was the case with embedded SQL, when the result of an SQL query (**select** statement) consists of more than one row, the simple **select into** statement cannot be used. To handle this situation, PL/SQL provides *cursors*. A PL/SQL cursor, just like an embedded SQL cursor, allows the program to fetch and process information from the database into the PL/SQL program, one row at a time. The cursors used for processing a query resulting in more than one row are called *explicit cursors*. These are in contrast to *implicit cursors*, which are automatically defined by PL/SQL for the **select into** statements that result in one or fewer rows and for the **insert**, **delete**, and **update** operations. The programmer need not be aware of the implicit cursors, as they are automatically created and used by PL/SQL.

Cursors can also have parameters. Such cursors are referred to as *parameterized cursors*. Having parameters makes cursors more flexible, and several similar queries can be coded into one cursor definition using the parameter mechanism.

A relatively new feature in PL/SQL is that of a *cursor variable*. In contrast to explicit cursors, which require a select statement to be specified in their declaration, cursor variables provide a pointer or reference to the cursor work area and thereby increase the flexibility of the use of cursors.

4.6.1 Explicit Cursors

The syntax for declaring a PL/SQL explicit cursor without parameters is

```
cursor <cname> [return <return-spec>] is
    <select-statement>;
```

where

- `<cname>` is the name given to the cursor.
- `<select-statement>` is the SQL select statement associated with the cursor.

The optional **return** clause specifies the row structure that is to be returned by the cursor. The **return** clause is usually specified so that the compiler can verify the usage of this cursor at various points in the program. Otherwise, there is a possibility of a run-time error if the cursor is not used properly. Here are some examples of cursor declarations:

```
cursor c1 return customers%rowtype is
  select * from customers;
cursor c2 is
  select pno,pname,price*markdown sale_price
  from   parts;
```

Cursor `c1` uses the **return** clause, which is consistent with the select list of the select statement in the SQL query associated with the cursor. Cursor **c2** uses a PL/SQL variable **markdown** in the select statement associated with the cursor.

The cursor definition may involve PL/SQL variables. These variables should not be preceded by a colon (`:`), as was done in embedded SQL. PL/SQL easily resolves the name conflicts. However, it is important to note that if a cursor definition has a PL/SQL variable with the same name as that of a database column that is relevant to the cursor, the database column name gets precedence and all occurrences of the name are treated as the database column, not the PL/SQL variable. For this reason, it is always advisable to have a naming convention for PL/SQL variables that differentiates them from database column names.

The **return** clause is also useful when cursors are defined in a PL/SQL package. This clause can be used in the package specification, and the actual SQL query that is associated with the cursor can be specified in the package body, as the following example illustrates:

```
package ppp is
  type cur_rec_type is record
   (pno   parts.pno%type,
    pname parts.pname%type,
    sale_price parts.price%type);

  cursor c2 return cur_rec_type;
  .
  .
  .
end ppp;
```

```
package body ppp is

  cursor c2 return cur_rec_type is
    select pno,pname,price*markdown sale_price
    from   parts;
  .
  .
  .
end ppp;
```

Once a cursor has been declared, it can be processed using the **open**, **fetch**, and **close** statements. The syntax for these statements is

```
open <cname>;
fetch <cname> into <Record-or-VariableList>;
close <cname>;
```

The record or the variable list into which the cursor rows are to be fetched must be compatible with the cursor row type. Otherwise, a run-time error can occur. It is always good programming practice to (1) open cursors only when they are going to be used and not much earlier and (2) close all cursors as soon as they are processed and not wait until later. By adhering to these practices, memory is optimally used.

To obtain information about a particular cursor that is being processed, *cursor attributes* can be used. There are four such attributes:

- `%found`. This attribute returns `true` if a record was successfully fetched from the cursor; otherwise it returns `false`.
- `%notfound`. This attribute returns `true` if a record was not successfully fetched from the cursor; otherwise it returns `false`.
- `%rowcount`. This attribute returns the number of records fetched from the cursor at the time it is used.
- `%isopen`. This cursor returns `true` if the cursor is open; otherwise it returns `false`.

The following example illustrates the use of the cursor statements and attributes:

```
declare
  cursor c1 is
    select cno,cname,city
    from   customers,zipcodes
    where  customers.zip = zipcodes.zip;
  c1_rec c1%rowtype;
begin
```

```
  if not c1%isopen then
    open c1;
  end if;
  fetch c1 into c1_rec;
  while c1%found loop
    dbms_output.put_line('Row Number ' || c1%rowcount || '> ' ||
                         c1_rec.cno || '  ' || c1_rec.cname  ||
                        '  ' || c1_rec.city);
    fetch c1 into c1_rec;
  end loop;
  close c1;
end;
/
```

Cursor `for loop`

PL/SQL provides a variation of the **for loop** to be used with cursors. This loop is very useful in situations where all rows of the cursor are to be processed. The syntax is

```
for <record_index> in <cname> loop
  <loop-body>;
end loop;
```

where

- `<record-index>` is a record variable that is implicitly declared by PL/SQL. The scope of this record variable is the `for loop` and cannot be accessed outside the `for loop`. The structure of the record is the same as that of a row of the cursor.
- `<cname>` is the cursor that is to be processed.

Within the body of this loop, the individual fields of the records can be accessed in the usual way. The loop terminates automatically when all rows of the cursor have been fetched. There is no need to **open**, **fetch**, or **close** the cursor, and there is no need to declare the record into which the cursor rows are to be fetched. The previous example is modified with a cursor `for loop` in the following:

```
declare
  cursor c1 is
    select cno,cname,city
    from   customers,zipcodes
    where  customers.zip = zipcodes.zip;
begin
```

```
    for c1_rec in c1 loop
      dbms_output.put_line('Row Number ' || c1%rowcount || '> ' ||
                           c1_rec.cno || '  ' || c1_rec.cname  ||
                           '  ' || c1_rec.city);
    end loop;
  end;
  /
```

Notice the economy of code when the cursor `for loop` is used.

An explicit cursor may also be "implicitly" defined within a cursor `for loop` as follows:

```
for i in (select * from employees) loop
  .
  .
  .
end loop;
```

Here, the cursor is not even declared in the **declare** section. In this case, there is no need to declare, open, fetch, or close the cursor.

4.6.2 Parameterized Cursors

PL/SQL allows for cursors to take input parameters. This feature makes the cursors more flexible. The syntax for declaring a PL/SQL explicit cursor with parameters is

```
cursor <cname>  (<parameter-list>)
  [return <return-spec>]
  is <select-statement>;
```

The parameters are specified immediately after the cursor name as a list within parentheses. An example of cursors with parameters is shown below:

```
cursor c3(city_in in zipcodes.city%type) is
  select orders.eno,ename,sum(qty*price) Sales
  from   employees,orders,odetails,parts,zipcodes
  where  employees.eno = orders.eno and
         orders.ono = odetails.ono and
         odetails.pno = parts.pno and
         employees.zip = zipcodes.zip and
         zipcodes.city = city_in
  group by orders.eno,ename;
```

Cursor `c3` involves a parameter `city_in`, which is used in the SQL select statement associated with the cursor. Given a city, this cursor returns the sales totals for every employee from that city. The **open** statement for such cursors will have the actual argument for the parameters as follows:

```
open c3('Wichita');
```

If a cursor loop is used to process this cursor, it would be done as follows:

```
for c3_rec in c3('Wichita') loop
  .
  .
  .
end loop;
```

4.6.3 Select for Update

PL/SQL cursors can also be used to perform updates (**update** and **delete**) on the database. The cursor, when used for this purpose, should be declared using the **for update** clause as follows:

```
cursor <cname> is
  <select-statement> for update;
```

The select statement should involve only one database table; otherwise it does not make much sense to perform an update on a row generated from more than one table. Once the cursor is declared in this manner, the following statements can be used to perform a delete of a row or a modification to the row.

```
update <table-name>
set    <set-clause>
where current of <cname>;

delete from <table-name>
where current of <cname>;
```

It is important to note that these two statements can be used only after the cursor is opened and a particular row has been fetched. Here is a simple example that uses the cursor mechanism to update the price of parts. In the following anonymous block, the price of every part whose quantity-on-hand value is more than 175 is set to 80 percent of its old price.

```
declare
  cursor c1 is
    select * from parts
    for update;
  c1_rec c1%rowtype;
```

```
begin
  for c1_rec in c1 loop
    if (c1_rec.qoh > 175) then
      update parts set price = 0.8 * price
      where current of c1;
    end if;
  end loop;
end;
/
```

4.6.4 Cursor Variables

In contrast to explicit cursors, cursor variables are not required to have the SQL select statement associated with them at the time of their declaration. Different SQL select statements can be associated with cursor variables at different times in the program, and these cursor variables can be passed as parameters to other program modules. In a sense, cursor variables are similar to PL/SQL variables, and explicit cursors are similar to PL/SQL constants. This results in the possibility of the cursor being opened in one procedure, and possibly a few rows fetched in the procedure, and the rest of the processing happening in another procedure.

To declare a cursor variable, first a type declaration must be made and then the variable must be declared. The syntax is

```
type ⟨cursor-var-type-name⟩ is ref cursor
  [return ⟨return-type⟩];
```

The optional **return** clause is used to constrain the type of select statement that will be associated with the cursor at a later time. If the **return** clause is missing, any select statement can be associated with the cursor. Cursor variables that are declared with the **return** clause are sometimes referred to as *constrained cursor variables.*

Cursor variables are opened using the following syntax:

```
open <cname> for <select-statement>;
```

This is the time when an SQL query is associated with a cursor variable. If the cursor variable is a constrained variable, the return type of the variable must be consistent with the select list used in the query in the `open` statement. Otherwise, a `rowtype_mismatch` exception will be generated by the system. Of course, if the cursor is not constrained, the `open` statement should succeed. The select statement must be explicitly stated; it should not be a value of a string variable. In this sense, the cursor variables are not a substitute for dynamic SQL (the `dbms_sql` package).

Once opened, a cursor variable is used in the same manner as explicit cursors. The `fetch` and `close` statements use the same syntax that is used for explicit cursors. All the cursor attributes are also available on cursor variables.

The example below illustrates the use of cursor variables. The procedure described here displays the table whose name is an input parameter. The table name must be one of the six tables of the mail-order database: `customers`, `employees`, `orders`, `odetails`, `parts`, or `zipcodes`. A cursor variable is declared whose return type is not stated in the declaration. Then, based on the table name, the appropriate select statement is used to open the cursor. The cursor is then processed.

```
create or replace procedure display_table
      (tname IN varchar2) as
  type cur_type is ref cursor;

  invalid_table_error exception;
  c1 cur_type;
  emp_rec  employees%rowtype;
  cust_rec customers%rowtype;
  zip_rec  zipcodes%rowtype;
  ord_rec  orders%rowtype;
  od_rec   odetails%rowtype;
  part_rec parts%rowtype;

begin
  if upper(tname) = 'CUSTOMERS' then
    open c1 for select * from customers;
  elsif upper(tname) = 'EMPLOYEES' then
    open c1 for select * from employees;
  elsif upper(tname) = 'ORDERS' then
    open c1 for select * from orders;
  elsif upper(tname) = 'ODETAILS' then
    open c1 for select * from odetails;
  elsif upper(tname) = 'PARTS' then
    open c1 for select * from parts;
  elsif upper(tname) = 'ZIPCODES' then
    open c1 for select * from zipcodes;
  else
    raise invalid_table_error;
  end if;
```

```
loop
  if upper(tname) = 'CUSTOMERS' then
    fetch c1 into cust_rec;
    exit when c1%notfound;
    dbms_output.put_line(cust_rec.cno || ' ' ||
                         cust_rec.cname || ' ' ||
                         cust_rec.street || ' ' ||
                         cust_rec.zip || ' ' ||
                         cust_rec.phone);
  elsif upper(tname) = 'EMPLOYEES' then
    fetch c1 into emp_rec;
    exit when c1%notfound;
    dbms_output.put_line(emp_rec.eno || ' ' ||
                         emp_rec.ename || ' ' ||
                         emp_rec.zip || ' ' ||
                         emp_rec.hdate);
  elsif upper(tname) = 'PARTS' then
    fetch c1 into part_rec;
    exit when c1%notfound;
    dbms_output.put_line(part_rec.pno || ' ' ||
                         part_rec.pname || ' ' ||
                         part_rec.qoh || ' ' ||
                         part_rec.price || ' ' ||
                         part_rec.olevel);
  elsif upper(tname) = 'ZIPCODES' then
    fetch c1 into zip_rec;
    exit when c1%notfound;
    dbms_output.put_line(zip_rec.zip || ' ' ||
                         zip_rec.city);
  elsif upper(tname) = 'ORDERS' then
    fetch c1 into ord_rec;
    exit when c1%notfound;
    dbms_output.put_line(ord_rec.ono || ' ' ||
                         ord_rec.cno || ' ' ||
                         ord_rec.eno || ' ' ||
                         ord_rec.received || ' ' ||
                         ord_rec.shipped);
  elsif upper(tname) = 'ODETAILS' then
    fetch c1 into od_rec;
    exit when c1%notfound;
```

```
      dbms_output.put_line(od_rec.ono || ' ' ||
                           od_rec.pno || ' ' ||
                           od_rec.qty);
    end if;
  end loop;
  close c1;

  exception
    when invalid_table_error then
      dbms_output.put_line('NOT A VALID TABLE NAME');
end;
/
```

The following is a sample SQL*Plus session to illustrate the above example.

```
SQL> execute display_table('customers');
1111 Charles 123 Main St. 67226 316-636-5555
2222 Bertram 237 Ash Avenue 67226 316-689-5555
3333 Barbara 111 Inwood St. 60606 316-111-1234

PL/SQL procedure successfully completed.

SQL> execute display_table('abcd');
NOT A VALID TABLE NAME

PL/SQL procedure successfully completed.
```

4.7 Records

A PL/SQL *record* is a composite data structure, similar to a record structure in a high-level programming language. PL/SQL records can be table-based, cursor-based, or programmer-defined.

4.7.1 Table-Based Records

A record whose structure is the same as that of a row in a database table is called a *table-based record*, a structure that is useful in situations where the application program is reading (or writing) rows from (to) database tables. The syntax to declare table-based records is

```
<record-var-name> <table-name>%rowtype;
```

where <record-var-name> is the variable name and <table-name> is the name of the table whose row structure is being used in the record definition. A possible usage of table-based records is as follows:

```
declare
  customer_rec customers%rowtype;
begin
  select *
  into   customer_rec
  from   customers
  where  cno = '1111';
  if (customer_rec.phone is null) then
    dbms_output.put_line('Phone number is absent');
  else
    dbms_output.put_line('Phone number is '|| customer_rec.phone);
  end if;
end;
```

The individual fields of the record variable are accessed in the usual way, using the dot notation. The above anonymous block retrieves the row corresponding to a customer into a record variable and then checks for the phone number in that row.

4.7.2 Cursor-Based Records

A record whose structure is based on the `select-list` of a cursor is called a *cursor-based* record. If the select list involves an expression other than a column name, an alias must be present; otherwise PL/SQL would have no way of naming the corresponding field in the cursor-based record. The syntax to define a cursor-based record is

```
<record-var-name> <cursor-name>%rowtype;
```

where <record-var-name> is the variable name and <cursor-name> is the name of the cursor upon which the record is based. A possible usage of cursor-based records is shown below:

```
declare
  cursor c1 is
    select orders.eno employee_no,
           ename employee_name,
           sum(price*qty) total_sales
    from   employees,orders,odetails,parts
    where  employees.eno = orders.eno and
```

```
          orders.ono = odetails.ono and
          odetails.pno = parts.pno
      group by orders.eno, ename;

    emp_sales_rec c1%rowtype;

  begin
    open c1;
    loop
      fetch c1 into emp_sales_rec;
      exit when c1%notfound;
      dbms_output.put_line(emp_sales_rec.employee_no || '   ' ||
                           emp_sales_rec.employee_name || '   ' ||
                           emp_sales_rec.total_sales);
    end loop;
    close c1;
  end;
  /
```

The above example declares a cursor-based record and then processes the cursor using the record. Notice the aliases used in the select list of the cursor and the same names used for the fields of the record.

4.7.3 Programmer-Defined Records

Programmer-defined records are similar to records in high-level programming languages. A **type** declaration is needed before record variables can be declared. The general syntax for the record type declaration is

```
type ⟨type-name⟩ is record
 (⟨field1⟩ ⟨datatype1⟩,
  ⟨field2⟩ ⟨datatype2⟩,
  .
  .
  .
  ⟨fieldN⟩ ⟨datatypeN⟩);
```

where ⟨*type-name*⟩ is the name given to the record type, ⟨*fieldI*⟩ is the name of the Ith field of the record, and ⟨*datatypeI*⟩ is the corresponding data type for the field. The data type could be almost any data type available in PL/SQL. An example follows.

```
declare
  type my_rec_type is record
    (number integer,
     name varchar2(20));
```

```
  r1 my_rec_type;
  r2 my_rec_type;
begin
  r1.number := 111;
  r1.name := 'jones';
  r2 := r1;
  dbms_output.put_line('Number = ' || r2.number ||
                       '  Name = ' || r2.name);
end
```

This example illustrates how a programmer-defined record is declared and used in an assignment statement.

4.8 PL/SQL Tables

PL/SQL tables are similar to database tables, except that they always consist of just one column indexed by binary integers. These tables have no bound and grow dynamically, much like database tables. They can also be likened to single-dimension arrays in high-level languages. They are also sparse—i.e., the rows that are defined in the PL/SQL table may not be sequential. The fact that PL/SQL tables are sparse leads to an interesting conclusion—namely, that the rows of a database table that has a single primary key attribute of type integer can be stored in the PL/SQL table indexed by the key value, thereby providing for direct access to these rows, much like a hash table.

The syntax for declaring a PL/SQL table type is

```
type ⟨table-type-name⟩ is table of ⟨datatype⟩
  index by binary_integer;
```

where ⟨*table-type-name*⟩ is the name given to the table type, and ⟨*datatype*⟩ is the data type of the elements of the table. This data type could include any scalar data type as well as any record data type whose fields are scalar. The data type cannot be another PL/SQL table type. The `%rowtype` and `%type` attributes can be used in specifying the data type of the elements of the PL/SQL table.

PL/SQL provides a set of operations that can be applied to PL/SQL tables to get information about the table as well as to delete rows from the table. These operations are summarized below along with a sample usage. (The operations are invoked using the dot notation, somewhat similar to invoking methods in an object-oriented language.)

- `count`. This operation returns the number of elements in the PL/SQL table.

```
n := the_table.count;
```

- `delete`. This operation deletes the specified row or all the rows between the specified indices from a PL/SQL table. The following invocation of the `delete` operation deletes the forty-third row in `the_table`:

  ```
  the_table.delete(43);
  ```

  The following invocation deletes all the rows between and including the indices −10 and 25:

  ```
  the_table.delete(-10,25);
  ```

- `exists`. This operation returns true if there exists a row in the specified index; otherwise it returns false.

  ```
  if the_table.exists(3) then
    ...
  ```

- `first`. This operation returns the lowest-valued index in the PL/SQL table containing an element. If the PL/SQL table is empty, `null` is returned.

  ```
  i := the_table.first;
  ```

- `last`. This operation returns the highest-valued index in the PL/SQL table containing an element. If the PL/SQL table is empty, `null` is returned.

  ```
  i := the_table.last;
  ```

- `next`. Given an index in a PL/SQL table, this operation returns the next-higher-valued index where an element exists. If such an element does not exist, `null` is returned.

  ```
  i := the_table.next(5)
  ```

- `prior`. Given an index in a PL/SQL table, this operation returns the next-lower-valued index where an element exists. If such an element does not exist, `null` is returned.

  ```
  i := the_table.prior(5)
  ```

A detailed example is shown below. The anonymous block retrieves information from the Oracle data dictionary table `user_tab_columns` and prints the relational schemes of tables whose names start with the letter "Z." The information is first retrieved into a PL/SQL table and then processed.

```
declare
  type dd_rec_type is record (
    table_name varchar2(30),
    column_name varchar2(30),
    data_type  varchar2(9));
  type dd_table_type is table of dd_rec_type
```

```
      index by binary_integer;
  dd_table dd_table_type;
  dd_rec dd_rec_type;
  cursor c1 is
     select table_name,column_name,data_type
     from   user_tab_columns
     where  table_name like 'Z%'
     order  by table_name,column_name;
  i binary_integer;
  prev varchar2(30);
  newentry boolean;

begin
  i := 0;
  open c1;
  loop
    fetch c1 into dd_rec;
    exit when c1%notfound;
    i := i + 1;
    dd_table(i) := dd_rec;
  end loop;
  close c1;
  dbms_output.put_line('Tables Starting with "Z"');
  dbms_output.put_line('------------------------');
  prev := '';
  newentry := false;
  for i in 1 .. dd_table.count loop
    if (i = 1) then
      dbms_output.put(dd_table(i).table_name || '(');
      prev := dd_table(i).table_name;
    elsif (prev != dd_table(i).table_name) then
      dbms_output.put_line(');');
      dbms_output.put(dd_table(i).table_name || '(');
      prev := dd_table(i).table_name;
      newentry := false;
    end if;
    if (newentry) then
      dbms_output.put(', ');
    end if;
    newentry := true;
    dbms_output.put(dd_table(i).column_name || ':');
    dbms_output.put(dd_table(i).data_type);
```

```
  end loop;
  dbms_output.put_line(');');
end;
/
```

The following is a sample run of the anonymous block in SQL*Plus, assuming that the block resides in the file p10.sql.

```
SQL> start p10
Tables Starting with "Z"
------------------------
ZIPCODES(CITY:VARCHAR2, ZIP:NUMBER);
ZZZ(COL1:NUMBER, COL2:NUMBER, COL3:VARCHAR2);

PL/SQL procedure successfully completed.

SQL>
```

4.9 Built-In Packages

PL/SQL provides several built-in packages. In this section, two very useful packages are discussed: package **dbms_output**, which is used for debugging purposes, and **dbms_sql**, which is used for executing dynamic SQL and PL/SQL statements.

4.9.1 The dbms_output Package

The **dbms_output** package allows the user to display information to the session's output device (usually the screen) as the PL/SQL program executes. The **put_line** procedure belonging to the **dbms_output** package has already been used many times in this chapter. This, and the remaining procedures that constitute the **dbms_output** package, are described here.

The **dbms_output** package works with a buffer into which information can be written using the **put**, **put_line**, and **new_line** procedures. This information can subsequently be retrieved using the **get_line** and **get_lines** procedures. Besides these procedures to write and read from the buffer, two additional procedures, **disable** and **enable**, are provided. These procedures, which disable and enable the buffering process, are discussed in detail next.

- **disable**. This procedure disables all calls to the **dbms_output** package, except the **enable** procedure. The statement has the following syntax:

```
dbms_output.disable;
```

An alternative way to disable the calls to the package is to issue the following command in SQL*Plus:

```
SQL> set serveroutput off
```

- `enable`. This procedure enables all calls to the `dbms_output` package. It takes as input an optional buffer size. The call is made as follows:

  ```
  dbms_output.enable(1000000);
  ```

  This call will initialize the buffer size to `1000000`. If the buffer size is not provided, as in

  ```
  dbms_output.enable;
  ```

  the default buffer size is `2000`. The package can also be enabled from SQL*Plus as follows:

  ```
  SQL> set serveroutput on size 1000000
  ```

  or

  ```
  SQL> set serveroutput on
  ```

- `new_line`. This procedure inserts an end-of-line marker in the buffer. The syntax is

  ```
  dbms_output.new_line;
  ```

- `put`. This procedure puts information into the buffer. The input to the procedure could be of type `varchar2`, `number`, or `date`. Examples are

  ```
  dbms_output.put(emp_rec.eno);
  dbms_output.put(emp_rec.hdate);
  dbms_output.put(emp_rec.ename);
  ```

- `put_line`. This procedure is the same as `put` except that an end-of-line marker is also placed.
- `get_line`. This procedure retrieves one line of information from the buffer. Even though the `put` and `put_line` procedures put information that is numeric, character string, or date type, the `get_line` procedure retrieves this in character string form. The procedure has the following specification:

  ```
  procedure get_line(line out varchar2,
                     status out integer);
  ```

The maximum size of the line can be 255. The **status** output indicates whether an error has occurred. Upon successful retrieval of a line from the buffer, **status** is set to 0; otherwise it is set to 1.

- **get_lines**. This procedure retrieves a specified number of lines from the buffer and returns them in a PL/SQL table of string type. The specification is as follows:

```
type string255_table is table of varchar2(255)
     index by binary_integer;
procedure get_lines(lines out string255_table,
                    nlines in out integer);
```

  The **nlines** parameter is the number of lines to be retrieved and also serves as the number of lines actually retrieved.

4.9.2 The dbms_sql Package

The **dbms_sql** package provides the ability to execute dynamically created SQL statements in PL/SQL. These statements are created as a character string and are sent to Oracle for syntax checking. After they are verified to be syntactically correct, they are sent for execution. The processing required is different for nonquery data manipulation statements such as **insert**, **delete**, and **update**, for data definition language (DDL) statements such as **create table** and **alter table**, and for query statements. The details are discussed here.

Executing Nonquery Statements

The steps involved in executing an **insert**, **delete**, or **update** statement are as follows:

1. *Open the cursor*. All database processing takes place using cursors in PL/SQL. For static PL/SQL, the cursor processing was either implicitly done by PL/SQL or was explicitly done by the programmer as discussed in an earlier section. Dynamic SQL statements must also be processed using cursors; hence the first step is to open a cursor. This is done using the following function call:

```
handle := dbms_sql.open_cursor;
```

   The **open_cursor** function takes no input and returns an integer cursor ID as output. This cursor ID must be used in subsequent references to the cursor. More than one SQL statement can be executed sequentially within the same cursor, or the same statement can be executed multiple times within the cursor.

2. *Parse the statement*. The next step is to *parse* the SQL statement. The SQL statement is stored in a string variable and is sent to the Oracle server for syntax checking. The **parse** procedure has the specification

```
procedure parse(handle in integer,
                stmt in varchar2,
                language in integer);
```

   where **handle** is the cursor ID that is returned by the **open_cursor** call, **stmt** is the string variable containing the SQL statement (without the terminating semicolon), and **language** is one of the following constants:

   - DBMS_SQL.V6 for Oracle Version 6.
   - DBMS_SQL.V7 for Oracle Version 7.
   - DBMS_SQL.NATIVE for the database to which the program is connected.

   If the SQL statement is not syntactically correct, an exception is raised.

3. *Bind any input variables*. After opening the cursor and parsing the statement, any placeholders in the SQL statement need to be bound to actual PL/SQL variables or constants. This is done with **bind_variable**, an overloaded procedure having the specifications

```
procedure bind_variable(handle in integer,
                        name in varchar2,
                        value in number);
procedure bind_variable(handle in integer,
                        name in varchar2,
                        value in varchar2);
procedure bind_variable(handle in integer,
                        name in varchar2,
                        value in date);
procedure bind_variable_char(handle in integer,
                             name in varchar2,
                             value in char);
```

   where **handle** is the cursor ID, **name** is the placeholder name in the dynamic SQL statement, and **value** is the PL/SQL constant or variable to be bound to the placeholder. Examples of usage are

```
dbms_sql.bind_variable(handle,':n',10);
dbms_sql.bind_variable(handle,':n',enum);
dbms_sql.bind_variable(handle,':c','jones');
dbms_sql.bind_variable(handle,':c',ename);
dbms_sql.bind_variable(handle,':d',hdate);
```

It is good practice to precede the placeholder names with a colon, as shown in the above examples.

4. *Execute the statement*. After the statement is parsed and any placeholders are assigned values, the statement is ready to be executed. The function **execute** is used for this purpose as follows:

   ```
   nrows := dbms_sql.execute(handle);
   ```

   where **handle** is the cursor ID and the function returns the number of rows processed.

5. *Close the cursor*. The final step is to close the cursor and release any resources used in the process. This is done as follows:

   ```
   dbms_sql.close_cursor(handle);
   ```

An example of executing a dynamic **update** statement is shown below:

```
declare
  handle integer;
  stmt varchar2(256);
  discount parts.price%type := 0.8;
  part_number parts.pno%type := 10506;
  nrows integer;
begin

  stmt := 'update parts set price = price * :fract' ||
          ' where pno = :pnum';

  handle := dbms_sql.open_cursor;
  dbms_sql.parse(handle,stmt,DBMS_SQL.V7);
  dbms_sql.bind_variable(handle,':fract',discount);
  dbms_sql.bind_variable(handle,':pnum',part_number);
  nrows := dbms_sql.execute(handle);
  dbms_output.put_line('number of rows updated = ' || nrows);
  dbms_sql.close_cursor(handle);

  exception
    when others then
      dbms_sql.close_cursor(handle);
end;
/
```

The steps involved in executing a data definition language statement such as **drop table** or **create table** is essentially the same as for **insert**, **delete**, or update except that the two steps **bind variable** and **execute** are not necessary. This is because placeholders are not allowed in dynamic DDL statements and the **execute** takes place at the time the statement is parsed. An example follows:

```
declare
  handle integer;
  stmt1 varchar2(256);
  stmt2 varchar2(256);
begin
  stmt1 := 'drop table zzz';
  stmt2 := 'create table zzz (col1 integer,' ||
           ' col2 number(4), col3 varchar2(30))';
  handle := dbms_sql.open_cursor;
  dbms_sql.parse(handle,stmt1,DBMS_SQL.V7);
  dbms_output.put_line('Table ZZZ dropped');
  dbms_sql.parse(handle,stmt2,DBMS_SQL.V7);
  dbms_output.put_line('Table ZZZ created');
  dbms_sql.close_cursor(handle);
  exception
    when others then
      dbms_sql.close_cursor(handle);
end;
/
```

Executing Queries

The steps involved in executing a dynamic query are more complicated. Additional steps to define output variables, fetch the rows, and return results to PL/SQL variables are needed. The sequence of steps required to process a dynamic query is as follows:

1. *Open the cursor*. Same as before.
2. *Parse the statement*. Same as before. Note that the **select** statement should not have the **into** clause because the results are processed differently in dynamic SQL.
3. *Bind any input variables*. Same as before.
4. *Define the output variables*. The output variables into which the results of the query are to be returned must be defined using the **define_column** procedure. The process is similar to binding input variables to placeholders except that the select list items are identified by positions (1, 2, 3, etc.), not by names. The specification of the **define_column** is overloaded as follows:

```
procedure define_column(handle in integer,
                        position in integer,
                        column in number);
procedure define_column(handle in integer,
                        position in integer,
                        column in varchar2,
                        col_size in integer);
procedure define_column(handle in integer,
                        position in integer,
                        column in date,
                        col_size in integer);
procedure define_column_char(handle in integer,
                        position in integer,
                        column in char,
                        col_size in integer);
```

where **handle** is the cursor ID, **position** is the position of the select list item that is being defined, **column** is the PL/SQL variable of appropriate type, and **col_size**, which is required, is the maximum size, in bytes, of the output data. Examples of its usage are

```
dbms_sql.define_column(handle,1,ccno);
dbms_sql.define_column(handle,2,ccname,30);
dbms_sql.define_column(handle,3,ccstreet,30);
dbms_sql.define_column(handle,4,ccdate,9);
```

5. *Execute the query*. Same as before.
6. *Fetch the rows*. The rows of the result of the query are fetched into a buffer using the **fetch_rows** function as follows:

```
if dbms_sql.fetch_rows(handle) = 0 then
      exit;
else
  .
  .
  .
```

The function returns the number of rows in the results of the query.

7. *Return the results to PL/SQL variables*. After **fetch_rows** is called, a call to the **column_value** procedure retrieves the values into PL/SQL variables. Typically, the same variable that was bound in the **define_column** call is used here. This procedure is also overloaded and has the specification

```
procedure column_value(handle in integer,
                       position in integer,
                       value out number);
procedure column_value(handle in integer,
                       position in integer,
                       value out varchar2);
procedure column_value(handle in integer,
                       position in integer,
                       value out date);
procedure column_value(handle in integer,
                       position in integer,
                       value out char);
```

where **handle** is the cursor ID, **position** is the position in the select list of the query, and **value** is the output variable for this select list item. Each of these functions has a fourth optional output parameter, called **error**, which returns any numeric error codes, and an optional fifth parameter, called **actual_length**, which returns the original length of the column value (before any possible truncation). Examples of **column_value** usage are

```
dbms_sql.column_value(handle,1,ccno);
dbms_sql.column_value(handle,2,ccname);
dbms_sql.column_value(handle,3,ccstreet);
dbms_sql.column_value(handle,4,ccdate);
```

8. *Close the cursor*. Same as before.

An example containing dynamic queries follows. A package called **dsql** is defined. It contains two procedures:

- **get_columns**. This procedure takes as input **startch**, a character, and returns information about all the columns of any database table in the database whose name starts with **startch**. The information is returned in a PL/SQL table of records with three fields: table name, column name, and data type. The number of elements in the PL/SQL table is also returned. The query is based on the data dictionary table **user_tab_columns**.
- **get_query_results**. This procedure takes as input
  - **query_string**, which has as its value an SQL select statement
  - **ncols**, the number of select list items in the SQL select statement
  - **column_types**, a PL/SQL table that contains the data type of each of the select list items

The procedure then executes the query and returns the results in the output parameter **result** along with the number of rows in the result in variable **nrows**. The **result** output parameter is a PL/SQL table of strings. The individual columns in a row of the result of the query are concatenated into a long string with the bar character (|) between two values.

```
-- p20.sql
create or replace package dsql as
  type dd_rec_type is record (
    table_name varchar2(30),
    column_name varchar2(30),
    data_type  varchar2(9));
  type dd_table_type is table of dd_rec_type
       index by binary_integer;
  type string1024_table is table of varchar2(1024)
       index by binary_integer;
  type string9_table is table of varchar2(9)
       index by binary_integer;
  type number_table is table of number
       index by binary_integer;

procedure get_columns(startch in char,
                      dd_table out dd_table_type,
                      n out number);

procedure get_query_results(query_string in varchar2,
                            ncols in number,
                            column_types in string9_table,
                            result out string1024_table,
                            nrows out number);

end dsql;
/
show errors

create or replace package body dsql as

procedure get_columns(startch in char,
                      dd_table out dd_table_type,
                      n out number) as
```

```
handle integer;
dbms_return integer;
tablename varchar(30);
colname varchar(30);
datatype varchar(9);
counter integer := 0;

begin

  handle := dbms_sql.open_cursor;
  dbms_sql.parse(handle,
    'select distinct table_name,column_name,data_type ' ||
    'from   user_tab_columns '                          ||
    'where  table_name like '''                         ||
    startch                                             ||
    '%'''                                               ||
    'order by table_name,column_name', DBMS_SQL.V7);

  dbms_sql.define_column(handle, 1, tablename, 30);
  dbms_sql.define_column(handle, 2, colname, 30);
  dbms_sql.define_column(handle, 3, datatype, 9);

  dbms_return := dbms_sql.execute(handle);

  counter := 0;
  loop
    if dbms_sql.fetch_rows(handle) = 0 then
      exit;
    else
      dbms_sql.column_value(handle, 1, tablename);
      dbms_sql.column_value(handle, 2, colname);
      dbms_sql.column_value(handle, 3, datatype);

      counter := counter + 1;
      dd_table(counter).table_name := tablename;
      dd_table(counter).column_name := colname;
      dd_table(counter).data_type := datatype;
    end if;
  end loop;
  n := counter;
```

```
  dbms_sql.close_cursor(handle);

exception
  when others then
    dbms_sql.close_cursor(handle);
    n := -1;
end get_columns;

procedure get_query_results(query_string in varchar2,
                            ncols in number,
                            column_types in string9_table,
                            result out string1024_table,
                            nrows out number) as

y1 string1024_table;
y2 number_table;
counter integer;
i integer;
handle integer;
dbms_return integer;
temp string1024_table;

begin

  for i in 1 .. ncols loop
    y1(i) := '';
    y2(i) := 0;
  end loop;

  counter := 0;
  handle := dbms_sql.open_cursor;
  dbms_sql.parse(handle,query_string,DBMS_SQL.V7);

  for i in 1 .. ncols loop
    if ((column_types(i) = 'VARCHAR2') or
        (column_types(i) = 'CHAR')) then
      dbms_sql.define_column(handle, i, y1(i) , 300);
    else
      dbms_sql.define_column(handle, i, y2(i));
    end if;
```

```
    end loop;

    dbms_return := dbms_sql.execute(handle);

    loop
      if dbms_sql.fetch_rows(handle) = 0 then
        exit;
      else
        for i in 1 .. ncols loop
          if ((column_types(i) = 'VARCHAR2') or
              (column_types(i) = 'CHAR')) then
            dbms_sql.column_value(handle, i, y1(i));
          else
            dbms_sql.column_value(handle, i, y2(i));
          end if;
        end loop;
        counter := counter + 1;
        temp(counter) := '';

        for i in 1 .. ncols loop
          if ((column_types(i) = 'VARCHAR2') or
              (column_types(i) = 'CHAR')) then
            temp(counter) := temp(counter) || rtrim(y1(i)) || '|';
          else
            temp(counter) := temp(counter) || trim(y2(i)) || '|';
          end if;
        end loop;
     end if;
    end loop;

    nrows := counter;
    result := temp;
    dbms_sql.close_cursor(handle);

    exception
      when others then
        dbms_sql.close_cursor(handle);
        nrows := -1;
  end get_query_results;
  end dsql;
```

```
/
show errors
```

The following package, called **dsql_driver**, contains two procedures to drive the two procedures in the **dsql** package.

```
-- p21.sql
create or replace package dsql_driver as
procedure drive_get_columns(startch in char);
procedure drive_get_query_results(
    query_string in varchar2,
    ncols in number,
    column_types in dsql.string9_table);
end dsql_driver;
/

create or replace package body dsql_driver as
procedure drive_get_columns(startch in char) as
  dd_table dsql.dd_table_type;
  i binary_integer;
  n number;
  prev varchar2(30);
  newentry boolean;
begin
  dsql.get_columns(startch,dd_table,n);
  dbms_output.put_line('N =  ' || n);

  dbms_output.put_line('Tables Starting with ' || startch);
  dbms_output.put_line('------------------------');
  prev := '';
  newentry := false;
  for i in 1 .. dd_table.count loop
    if (i = 1) then
      dbms_output.put(dd_table(i).table_name || '(');
      prev := dd_table(i).table_name;
    elsif (prev != dd_table(i).table_name) then
      dbms_output.put_line(');');
      dbms_output.put(dd_table(i).table_name || '(');
      prev := dd_table(i).table_name;
      newentry := false;
    end if;
```

```
      if (newentry) then
        dbms_output.put(', ');
      end if;
      newentry := true;
      dbms_output.put(dd_table(i).column_name || ':');
      dbms_output.put(dd_table(i).data_type);
    end loop;
    dbms_output.put_line(');');
  end;

  procedure drive_get_query_results
      (query_string in varchar2,
       ncols in number,
       column_types in dsql.string9_table) as
  result dsql.string1024_table;
  nrows number;
  i binary_integer;

  begin
    dsql.get_query_results(query_string,ncols,column_types,
                           result,nrows);
    for i in 1 .. nrows loop
      dbms_output.put_line(result(i));
    end loop;
  end;

  end dsql_driver;
  /
  show errors
```

The following anonymous PL/SQL block calls the driver procedure for the `get_query_results` procedure.

```
-- p22.sql
declare
 query_string varchar2(256);
 ncols number;
 column_types dsql.string9_table;
begin
  query_string := 'select cno,cname,city ' ||
                  'from customers,zipcodes ' ||
```

```
                    'where customers.zip = zipcodes.zip';
  ncols := 3;
  column_types(1) := 'NUMBER';
  column_types(2) := 'VARCHAR2';
  column_types(3) := 'VARCHAR2';

  dsql_driver.drive_get_query_results(query_string,
                                      ncols,
                                      column_types);
end;
/

SQL> execute dsql_driver.drive_get_columns('Z');
N =  2
Tables Starting with Z
------------------------
ZIPCODES(CITY:VARCHAR2, ZIP:NUMBER);

PL/SQL procedure successfully completed.

SQL> start p22
1111|Charles|Wichita|
2222|Bertram|Wichita|
3333|Barbara|Fort Dodge|

PL/SQL procedure successfully completed.

SQL>
```

4.10 Error Handling

PL/SQL implements run-time error handling via *exceptions* and *exception handlers*. Exceptions can be associated with Oracle system errors or with application program errors. When an error occurs during the execution of a PL/SQL program, an exception is *raised*. Immediately, program control is transferred to the `exception` section of the block in which the exception was raised. If such a section exists, and if there is code present to handle the exception, the exception is handled and the program returns to the environment that called the block in which the error occurred. Otherwise, program control is passed on to the enclosing block's exception handler, if there is one.

Exceptions can be of two types: *system exceptions* and *user-defined exceptions*. System exceptions are raised automatically by PL/SQL, and they correspond to errors in PL/SQL or Oracle database processing. Some commonly occurring system exceptions have been given names by PL/SQL and are listed below:

- `CURSOR_ALREADY_OPENED` (SQLCODE = −6511). Attempt to open cursor that is already open.
- `DUP_VAL_ON_INDEX` (SQLCODE = −1). Attempt to store duplicate value in a unique index column.
- `INVALID_CURSOR` (SQLCODE = −1001). Attempt to use a cursor that does not exist or is not open.
- `INVALID_NUMBER` (SQLCODE = −1722). Attempt to convert a string into a number using the `to_number` function failed.
- `LOGIN_DENIED` (SQLCODE = −1017). Invalid user name or password when attempting to connect to database.
- `NO_DATA_FOUND` (SQLCODE = +100). Attempt to access uninitialized row in a PL/SQL table or `select into` resulted in no row.
- `TOO_MANY_ROWS` (SQLCODE = −1422). `select into` resulted in more than one row.
- `VALUE_ERROR` (SQLCODE = −6502). Error during conversion of data.
- `ZERO_DIVIDE` (SQLCODE = −1476). Divide by zero error.

System errors that have not been given names can be handled using the `when others` clause in the exception section. It is useful to print the values of the variables `sqlcode` and `sqlerrm` to see the error code and the error message associated with the error. These variables are available to any PL/SQL program as they are declared in the `standard` package of PL/SQL.

The exception section of a PL/SQL block contains code to handle the exceptions. The syntax is

```
when <exception-name> then
  <Error-Handling-Code>;
```

where the name of the exception is mentioned after the `when` keyword. If the name is not known, `others` can be used to trap such exceptions. Any number of these `when` clauses can be used. If the error-handling code is the same for more than one exception, the `when` clauses can be combined by placing an `or` between the exception names.

User-defined exceptions are also treated in a similar manner, except that the user has to define the exception first and then raise the exception at the appropriate point in the program. User-defined exceptions are declared using the syntax

```
<exception-name> exception;
```

and are raised using the syntax

```
raise <exception-name>;
```

An example illustrating some of the above concepts is shown below.

```
create or replace procedure insert_odetails
  (onum in integer, pnum in integer, qty in integer) as

  invalid_quantity exception;
begin
  if (qty <= 0) then
    raise invalid_quantity;
  end if;

  insert into odetails values (onum,pnum,qty);

  exception
    when dup_val_on_index then
      dbms_output.put_line('PRIMARY KEY VIOLATION');
      dbms_output.put_line(sqlcode || '--' || sqlerrm);

    when invalid_quantity then
      dbms_output.put_line('Quantity is invalid');

    when others then
      dbms_output.put_line('OTHER ERROR');
      dbms_output.put_line(sqlcode || '--' || sqlerrm);
end;
/
```

The above stored procedure tries to insert a row in the `odetails` table. If the quantity value is negative or zero, a user-defined exception is raised. If a primary key violation takes place, the system exception **DUP_VAL_ON_INDEX** is raised. If a foreign key violation takes place, the **when others** clause executes and an appropriate error message is displayed. The following is a screen capture of an SQL*Plus session illustrating the various possibilities.

```
SQL> select * from odetails;

       ONO        PNO        QTY
---------- ---------- ----------
      1020      10506          1
      1020      10507          1
      1020      10508          2
      1020      10509          3
      1021      10601          4
      1022      10601          1
      1022      10701          1
      1023      10800          1
      1023      10900          1
      2000      10900        140

10 rows selected

SQL> execute insert_odetails(1234,1111,-5);
Quantity is invalid

PL/SQL procedure successfully completed.

SQL> execute insert_odetails(2000,10900,10);
PRIMARY KEY VIOLATION
-1--ORA-00001: unique constraint (BOOK.SYS_C0068915)
violated

PL/SQL procedure successfully completed.

SQL> execute insert_odetails(2000,11001,10);
OTHER ERROR
100--ORA-01403: no data found
ORA-01403: no data found
ORA-06512: at
```

```
"BOOK.INSERT_ODETAILS", line 5
ORA-04088: error during execution of trigger
'BOOK.INSERT_ODETAILS'

PL/SQL procedure successfully completed.
SQL>
```

4.11 PL/SQL Access to Oracle8 Objects

Object-oriented features of Oracle8 PL/SQL language are briefly introduced in this section. Object variables can be declared and used in PL/SQL based on object types defined in the database. The structure of the objects can be easily traversed using the dot notation, objects can be modified, and, if needed, the database can be updated using the modified objects. Examples of object-type method implementations are presented in this section. Accessing varying arrays in PL/SQL, and manipulating/querying of nested tables are also presented.

4.11.1 Declaring and Initializing Objects

PL/SQL object variables are declared in the same manner as ordinary variables by following the variable name by the object type name. The variables may be given an initial value at the time of declaration using the object type constructors. For example, the following declaration declares a **person_type** object variable **p** and initializes it.

```
p person_type := person_type('aaa',
    address_type('sss','ccc','sss',11111),
    phones_varray_type(null,null,null));
```

The variable, once initialized, can be used in other PL/SQL statements, and its attributes can be accessed using the dot notation. The following PL/SQL anonymous block creates a **person_type** object, initializes it, updates its attributes, and calls a procedure to display the object.

```
declare
  p person_type := person_type('aaa',
   address_type('sss','ccc','sss',11111),
   phones_varray_type(null,null,null));
  procedure display_person(p in person_type) is
```

```
    begin
      if (p is not null) then
        dbms_output.put_line('Name: ' || p.name);
        dbms_output.put_line('Street: ' || p.address.street);
        dbms_output.put_line('City: ' || p.address.city);
        dbms_output.put_line('State: ' || p.address.state);
        dbms_output.put_line('Zip: ' || p.address.zip);
        if (p.phones(1) is not null) then
          dbms_output.put_line('Phone 1: ' || p.phones(1));
        end if;
        if (p.phones(2) is not null) then
          dbms_output.put_line('Phone 2: ' || p.phones(2));
        end if;
        if (p.phones(3) is not null) then
          dbms_output.put_line('Phone 3: ' || p.phones(3));
        end if;
      end if;
    end;
begin
  p.name := 'D. Maul';
  p.address.street := '123 Kenobi St.';
  p.address.city := 'Death Star';
  p.address.state := 'Tattoine';
  p.address.zip := '66666';
  p.phones(1) := '111-1234';
  p.phones(2) := '111-1235';
  p.phones(3) := null;
  display_person(p);
end;
/
show errors
```

Notice the use of the `is null` predicate on both the object variable as well as its attribute. Object variables that are not initialized are assigned the `null` reference.

4.11.2 Object Type Method Implementation

Methods associated with object types are specified in PL/SQL. Recall the two methods `cost` and `total_cost` specified in the object type declarations for `odetails_type` and `o_order_type` respectively in Chapter 2. The `create type` `body` statement is used to specify the implementation of methods for object types. The PL/SQL code for the two methods is shown below:

```
create or replace type body odetails_type as
member function cost return number is
  p parts.price%type;
begin
  select price into p from parts where pno = self.pno;
  return p * self.qty;
end;
end;
/
show errors

create or replace type body o_order_type as
  member function total_cost return number is
    i          integer;
    item       odetails_type;
    total      number := 0;
    item_cost  number;
  begin
    for i in 1..self.odetails.count  loop
      item := self.odetails(i);
      item_cost := item.cost();
      total := total + item_cost ;
    end loop;
    return total;
  end;
end;
/
show errors
```

Notice the use of the `self` keyword, which allows the method to refer to the attributes of the object on which the method is applied. Nested tables in the database can be treated as PL/SQL tables when accessed within PL/SQL. Hence, the syntax for accessing an individual item within the nested table `odetails` is `self.odetails(i)`. Also notice the call to `cost()` in the `total_cost` method where the individual line item costs are summed up to produce the total cost of an order.

4.11.3 Accessing Database Objects in PL/SQL

Database objects and object tables can be accessed within PL/SQL with ease. Several examples are presented here.

Example 4.11.1 The following PL/SQL anonymous block queries the `o_employees` table and displays employee details. It employs a standard PL/SQL cursor and uses the dot notation to access the attributes within the object structure.

```
declare
  p person_type;
  enum o_employees.eno%type;
  cursor c is
    select eno,person from o_employees;

begin
  open c;
  loop
    fetch c into enum, p;
    exit when c%notfound;
    dbms_output.put('ENO: ' || enum);
    dbms_output.put('   ENAME: ' || p.name);
    dbms_output.put_line('   ZIP: ' || p.address.zip);
  end loop;
  close c;
end;
/
show errors
```

Example 4.11.2 The following PL/SQL anonymous block queries the nested table `odetails` within the `o_orders` table and prints all the line item details for order 1020.

```
declare
  onum o_orders.ono%type;
  cursor c is
    select nt.pno, nt.qty
    from   THE(select o.odetails
               from  o_orders o
               where o.ono = onum) nt;

  pnum parts.pno%type;
```

```
  qtty number;

begin
  onum := 1020;

  open c;
  loop
    fetch c into pnum,qtty;
    exit when c%notfound;
    dbms_output.put_line('PNO = ' || pnum || '  QTY = ' || qtty);
   end loop;
end;
/
show errors
```

Notice the **THE** operator that is applied to the nested table to flatten its rows for access in the outer query.

Example 4.11.3 The following PL/SQL anonymous block contains a function that takes an employee number and returns the total sales for that employee. This function queries the `o_orders` table using a PL/SQL cursor. Since the `o_orders` table is an object table, it has no column names. So it is not possible to select any named columns from this table. To access the row objects, one must use the **value** operator, which takes the table alias as input and returns the row object.

```
declare
  enum o_employees.eno%type;
  total number(10,2);

  function total_emp_sales(emp_no in employees.eno%type)
    return number is
  sales number := 0.0;
  cursor c is
    select value(o)
    from   o_orders o
    where  o.eno = emp_no;
  od o_order_type;
```

```
    begin
      open c;
      loop
        fetch c into od;
        exit when c%notfound;
        sales := sales + od.total_cost();
      end loop;
      return (sales);
    end;

  begin
    enum := 1001;
    total := total_emp_sales(enum);
    dbms_output.put_line('Total sales for employee ' ||
                           enum   || ' is ' || total);
  end;
  /
  show errors
```

Notice the call to the method `total_cost`, which computes the total sales value for a particular order. The total sales for each order are summed up to produce the total sales for the employee. The anonymous PL/SQL block invokes the function `total_emp_sales` and displays the total sales for employee `1020`.

4.11.4 Accessing Varying Arrays in PL/SQL

Recall that it was not possible to query and access varying array attributes of objects in SQL. PL/SQL provides an easy way to access varying arrays by allowing varying array objects in the database to be read into PL/SQL variables. The following PL/SQL anonymous block reads the `phones` varying array for employee `1002` and displays them.

```
declare
  enum o_employees.eno%type;
  phs o_employees.person.phones%type;
begin
  enum := 1002;

  select e.person.phones
  into   phs
```

```
  from    o_employees e
  where   e.eno = enum;

  for i in 1..3 loop
    if (phs(i) is not null) then
      dbms_output.put_line('Phone for employee ' ||
                           enum   || ' is ' || phs(i));
    end if;
  end loop;
end;
/
show errors
```

If the varying arrays are to be updated, the updates can be done in PL/SQL and the varying array can then be stored back in the database. The following PL/SQL anonymous block illustrates the addition of a new phone number for employee 1002.

```
declare
  enum o_employees.eno%type;
  phs o_employees.person.phones%type;
begin
  enum := 1002;

  select e.person.phones
  into   phs
  from   o_employees e
  where  e.eno = enum;

  phs(2) := '999-999-0000';

  update o_employees e
  set    e.person.phones = phs
  where  e.eno = enum;
end;
/
show errors
```

Note that it is not possible to access the elements within the varying array directly in an SQL query or update statement. Instead, the varying array must be retrieved into a PL/SQL variable, updated, and then written back to the database

4.11.5 Built-In Methods for Collection Objects

All of the PL/SQL table operators presented in Section 4.8 are also applicable to varying array and nested table objects. In addition to these, the following two additional methods are applicable to collection objects:

- The **extend** method adds elements at the end of a nested table. This method has three variations:

  ```
  extend      : adds a null element at the end
  extend(n)   : adds n null elements at the end
  extend(n,i) : adds n copies of element i at the end
  ```

  The **extend** method should not be applied to a varying array, since its size is fixed. However, an application of **extend** to a varying array is legal and it does not change the varying array.

- The **trim** method deletes elements at the end of a nested table. This method has two variations:

  ```
  trim    : deletes the last element
  trim(n) : deletes the last n elements
  ```

These built-in methods can be used only in the procedural PL/SQL code and not in SQL. An example of the **count** method is shown below in the anonymous PL/SQL block, which queries the **o_employees** table and prints the employee numbers and the number of phone number entries for each employee.

```
declare
  cursor c is
    select e.eno, e.person.phones
    from   o_employees e;
  enum o_employees.eno%type;
  phs  o_employees.person.phones%type;
begin
  open c;
  loop
    fetch c into enum, phs;
    exit when c%notfound;
    dbms_output.put_line('Employee ' ||
        enum || ' has ' ||
        phs.count || ' phone numbers');
  end loop;
```

```
  close c;
end;
/
show errors
```

Exercises

Mail-Order Database Problems

4.1 Write a PL/SQL procedure that finds the five employees with the highest sales figures in terms of dollars and prints their numbers and names along with the total sales for each.

4.2 Write a PL/SQL procedure that performs an update of a zip code value. It takes the old and new values of the zip code and changes all occurrences of the old value to the new throughout the database.

4.3 Assume that the `odetails` table has an additional column, called `cost`, whose value is the product of the quantity and price of the part being ordered. Also assume that the `orders` table has an additional column, called `order_cost`, whose value is the sum of the `cost` values for each part in the order. Write a PL/SQL procedure that processes an update to the `price` value of a part. The procedure takes the part number and new price as input and performs an update to the `price` column of the `parts` table along with appropriate changes to the `cost` and `order_cost` values.

4.4 Write a PL/SQL procedure that takes as input two parameters: (1) `conditions`, a PL/SQL table containing several selection conditions as strings, and (2) `nconds`, which contains the number of conditions in `conditions`. The procedure then computes the query

```
select customers.cno,cname,employees.eno,ename
from customers,orders,employees
where customers.cno = orders.cno and
      employees.eno = orders.eno and
      C;
```

where `C` is the conjunction of the conditions in the input parameter. Some examples of the input conditions are

```
customers.zip = 60606
customers.zip = employees.zip
cname like 'C%'
```

The results of the query are sent to the standard output. Write a PL/SQL anonymous block to test this procedure.

Grade Book Database Problems

4.5 Write a PL/SQL procedure that takes as input the term, line number, and component name for a particular course and processes the student scores for this component. The scores are assumed to be in a temporary table called `temp_scores` with two columns: `sid` and `points`. The procedure should add each of the scores mentioned in the temporary table into the `scores` table. If the term, line number, or component name is invalid, the procedure should simply return. If the student ID is invalid or the score is outside the range of allowed values, the procedure should send an error message to the standard output and continue processing the remaining scores. Write a PL/SQL anonymous block to test this procedure.

4.6 Write a PL/SQL procedure that takes as input the term and line number for a particular course and processes updates to the student scores for this course. The updates to the scores are assumed to be in a temporary table called `temp_updates` with three columns: `compname`, `sid`, and `change`. The `change` column is a positive or negative number indicating the change to be made to the current score. If the term or line number of the course is invalid, the procedure should simply return. Otherwise, the procedure should process each of the updates. If the component name of the student ID is invalid or if the updated score is outside the range of allowed values, the procedure should send an error message to the standard output and continue processing the remaining updates. Write a PL/SQL anonymous block to test this procedure.

4.7 Write a PL/SQL procedure that finds the student with the highest overall average in every course. In case there is more than one student tied for the highest average, the procedure should return all of the averages. The results should be returned in a PL/SQL table of records, where each record has the fields term, line number, course title, student ID, student name, and overall average. Also, write an anonymous PL/SQL block that makes a call to the procedure and prints the results to the standard output.

4.8 Write a trigger that fires when a row is deleted from the `enrolls` table. The trigger should record the dropped student's scores in a temporary table, called `deleted_scores`, and cascade the deletes to ensure that the referential integrity constraints are maintained.

4.9 Write a PL/SQL procedure that finds the course numbers, titles, terms, line numbers, and total enrollments for courses with the 10 highest enrollments. The procedure should send the results to the standard output.

4.10 Write a PL/SQL stored procedure that takes the name of a database table as input and prints the number of columns and rows for that table to the standard output.

Investment Portfolio Database Problems

4.11 Write a PL/SQL stored procedure that takes as input a security symbol and produces a ratings list for that security symbol in the same format as Exercise 3.12.

4.12 Write a PL/SQL stored procedure that produces a listing of the top five rated securities based on the consensus mean. (Refer to Exercise 3.12 for a definition of the consensus mean.)

4.13 Write a PL/SQL stored procedure to produce a portfolio view for a member. The procedure should take as input the member id and produce a report of the format shown in Exercise 3.11.

Mail-Order Database Problems (Object Version)

4.14 Write a PL/SQL stored procedure that produces an invoice report for a particular order. The order number is an input parameter to this procedure. The report is to be sent to display. The format of the report should be:

```
Customer: Bertram          Customer Number: 2222
Street  : 237 Ash Avenue
City    : Wichita
ZIP     : 67226
Phone   : 316-689-5555
--------------------------------------------------------------
Order No: 1022
Taken By: Smith (1001)
Received On: 13-FEB-95
Shipped  On: 20-FEB-95

Part No.              Part Name    Quan.   Price     Ext
-------------------------------------------------------------
   10601          Sleeping Beauty      1     24.99     24.99
   10701     When Harry Met Sally      1     19.99     19.99
-------------------------------------------------------------
                                TOTAL:                44.98
-------------------------------------------------------------
```

4.15 Write a PL/SQL stored procedure that prints all customer information to display. The format of the output is as follows:

```
CNO   CNAME       STREET            ZIP     PHONES
-----------------------------------------------------
1111  Charles     123 Main St.      67226   316-636-5555
                                            316-666-1234
2222  Bertram     237 Ash Avenue    67226   316-689-5556
                                            316-666-1233
                                            316-666-1235
3333  Barbara     111 Inwood St.    60606   316-111-1234
-----------------------------------------------------
```

4.16 Write a PL/SQL stored procedure that computes and prints the names of employees with the five highest sales totals. The output should contain the sales total and should be sorted in decreasing order of sales total.

4.17 Write a PL/SQL anonymous block that prompts the user for an area code and prints the names and addresses of all customers who have at least one phone number with that particular area code.

4.18 Write a PL/SQL anonymous block that prompts the user for a part number and prints the order number of all orders in which the particular part was ordered along with the quantity. At the end, it should print a total quantity of the part ordered in all orders.

CHAPTER

5

Oracle JDBC

Oracle supports the JDBC API by providing drivers that work with the Oracle database server. JDBC consists of Java classes that make database access from a Java environment easy and powerful. In this chapter, the JDBC API is introduced. Packed with examples, this chapter shows how to connect to the Oracle database, issue SQL statements, and process results. Invoking Oracle stored procedures and obtaining metadata via the JDBC classes are also discussed.

5.1 What Is JDBC?

JDBC[1] is an Application Programming Interface (API) that enables database access in Java. It consists of a set of classes and interfaces written in Java that allow the programmer to send SQL statements to a database server for execution and, in the case of an SQL query, to retrieve query results.

Writing database applications in Java using JDBC has at least two advantages: (1) portability across database servers and (2) portability across hardware architectures. The portability across database servers is a consequence of the JDBC API. Various database vendors (Oracle, Sybase, and Informix, to name a few) provide JDBC drivers, which are basically implementations of the JDBC API for their database engines. The JDBC drivers take care of the server dependencies, and the applications written in Java using JDBC are independent of the database server. The portability

1. JDBC is a trademark name and not an acronym. However, it is thought of as Java Database Connectivity.

across hardware platforms is a result of the Java language. Hence, the combination of Java and JDBC to develop database applications is an ideal match, as it is possible for the applications to be written once and run anywhere.

5.2 A Simple JDBC Program

A simple Java program that accesses an Oracle database using JDBC is shown below.

```
import java.sql.*;
import java.io.*;
class simple {
  public static void main (String args [])
      throws SQLException, IOException {

    try {
      Class.forName ("oracle.jdbc.driver.OracleDriver");
    } catch (ClassNotFoundException e) {
        System.out.println ("Could not load the driver");
      }
    String user, pass;
    user = readEntry("userid  : ");
    pass = readEntry("password: ");
    Connection conn = DriverManager.getConnection(
                "jdbc:oracle:oci8:"+user+"/"+pass);

    Statement stmt = conn.createStatement ();

    ResultSet rset = stmt.executeQuery
           ("select eno,ename,zip,hdate from employees");
    while (rset.next ()) {
      System.out.println(rset.getString(1) + "   " +
                         rset.getString(2) + "   " +
                         rset.getString(3) + "   " +
                         rset.getString(4));
    }
    stmt.close();
    conn.close();
  }
```

```
    //readEntry function -- to read input string
    static String readEntry(String prompt) {
      try {
        StringBuffer buffer = new StringBuffer();
        System.out.print(prompt);
        System.out.flush();
        int c = System.in.read();
        while(c != '\n' && c != -1) {
          buffer.append((char)c);
          c = System.in.read();
        }
        return buffer.toString().trim();
      } catch (IOException e) {
        return "";
        }
    }
}
```

The above program executes the SQL query

```
select eno,ename,zip,hdate
from   employees;
```

and prints the results of the query to the standard output. The function `readEntry` prints the prompt to standard output and reads a string and returns it. This function is used throughout the chapter.

5.3 Developing JDBC Applications

The following basic steps are involved in developing JDBC applications:

1. Import the JDBC classes (`java.sql.*`).
2. Load the JDBC drivers.
3. Connect to the database.
4. Interact with the database using JDBC.
5. Disconnect from the database.

5.3.1 Loading the JDBC Drivers

A Java program can load several JDBC drivers at any time. This allows for the possibility of the program interacting with more than one database running on possibly different servers. The syntax to load Oracle JDBC drivers[2] is

```
Class.forName("oracle.jdbc.driver.OracleDriver")
```

5.3.2 Connecting to the Database

A connection to the database is established via the `DriverManager` class. The `DriverManager` class provides a basic service for managing a set of JDBC drivers. Once the JDBC drivers are loaded, the `getConnection` method can be applied to the `DriverManager` class as follows.

```
Connection conn = DriverManager.getConnection(url);
```

where `url` is of the form

```
jdbc:oracle:drivertype:user/password@database
```

The `drivertype` is `oci7`, `oci8`, or `thin` depending on the version of Oracle OCI being used; `thin` is used in an `applet`. The `@database` phrase is optional, because there is a default database associated with the installation. If it is specified, it must be one of the following:

- An SQL*Net name-value pair.
- (For JDBC OCI) An entry in the `tnsnames.ora` file.
- (For JDBC Thin) A string of the form `host:port:sid`.

When `getConnection` is called, the `DriverManager` will attempt to locate a suitable driver from among those loaded at initialization and those loaded explicitly using the same `classloader` as the current `applet` or application. After it finds a suitable driver, it returns a `Connection` object. Once the connection is established, all the interactions with the database are then performed via this connection object.

2. Use `oracle.jdbc.dnlddriver.OracleDriver` for the driver name when the Java code corresponds to an `applet`.

5.3.3 The Connection Object

A Connection represents a session with a specific database. All SQL statements are executed and results are returned within the context of a Connection. A single Java application can have any number of connections with a single database or multiple databases.

A Connection's database is able to provide information describing its tables, its supported SQL grammar, its stored procedures, the capabilities of this connection, etc. This information is obtained with the getMetaData method.

An important point to note is that, by default, the Connection object automatically commits changes after executing each statement. If auto-commit has been disabled, an explicit commit must be done or database changes will not be saved. Another point to note is that the Connection class is an interface. Hence Connection objects cannot be created explicitly; they can be created only by using the getConnection method on the DriverManager class.

Once a connection is established, the Connection object is used to send SQL statements to the database server. JDBC provides three classes for sending SQL statements to the database server:

- Statement, used for SQL statements without parameters.
- PreparedStatement, used in situations where the same statement, with possibly different parameters, is to be executed multiple times. The PreparedStatement normally contains a pre-compiled SQL statement. It has the potential to be more efficient than the Statement object, as it is pre-compiled and stored for future use.
- CallableStatement, used for executing stored procedures.

The Connection class has three methods to create instances of these classes:

1. createStatement: SQL statements without parameters are normally executed using Statement objects. The createStatement method has the following specification:

   ```
   public abstract Statement createStatement()
     throws SQLException
   ```

   When invoked on a Connection object, the createStatement method returns a new Statement object. If the same SQL statement is to be executed many times, it is more efficient to use an instance of the class PreparedStatement described next.

2. prepareStatement: An SQL statement with or without IN parameters can be pre-compiled and stored in a PreparedStatement object. This object can then

be used to efficiently execute this statement multiple times. The **prepareStatement** method has the specification

```
public abstract PreparedStatement
   prepareStatement(String sql) throws SQLException
```

where **sql** is an SQL statement that may contain one or more **'?' IN** parameter placeholders. The method, when invoked on a **Connection** object, returns a new **PreparedStatement** object containing the pre-compiled statement.

3. **prepareCall**: An SQL stored procedure call is handled by creating a **CallableStatement** for it. The **CallableStatement** provides methods for setting up its **IN** and **OUT** parameters, and methods for executing it. The **prepareCall** method, when invoked on a **Connection** object, returns a **CallableStatement** and has the specification

```
public abstract CallableStatement
  prepareCall(String sql) throws SQLException
```

where **sql** is an SQL statement that may contain one or more **'?'** parameter placeholders. Typically this statement is a JDBC function call escape string.

Examples of these three methods are given in subsequent sections. There are some other useful methods in the **Connection** class:

1. **close**: In some cases, it is desirable to immediately release a **Connection** object's database and JDBC resources instead of waiting for them to be automatically released; the **close** method provides this immediate release. Its specification is

```
public abstract void close() throws SQLException
```

Note that a **Connection** object is automatically closed when it is garbage collected.

2. **setAutoCommit**: If a connection is in auto-commit mode, then all its SQL statements will be executed and committed as individual transactions. Otherwise, its SQL statements are grouped into transactions that are terminated by either **commit** or **rollback**. By default, new connections are in auto-commit mode. The commit occurs when the statement completes or the next execute occurs, whichever comes first. In the case of statements returning a **ResultSet**, the statement completes when the last row of the **ResultSet** has been retrieved or the **ResultSet** has been closed. The **setAutoCommit** method sets or resets the auto-commit mode and has the following specification:

```
public abstract void setAutoCommit
        (boolean autoCommit) throws SQLException
```

where `autoCommit` should be set to `true` to enable auto-commit and to `false` to disable auto-commit.

3. `commit`: This method should be used only if the auto-commit mode is set to `false`. `commit` makes all changes made since the previous commit/rollback permanent and releases any database locks currently held by the `Connection`. It has the following specification:

```
public abstract void commit() throws SQLException
```

4. `rollback`: This method drops all changes made since the previous commit/rollback and releases any database locks currently held by the `Connection`. It has the following specification:

```
public abstract void rollback() throws SQLException
```

   This method should also be used only when the auto-commit mode is set to `false`.

5. `getMetaData`: A `Connection`'s database is able to provide information describing its tables, its supported SQL grammar, its stored procedures, the capabilities of this `Connection`, etc. This information is made available through a `DatabaseMetaData` object. It can be obtained using the `getMetaData` method, which has the following specification:

```
public abstract DatabaseMetaData getMetaData()
  throws SQLException
```

   The `DatabaseMetaData` object is discussed in a later section.

5.4 Nonquery SQL Statements

To execute a nonquery SQL statement from a Java program using JDBC, one of the following three statement objects must be used:

- `Statement`
- `PreparedStatement`
- `CallableStatement`

This section describes how these three classes are used to execute SQL DDL or nonquery statements.

5.4.1 Using the Statement Object

The **Statement** class is used for executing SQL statements without parameters. The SQL statement can be a DDL statement such as **create table**, a nonquery statement such as **insert**, **delete**, or **update**, or an SQL query (**select** statement). The mechanism to handle an SQL **select** statement is explained in a subsequent section.

The **createStatement** method of the **Connection** class is used to instantiate a **Statement** object. The syntax for doing so is

```
Statement s = conn.createStatement();
```

where **conn** is a previously created **Connection** object. You can create as many **Statement** objects as you wish in a Java program. In most normal cases,[3] it is sufficient to create just one instance of the **Statement** object.

Once the **Statement** object has been created, its **executeUpdate** method can be invoked to execute a nonquery SQL statement. Its specification is

```
public abstract int executeUpdate(String sql)
  throws SQLException
```

where **sql** is a string variable containing the nonquery SQL statement. This method returns either the row count for **insert**, **update**, or **delete** or 0 for SQL DDL statements that return nothing.

Example 5.4.1 The following function performs an **insert** into the **catalog** table of the grade book database.

```
void add_catalog(Connection conn)
  throws SQLException, IOException {

  Statement stmt = conn.createStatement();

  String cnum   = readEntry("Course Number: ");
  String ctitle = readEntry("Course Title : ");
  String query = "insert into catalog values (" +
          "'" + cnum + "','" + ctitle + "')";
  try {
    int nrows = stmt.executeUpdate(query);
  } catch (SQLException e) {
      System.out.println("Error Adding Catalog Entry");
```

3. There are situations, such as performing multiple queries at the same time, when more than one instance of this class would have to be created.

```
      while (e != null) {
        System.out.println("Message:"+e.getMessage());
        e = e.getNextException();
      }
      return;
    }
  stmt.close();
  System.out.println("Added Catalog Entry");
}
```

The above function receives an open connection object as input. It first reads from standard input the course number and course title, then creates a **String** object, called **query**, which contains as its value the **insert** statement,[4] then creates a **Statement** object, and finally invokes the **executeUpdate** method on the **Statement** object with the SQL statement in **query**. The error checking is explained in a separate section. The **try–catch** mechanism of Java is used extensively to trap any errors that are encountered.

Example 5.4.2 The following function creates a table from within a Java program using JDBC.

```
void create_table(Connection conn)
  throws SQLException, IOException {
  String query =  "create table deleted_scores (" +
           "sid      varchar2(5) not null," +
           "term     varchar2(10) not null," +
           "lineno   number(4) not null," +
           "compname varchar2(15) not null," +
           "points   number(4) check(points >= 0))";

  Statement stmt = conn.createStatement ();
  try {
    stmt.executeUpdate(query);
  } catch (SQLException e) {
      System.out.println("Could not create table");
      while (e != null) {
        System.out.println("Message:"+e.getMessage());
        e = e.getNextException();
      }
```

4. An important point to note is that the statement is not terminated with the traditional semicolon.

```
      return;
    }
  System.out.println("Table created");
  stmt.close();
}
```

This is a similar example, except that the SQL statement that is sent to the database server for execution is a DDL statement.

Example 5.4.3 The following function deletes a student row from the `enrolls` table of the grade book database.

```
void drop_student(Connection conn,
                  String term_in, String ls)
    throws SQLException, IOException {

  String id = readEntry("Student ID to drop: ");
  String query0 = "insert into deleted_scores " +
    "select * from scores where sid = '" + id +
    "' and term = '" + term_in + "' and lineno = " + ls;
  String query1 = "delete scores where sid = '" + id +
    "' and term = '" + term_in + "' and lineno = " + ls;
  String query2 = "delete enrolls where sid = '" + id +
    "' and term = '" + term_in + "' and lineno = " + ls;

  conn.setAutoCommit(false);
  Statement stmt = conn.createStatement ();
  int nrows;
  try {
    nrows = stmt.executeUpdate(query0);
    nrows = stmt.executeUpdate(query1);
    nrows = stmt.executeUpdate(query2);
  } catch (SQLException e) {
      System.out.println("Could not drop student");
      while (e != null) {
        System.out.println("Message: "+e.getMessage());
        e = e.getNextException();
      }
      conn.rollback();
      return;
    }
```

```
    System.out.println("Dropped student");
    conn.commit();
    conn.setAutoCommit(true);
    stmt.close();
}
```

This function first disables the auto-commit mode for the connection. It then copies the rows from the **scores** tables that correspond to the student being dropped into a backup table called **deleted_scores**. After that, to maintain the referential integrity constraint, it deletes all the rows in the **scores** table before deleting the student row from the **enrolls** table.

5.4.2 Using the PreparedStatement Object

The **PreparedStatement** object is used in situations where the same SQL statement, with possibly different parameters, has to be executed a number of times. The **PreparedStatement** class is derived from the **Statement** class discussed earlier. Unlike the **Statement** object, a **PreparedStatement** object is created with an SQL statement. As a result, the **PreparedStatement** object contains not just an SQL statement but an SQL statement that is pre-compiled. This results in efficient execution of the statement, especially if it has to be repeatedly executed.

Usually, the **PreparedStatement** object is used with SQL statements that have parameters. This has the advantage that the same statement can be supplied with different values at different times and have it executed efficiently each time, without recompilation.

The **prepareStatement** method of the **Connection** class is used to create an instance of the **PreparedStatement** class. It has the syntax

```
public abstract PreparedStatement
  prepareStatement(String sql) throws SQLException
```

where **sql** is an SQL statement that may contain one or more **'?' IN** parameter placeholders. It returns a new **PreparedStatement** object containing the pre-compiled statement. An SQL statement with or without **IN** parameters can be pre-compiled and stored in a **PreparedStatement** object. This object can then be used to efficiently execute this statement multiple times.

Once the statement is prepared, its parameters must be set before it can be executed. The input parameters for a **PreparedStatement** object are set using the **setXXX** method, where **XXX** is a Java primitive type. The syntax for the **setString** method is

```
public abstract void setString
  (int parameterIndex,
   String x) throws SQLException
```

where **parameterIndex** is the index of the parameter (starting at 1), and **x** is the value to be assigned to the parameter. This method sets a parameter to a Java **String** value. The driver converts this to an Oracle SQL **VARCHAR** when it sends it to the database. The other **setXXX** methods are similar.

After providing the input parameters for the **PreparedStatement** object, it can be executed using the **executeUpdate** or **executeQuery** method.

Example 5.4.4 The following function executes a sequence of **inserts** into the **students** table of the grade book database.

```
void add_students(Connection conn)
    throws SQLException, IOException {

  String id, ln, fn, mi;
  PreparedStatement stmt = conn.prepareStatement(
    "insert into students values (?, ?, ?, ?)"  );
  do {
    id = readEntry("ID (0 to stop): ");
    if (id.equals("0"))
      break;
    ln = readEntry("Last  Name    : ");
    fn = readEntry("First Name    : ");
    mi = readEntry("Middle Initial: ");
    try {
      stmt.setString(1,id);
      stmt.setString(2,fn);
      stmt.setString(3,ln);
      stmt.setString(4,mi);
      stmt.executeUpdate();
    } catch (SQLException e) {
      System.out.println("Error adding student");
    }
  } while (true);
  stmt.close();
}
```

The function repeatedly reads information about new students and inserts it into the **students** table. The loop stops when the user enters an ID of 0. Since the same statement with different values for the columns is to be executed many times, the **PreparedStatement** object is used.

5.4.3 Using the CallableStatement Object

The **CallableStatement** object is used to execute PL/SQL stored procedures and anonymous blocks. The call to the stored procedure or function or anonymous PL/SQL block is written in an escape syntax in one of the following forms:

```
{call procedure_name(?, ?, ..., ?)}
{? = call function_name(?, ?, ..., ?)}
("begin proc (:1, :2, ..., :n); end;")
("begin :1 := func(:1,:2, ..., :n); end;")
("anonymous-block")
```

The first two forms are recommended for portability purposes, and the last three are Oracle-specific. The **anonymous-block** may contain any number of parameter placeholders as in the other forms.

The **CallableStatement** class is derived from **PreparedStatement**, thereby inheriting many of its methods. A **CallableStatement** object is instantiated by calling the **prepareCall** method on a JDBC **Connection** object whose specification is shown below:

```
public abstract CallableStatement
   prepareCall(String sql) throws SQLException
```

where **sql** is an SQL statement that may contain one or more **'?'** parameter placeholders.

The **CallableStatement** class provides methods for setting up its **IN** and **OUT** parameters, and methods for executing PL/SQL stored procedures and anonymous blocks. The **IN** parameters are set in the same manner as in the case of **Prepared-Statement**, using the **setXXX** methods. The **java.sql.Types** type for each of the **OUT** parameters must be registered before the **CallableStatement** object can be executed. This is done using

```
public abstract void
  registerOutParameter(int parameterIndex,
                       int sType) throws SQLException
```

where

- **parameterIndex** is the index of the parameter (the first parameter is 1, the second is 2, etc.).
- **sType** is SQL type code defined by **java.sql.Types**.

For parameters of type NUMERIC or DECIMAL, the following version of registerOutParameter that accepts a scale value must be used:

```
public abstract void
  registerOutParameter(int parameterIndex,
                       int sType,
                       int scale) throws SQLException
```

In this situation

- parameterIndex is the same as before.
- sType is a NUMERIC or DECIMAL constant found in java.sql.Types.
- scale is a value greater than or equal to zero representing the desired number of digits to the right of the decimal point.

The OUT parameters are read using the getXXX method provided by the CallableStatement class. It is important to note that when reading the value of an OUT parameter, the getXXX method whose Java type XXX corresponds to the parameter's registered SQL type must be used.

Example 5.4.5 The following example makes calls to the stored procedures add_orders and add_order_details of the process_orders package discussed in the PL/SQL chapter.

```
import java.sql.*;
import java.io.*;
class call3 {
  public static void main (String args [])
      throws SQLException, IOException {
    try {
      Class.forName ("oracle.jdbc.driver.OracleDriver");
    } catch (ClassNotFoundException e) {
        System.out.println ("Could not load the driver");
      }
    String user, pass;
    user = readEntry("userid  : ");
    pass = readEntry("password: ");
    Connection conn = DriverManager.getConnection
      ("jdbc:oracle:oci8:"+user+"/"+pass);

    int enum = readNumber("Enter the employee number: ");
    int cnum = readNumber("Enter the customer number: ");
```

```
    int onum = readNumber("Enter the order    number: ");
    CallableStatement stmt = conn.prepareCall
      ("{call process_orders.add_order(?,?,?,?)}");
    stmt.setInt(1,onum);
    stmt.setInt(2,cnum);
    stmt.setInt(3,enum);
    stmt.setNull(4,Types.DATE);
    conn.setAutoCommit(false);
    try {
      stmt.executeUpdate();
    } catch (SQLException e) {
        System.out.println("Could not add order");
        conn.rollback();
        return;
      }
    stmt = conn.prepareCall
      ("{call process_orders.add_order_details(?,?,?)}");
    do {
      int pnum = readNumber("Enter the part number (0 to stop): ");
      if (pnum == 0)
        break;
      int qty = readNumber("Enter the quantity   : ");
      stmt.setInt(1,onum);
      stmt.setInt(2,pnum);
      stmt.setInt(3,qty);
      try {
        stmt.executeUpdate();
      } catch (SQLException e) {
          System.out.println("Could not add odetail");
        }
    } while (true);
  conn.commit();
  conn.setAutoCommit(true);
  stmt.close();
  conn.close();
  }
  //readNumber function -- to read input number
  static int readNumber(String prompt)
        throws IOException {
    String snum;
```

```
        int num = 0;
        boolean numok;
        do {
          snum = readEntry(prompt);
          try {
            num = Integer.parseInt(snum);
            numok = true;
          } catch (NumberFormatException e) {
              numok = false;
              System.out.println("Invalid number; enter again");
            }
        } while (!numok);
        return num;
      }
    }
```

The program reads the information about a new order from the standard input and makes a call to the `add_order` stored procedure using a `CallableStatement` object. It then repeatedly reads the order details information and makes a call to the `add_order_details` stored procedure. Note that both stored procedures called have only input parameters. Also note the use of the `setNull` method to set the value of an `IN` parameter to `null`.

Example 5.4.6 The following program makes a call to a stored function, `get_city`, which takes as input a customer number and returns the city for the customer.

```
import java.sql.*;
import java.io.*;
class call1 {
  public static void main (String args [])
      throws SQLException, IOException {
    try {
      Class.forName ("oracle.jdbc.driver.OracleDriver");
    } catch (ClassNotFoundException e) {
        System.out.println ("Could not load the driver");
      }
    String user, pass;
    user = readEntry("userid  : ");
    pass = readEntry("password: ");
    Connection conn = DriverManager.getConnection
      ("jdbc:oracle:oci8:"+user+"/"+pass);
```

```
      String cnum = readEntry(
        "Enter the customer number to find city: ");
      CallableStatement stmt =
        conn.prepareCall ("{? = call get_city (?)}");
      stmt.setString(2,cnum);
      stmt.registerOutParameter(1,Types.VARCHAR);
      stmt.execute();
      String city = stmt.getString(1);
      if (stmt.wasNull())
        System.out.println("Customer's city = Null");
      else
        System.out.println("Customer's city = "+stmt.getString(1));
      stmt.close();
      conn.close();
    }
  }
```

Note the `registerOutParameter` method invocation for the return value of the function. Also note the use of the `wasNull` method of the `Statement` object to check to see if the last value retrieved using a `getXXX` method was `null` or not.

5.5 Executing SQL Queries

An SQL query can be executed using any of the three statement objects: `Statement`, `PreparedStatement`, or `CallableStatement`. The `executeQuery` method must be used to execute the query. Its syntax when used on a `Statement` object is

```
public abstract ResultSet
  executeQuery(String sql) throws SQLException
```

and when used on the `PreparedStatement` and `CallableStatement` objects is

```
public abstract ResultSet
  executeQuery() throws SQLException
```

where `sql` is an SQL `select` statement. This method executes an SQL statement that returns a single `ResultSet` object. The `ResultSet` class is discussed next.

5.5.1 The ResultSet Class

The ResultSet class provides access to a table of data generated by executing a query. The table rows are retrieved in sequence, and within a row the column values can be accessed in any order. A ResultSet object maintains a cursor pointing to its current row of data. Initially the cursor is positioned before the first row. The next method moves the cursor to the next row. Therefore, it is important to use the next method before any of the rows are retrieved.

To retrieve the current row's column values, the getXXX methods are used, where XXX is a Java type. The column values can be retrieved either by using the index number of the column or by using the name of the column. In general, using the column index will be more efficient. Columns are numbered from 1. For the getXXX methods, the JDBC driver attempts to convert the underlying data to the specified Java type and returns a suitable Java value. See the online JDBC documentation for allowable mappings from SQL types to Java types with the ResultSet.getXXX methods.

Column names used as input to getXXX methods are case insensitive. When performing a getXXX using a column name, if several columns have the same name, then the value of the first matching column will be returned. The column name option is designed to be used when column names are used in the SQL query.

A ResultSet is automatically closed by the Statement that generated it when that Statement is closed, or re-executed, or when it is used to retrieve the next result from a sequence of multiple results. This is important to note in situations where more than one ResultSet is worked with at the same time. Since only one ResultSet is active for a Statement object, two or more Statement objects will become necessary in such situations.

5.5.2 ResultSet Methods

The methods provided for the ResultSet class are summarized below:

- next: This method positions the cursor to the next row in the ResultSet. It has the following specification:

  ```
  public abstract boolean next() throws SQLException
  ```

  A ResultSet is initially positioned before its first row; the first call to next makes the first row the current row; any subsequent call moves the cursor to the next row. It returns true if the next row is defined; otherwise it returns false.

- close: This method explicitly closes a ResultSet and releases any JDBC resources. It has the following specification:

```
public abstract void close() throws SQLException
```

Note that a `ResultSet` is automatically closed by the statement that generated it when that statement is closed or re-executed, or when it is used to retrieve the next result from a sequence of multiple results. A `ResultSet` is also automatically closed when it is garbage collected.

- `wasNull`: This method is used to check whether the previous column value read is `null` or not. It has the following specification:

  ```
  public abstract boolean wasNull() throws SQLException
  ```

  A column may have the value of SQL `null`; `wasNull` returns `true` if the last column read had this special value, and `false` otherwise. Note that a call to `getXXX` on a column to try to read its value must be made prior to the call to `wasNull()`.

- `getString`: This is one of many `getXXX` methods used to retrieve column values of the current row in a `ResultSet`. It has two versions. The first is

  ```
  public abstract String getString(int columnIndex)
    throws SQLException
  ```

  which takes a `columnIndex` as input (value of 1 or more) and returns the column value for that index as a Java `String` object. The second is

  ```
  public abstract String getString(String columnName)
    throws SQLException
  ```

  which takes the `columnName` as input and returns the column value as a Java `String`. In both cases, if the value is SQL `null`, the result is Java `null`.

- `getMetaData`: This method is used to obtain information about the `ResultSet` other than the rows. It has the following specification:

  ```
  public abstract ResultSetMetaData getMetaData()
    throws SQLException
  ```

  The number, types, and properties of the columns of a `ResultSet` are provided by this method. The metadata of a `ResultSet` are discussed later in this chapter.

- `findColumn`: This method returns the index of a column given its name. It has the following specification:

  ```
  public abstract int findColumn(String columnName)
    throws SQLException
  ```

Figure 5.1 Class report (gradebook database).

SID	LNAME	FNAME	EXAM1(400/40)	FINAL(500/60)	AVG	GRADE
9002	Blake	Gary	360	490	94.8	A
9000	Jones	Tony	300	300	66.0	D
9001	Smith	Charlie	380	400	86.0	B

5.5.3 An SQL Query Example

Consider the gradebook database and the problem of printing a class report (Figure 5.1) that contains a listing of all students along with their scores for each component and their course average and final grade.

The following function (`print_report`) generates this report. It takes as input an open connection to the database and the term and line number for the course for which the report is to be printed.

```
void print_report(Connection conn,
                  String term_in, String ls)
     throws SQLException, IOException {

  String query0 = "select a, b, c, d from courses " +
    "where term = '" + term_in + "' and lineno = " + ls;

  String query1 = "select compname, maxpoints, weight " +
    "from components where term = '" + term_in +
    "' and lineno = " + ls;

  String query2 = "select E.sid, S.lname, S.fname " +
    "from enrolls E, students S " +
    "where S.sid = E.sid and " +
    "E.term = '" + term_in + "' and " +
    "E.lineno = " + ls + " order by lname, fname";

  String query3 = "select points " + "from scores " +
     "where term = '" +  term_in + "' and " +
     "lineno = " + ls + " and " +
     "sid = ? and " +    // substitute ? by sid
     "compname = ?";  // substitute ? by compname
```

```
double total;
int scaleA, scaleB, scaleC, scaleD;
// Read the grade cut off points from courses
Statement stmt = conn.createStatement ();
ResultSet rset0;
try {
  rset0 = stmt.executeQuery(query0);
} catch (SQLException e) {
    System.out.println("Problem reading scales");
    while (e != null) {
      System.out.println("Message:"+e.getMessage());
      e = e.getNextException();
    }
    return;
  }
rset0.next();
scaleA = rset0.getInt(1);
scaleB = rset0.getInt(2);
scaleC = rset0.getInt(3);
scaleD = rset0.getInt(4);

System.out.print("SID  LNAME       FNAME     ");
// Read the component information into arrays
ResultSet rset1;
try {
  rset1 = stmt.executeQuery(query1);
} catch (SQLException e) {
    System.out.println("Problem reading components");
    while (e != null) {
      System.out.println("Message:"+e.getMessage());
      e = e.getNextException();
    }
    return;
  }
String comp_names[] = new String[20];
double comp_maxpoints[] = new double[20];
double comp_weight[] = new double[20];
int ncomps=0;
```

```
while (rset1.next()) {
  System.out.print(rset1.getString(1)+"("+
                   rset1.getString(2)+"/"+
                   rset1.getString(3)+")  ");
  comp_names[ncomps] = rset1.getString(1);
  comp_maxpoints[ncomps] = rset1.getDouble(2);
  comp_weight[ncomps] = rset1.getDouble(3);
  ncomps++;
}

System.out.println("AVG    GRADE");
// Read the students enrolled in the class
// For each student and for each grade component,
// read the score, print and keep total
ResultSet rset2;
try {
  rset2 = stmt.executeQuery(query2);
} catch (SQLException e) {
    System.out.println("Problem reading students");
    while (e != null) {
      System.out.println("Message:"+e.getMessage());
      e = e.getNextException();
    }
    return;
  }

PreparedStatement stmt2 =
  conn.prepareStatement(query3);
while (rset2.next()) {
  total = 0.0;
  System.out.print(rset2.getString(1)+" ");
  System.out.print(rset2.getString(2));
  for (int k=0;k < (12-rset2.getString(2).length()); k++)
    System.out.print(" ");
  System.out.print(rset2.getString(3));
  for (int k=0;k < (12-rset2.getString(3).length()); k++)
    System.out.print(" ");
  for (int i=0; i < ncomps; i++) {
    stmt2.setString(1,rset2.getString(1));
    stmt2.setString(2,comp_names[i]);
```

```
        ResultSet rset3;
        try {
          rset3 = stmt2.executeQuery();
        } catch (SQLException e) {
            System.out.println("Problem reading scores");
            while (e != null) {
              System.out.println("Message:"+e.getMessage());
              e = e.getNextException();
            }
            return;
          }
        try {
          rset3.next();
        } catch (SQLException e) {
            System.out.println("No entry for " +
              rset2.getString(3) + " in " + comp_names[i]);
            while (e != null) {
              System.out.println("Message:"+e.getMessage());
              e = e.getNextException();
            }
            continue;
          }
        total = total + ((rset3.getDouble(1)/comp_maxpoints[i])*
                 comp_weight[i]);
        System.out.print(rset3.getString(1));
      }

      // Print the total and grade.
      Double tot = new Double(total);
      for (int k2=0;k2 < (6-tot.toString().length()); k2++)
        System.out.print(" ");
      System.out.print(total + "      ");
      if (total >= scaleA) System.out.println("A");
      else if (total >= scaleB) System.out.println("B");
      else if (total >= scaleC) System.out.println("C");
      else if (total >= scaleD) System.out.println("D");
      else System.out.println("F");
  }
  stmt.close();
}
```

The procedure performs the following steps:

- Execute `query0` to obtain the cut-off points for the grades. This is a simple query with no parameters and is executed by using a `Statement` object.
- Execute `query1` to obtain the information about the grade components for the course. This information is printed to the report and is also stored in Java arrays for later use.
- Execute `query2` to get the students enrolled in the course.
- For each student in the result set of `query2` and for each component for the course, using nested loops, execute `query3` to obtain the score. After obtaining the score, print it to the report and update the total for the student. Since `query3` is to be executed many times, a `PreparedStatement` object is used. At the end of the inner loop, print the student's average and grade.

5.5.4 ResultSet Metadata

The `ResultSetMetaData` class provides the ability to find out about the types and properties of columns in a `ResultSet` object. This is a very useful feature, especially when the query being executed is not known at compile time, as is the case with dynamic SQL.

The `ResultSetMetaData` object can be created by invoking the `getMetaData` method on a `ResultSet` object as follows:

```
ResultSetMetaData rsetmd = rset.getMetaData();
```

where `rset` is a previously defined `ResultSet` object. The `rsetmd` object now contains all the metadata information about the `ResultSet rset`. The metadata information can be extracted using one of many `ResultSetMetaData` methods shown below:

- `getColumnCount`: This method returns the number of columns in the result set. Its specification is

  ```
  public abstract int getColumnCount()
   throws SQLException
  ```

- `isNullable`: This method checks to see if a particular column can have a `null` value or not. It has the specification

  ```
  public abstract int isNullable(int column)
   throws SQLException
  ```

where `column` is the column index. The return value is one of the following integer constants defined in this class: `columnNoNulls`, `columnNullable`, or `columnNullableUnknown`.

- `getColumnDisplaySize`: This method returns the column's normal maximum width. It has the specification

  ```
  public abstract int getColumnDisplaySize(int column)
   throws SQLException
  ```

  where `column` is the column index.

- `getColumnLabel`: This method returns the suggested column title for use in printouts and displays. It has the specification

  ```
  public abstract String getColumnLabel(int column)
   throws SQLException
  ```

  where `column` is the column index.

- `getColumnName`: This method returns the column name for a given column index. It has the specification

  ```
  public abstract String getColumnName(int column)
   throws SQLException
  ```

  where `column` is the column index.

- `getPrecision`: This method returns a column's number of decimal digits. It has the specification

  ```
  public abstract int getPrecision(int column)
   throws SQLException
  ```

  where `column` is the column index.

- `getScale`: This method returns a column's number of decimal digits to the right of the decimal point. It has the specification

  ```
  public abstract int getScale(int column)
    throws SQLException
  ```

  where `column` is the column index.

- `getTableName`: This method returns the name of the table for the given column. If not applicable, it returns the empty string object. It has the specification

  ```
  public abstract String getTableName(int column)
    throws SQLException
  ```

where `column` is the column index.

- `getColumnType`: This method returns the column's SQL type. See `java.sql.Types` for a list of SQL types. This method has the specification

```
public abstract int getColumnType(int column)
  throws SQLException
```

  where `column` is the column index.

- `getColumnTypeName`: This method returns the column's data source specific type name. It has the specification

```
public abstract String getColumnTypeName(int column)
  throws SQLException
```

  where `column` is the column index.

Example 5.5.1 The following is a Java program that interprets SQL queries and prints the results. The user may enter the SQL `select` statement on the `SQL>` prompt on one or more lines. (The `SQL>` prompt is echoed after each carriage return.) The query must be terminated with a semicolon. The display showing the results of the query is similar to the SQL*Plus display. Several `ResultSetMetaData` methods are invoked to display the results. The user may exit the program by typing `exit` and a semicolon.

```
import java.sql.*;
import java.io.*;
class meta3 {
public static void main (String args [])
    throws SQLException, IOException {

  try {
    Class.forName ("oracle.jdbc.driver.OracleDriver");
  } catch (ClassNotFoundException e) {
      System.out.println ("Could not load the driver");
    }

  String user, pass;
  user = readEntry("userid  : ");
  pass = readEntry("password: ");
  Connection conn = DriverManager.getConnection(
     "jdbc:oracle:oci8:"+user+"/"+pass);
```

```
System.out.println("Welcome to the SQL Interpreter\n");
System.out.print("SQL> ");
Statement stmt = conn.createStatement ();
do {
  String query = readQuery();
  if (query .equals("exit"))
    break;
  ResultSet rset;
  try {
    rset = stmt.executeQuery(query);
  } catch (SQLException e) {
      System.out.println("Not well formed query");
      continue;
    }
  ResultSetMetaData rsetmd = rset.getMetaData();
  int nCols;
  nCols = rsetmd.getColumnCount();
  for (int i = 1; i <= nCols; i++) {
    System.out.print(rsetmd.getColumnName(i));
    int colSize = rsetmd.getColumnDisplaySize(i);
    for (int k=0;
         k < colSize-rsetmd.getColumnName(i).length();
         k++)
      System.out.print(" ");
  }
  System.out.println("");
  while (rset.next ()) {
    for (int i = 1; i <= nCols; i++) {
      String val = rset.getString(i);
      if (rset.wasNull())
        System.out.print("null");
      else
        System.out.print(rset.getString(i));
      int colSize;
      if (rset.wasNull()) colSize = 4;
      else colSize = rsetmd.getColumnDisplaySize(i);
      if (rset.wasNull()) {
        for (int k=0; k < colSize-4; k++)
          System.out.print(" ");
```

```
          }
          else {
            for (int k=0;
                 k < colSize-rset.getString(i).length();
                 k++)
              System.out.print(" ");
          }
        }
        System.out.println("");
      }
    } while (true);
    stmt.close();
    conn.close();
    System.out.println("Thank you for using the SQL"+
                       " Interpreter\n");
  }
  //readQuery function
  static String readQuery() {
     try {
       StringBuffer buffer = new StringBuffer();
       System.out.flush();
       int c = System.in.read();
       while(c != ';' && c != -1) {
          if (c != '\n')
            buffer.append((char)c);
          else {
            buffer.append(" ");
            System.out.print("SQL> ");
            System.out.flush();
          }
          c = System.in.read();
        }
        return buffer.toString().trim();
      } catch (IOException e) {
        return "";
        }
    }
  }
```

Note: `null` values are checked before printing them using the `wasNull()` method. The following is a screen capture of a session with the above program.

```
[/home/book/jdbc][3:40pm] java meta3
userid  : book
password: book
Welcome to the SQL Interpreter

SQL> select cno,cname
SQL> from customers;
CNO                   CNAME
1111                  Charles
2222                  Bertram
3333                  Barbara
9999                  Johnny
SQL> select cno,cname,city
SQL> from customers,zipcodes
SQL> where customers.zip = zipcodes.zip;
CNO              CNAME                CITY
1111             Charles              Wichita
2222             Bertram              Wichita
3333             Barbara              Fort Dodge
9999             Johnny               null
SQL> select cno,zip
SQL> from customers;
CNO                   ZIP
1111                  67226
2222                  67226
3333                  60606
9999                  99999
SQL> select cno,city
SQL> from customers;
Not well formed query
SQL> exit;
Thank you for using the SQL Interpreter

[/home/book/jdbc][3:41pm]
```

5.5.5 Oracle REFCURSOR Type

The Oracle JDBC driver supports bind variables of type **REF CURSOR**, a reference to a cursor that is represented by a JDBC **ResultSet**. Using the **getCursor** method of the **CallableStatement** object, you can convert a **REF CURSOR** value returned by a PL/SQL procedure/function into a JDBC **ResultSet**. You must import classes from the **oracle.jdbc.driver** package to work with **REF CURSOR** values.

Example 5.5.2 The following is a PL/SQL package specification containing one function, called **get_courses**, which takes as input a **term** value and returns a reference to a cursor that contains the line number, course number, and course title for all courses taught in a given term.

```
create or replace package refcursor_jdbc as
  type refcurtype is ref cursor;
  function get_courses (term_in varchar2)
           return refcurtype;
end refcursor_jdbc;
/
show errors
create or replace package body refcursor_jdbc as
  function get_courses (term_in varchar2)
           return refcurtype as
    rc refcurtype;
  begin
   open rc for
     select lineno, courses.cno, ctitle
     from   courses, catalog
     where  courses.cno = catalog.cno and
            courses.term = term_in;
   return rc;
  end;
end refcursor_jdbc;
/
show errors
```

Once this package has been defined in the Oracle database, it can be accessed within a JDBC program. The following is a Java program that reads the value of **term** from standard input and makes a call to the **get_courses** function discussed earlier. It then processes the results and prints the courses on the screen.

```
import java.sql.*;
import java.io.*;
import oracle.jdbc.driver.*;

class refcur {
  public static void main (String args [])
       throws SQLException, ClassNotFoundException {

    try {
      Class.forName ("oracle.jdbc.driver.OracleDriver");
    } catch (ClassNotFoundException e) {
        System.out.println ("Could not load the driver");
      }

    String user, pass;
    user = readEntry("userid  : ");
    pass = readEntry("password: ");
    Connection conn = DriverManager.getConnection
       ("jdbc:oracle:oci8:"+user+"/"+pass);

    String term_in = readEntry("Enter Term: ");

    CallableStatement cstmt = conn.prepareCall
        ("{ ? = call refcursor_jdbc.get_courses (?)}");

    cstmt.registerOutParameter (1, OracleTypes.CURSOR);
    cstmt.setString (2, term_in);
    cstmt.execute ();
    ResultSet rset = (ResultSet)cstmt.getObject(1);
    System.out.println("Courses offered during " +
                       term_in + " are:");
    while (rset.next ()) {
      System.out.print(rset.getString(1) + "  ");
      System.out.print(rset.getString(2) + "  ");
      System.out.println(rset.getString(3));
    }
    cstmt.close();
    conn.close();
  }
}
```

Notice the statement

```
cstmt.registerOutParameter (1, OracleTypes.CURSOR);
```

which registers the data type of the return value of the function to be `OracleTypes.CURSOR`. Also notice the use of the `getObject` method to obtain the result set corresponding to the cursor reference. The following is the screen capture of a sample run of the above program.

```
[~book/jdbc][12:41pm] java refcur
userid  : book
password: book
Enter Term: F96
Courses offered during F96 are:
1031  CSC226  INTRODUCTION TO PROGRAMMING I
1032  CSC226  INTRODUCTION TO PROGRAMMING I
[~book/jdbc][12:42pm]
```

5.5.6 Processing Multiple `ResultSets`

An example of executing an anonymous PL/SQL block that contains several `REF CURSOR` values is shown here. This results in multiple `ResultSet` objects that need to be processed sequentially.

Example 5.5.3 An anonymous PL/SQL block that contains three cursor references is executed from within a Java program. The program reads in a customer number and executes the anonymous PL/SQL block. The first cursor reference contains a cursor that returns the total number of orders for the particular customer, the second cursor reference contains a cursor that returns the order number and receive date for orders for the given customer, and the third cursor reference contains a cursor for the order details for each order for the given customer. Once this PL/SQL block is executed, the three result sets are retrieved in sequence and processed. The Java program follows:

```
import oracle.jdbc.driver.*;
import java.sql.*;
import java.io.*;

class call2 {
 public static void main (String args [])
     throws SQLException, IOException {
```

```
try {
  Class.forName ("oracle.jdbc.driver.OracleDriver");
 } catch (ClassNotFoundException e) {
     System.out.println ("Could not load the driver");
   }

String user, pass;
user = readEntry("userid  : ");
pass = readEntry("password: ");
Connection conn = DriverManager.getConnection
   ("jdbc:oracle:oci8:"+user+"/"+pass);

String cnum = readEntry("Enter customer number: ");
CallableStatement cstmt;
ResultSet rset;

cstmt = conn.prepareCall
 ("begin " +
  "open ? for select count(*) from orders " +
    "where cno = ?;" +
  "open ? for select ono,received from orders " +
    "where cno = ?;" +
  "open ? for select orders.ono,parts.pno,pname,qty " +
    "from orders,odetails,parts where " +
    "orders.ono = odetails.ono and " +
    "odetails.pno = parts.pno " +
    "and cno = ?;" +  "end;");

cstmt.setString(2,cnum);
cstmt.setString(4,cnum);
cstmt.setString(6,cnum);
cstmt.registerOutParameter (1, OracleTypes.CURSOR);
cstmt.registerOutParameter (3, OracleTypes.CURSOR);
cstmt.registerOutParameter (5, OracleTypes.CURSOR);
cstmt.execute ();

rset = ((OracleCallableStatement)cstmt).getCursor(1);
while (rset.next ()) {
  System.out.println ("Customer has " +
                  rset.getString(1) + " orders");
```

```
      }
      System.out.println("The orders are:");
      rset = ((OracleCallableStatement)cstmt).getCursor(3);
      while (rset.next ()) {
        System.out.print("Order Number " +rset.getString(1));
        System.out.println(":Received on " +rset.getDate(2).toString());
      }
      System.out.println("The order details are:");
      System.out.println("ONO   PNO    PNAME    QUANTITY");
      rset = ((OracleCallableStatement)cstmt).getCursor(5);
      ResultSetMetaData rsetmd = rset.getMetaData();
      while (rset.next ()) {
        System.out.print(rset.getString(1));
        System.out.print(" " + rset.getString(2));
        System.out.print(" " + rset.getString(3));
        for (int k=0;
             k<(rsetmd.getColumnDisplaySize(3)-
                rset.getString(3).length()); k++)
          System.out.print(" ");
        System.out.println(" " + rset.getString(4));
      }
      cstmt.close();
      conn.close();
    }
  }
```

Note the use of the statement

```
rset = ((OracleCallableStatement)cstmt).getCursor(1);
```

The `getCursor` method is not available for a `CallableStatement` object, hence the cast. The following is a screen capture of a sample run of the above program.

```
[~book/jdbc][12:10pm] java call2
userid  : book
password: book
Enter the customer number: 1111
Customer has 5 orders
The orders are:
Order Number 1020:Received on 1994-12-10
Order Number 1021:Received on 1995-01-12
Order Number 2000:Received on 1998-01-26
```

```
Order Number 3005:Received on 1998-02-19
Order Number 3000:Received on 1998-02-19
The order details are:
ONO  PNO    PNAME                          QUANTITY
1020 10506 Land Before Time I                  1
1020 10507 Land Before Time II                 1
1020 10508 Land Before Time III                2
1020 10509 Land Before Time IV                 3
1021 10601 Sleeping Beauty                     4
3000 10506 Land Before Time I                 20
2000 10900 Dr. Zhivago                       140
3000 10507 Land Before Time II                20
3005 10506 Land Before Time I                 10
3005 10507 Land Before Time II                10
[~book/jdbc][12:10pm]
```

5.6 Grade Book Application

An application developed for the grade book database is introduced here. It is a terminal-based application having the following main menu:

```
    Main Menu

(1) Add Catalog
(2) Add Course
(3) Add Students
(4) Select Course
(q) Quit
```

The user options at the main menu level are as follows:

- `Add Catalog`: Requests information about new catalog entry and adds an entry to the `catalog` table.
- `Add Course`: Requests information about new courses and adds an entry to the `course` table.
- `Add Students`: Repeatedly requests information about new students and adds entries to the `students` table. The processing is stopped when the user types in 0 for `sid`.

- `Select Course`: This option asks for the term and then lists all the courses taught in that term and asks the user to select a particular course (line number) and displays the following sub-menu.

```
            SELECT COURSE SUB-MENU


    (1) Add Students to Course
    (2) Add Course Components
    (3) Add Student Scores
    (4) Modify Student Score
    (5) Drop Student from Course
    (6) Print Course Report
    (q) Quit
```

These sub-menu options are valid for a given course offering:

- `Add Enrolls`: Repeatedly requests `sid` values and inserts into `enrolls` table.
- `Add Course Components`: Requests information about a component and inserts into `components` table.
- `Add Scores`: This option first lists all the components for the course and asks the user to choose one. It then displays each student's name and requests the student's score for the selected component. These scores are inserted into the `scores` table.
- `Modify Scores`: Requests `sid` and `compname` values, then displays old score and requests new score. Finally, performs an update in the `scores` table.
- `Delete Enrolls`: Requests `sid` value and then deletes row from `enrolls` table.
- `Report`: Generates a course report.

Many of the functions required to implement this application have already been discussed. Some of the remaining functions are discussed next.

5.6.1 Function `select_course`

The following is the `select_course` function, which asks the user for the term and displays all the courses taught in that term. The user is then asked to select one of these courses for manipulation. A sub-menu is shown for the selected course, and various options are processed. The function takes as input an open connection to the database.

```
void select_course(Connection conn)
 throws SQLException, IOException {

 String query1 = "select distinct lineno," +
   "courses.cno,ctitle from courses,catalog " +
   "where courses.cno = catalog.cno and term = '";
 String query;
 String term_in = readEntry("Term: ");
 query = query1 + term_in + "'";

 Statement stmt = conn.createStatement ();
 ResultSet rset = stmt.executeQuery(query);
 System.out.println("");
 while (rset.next ()) {
   System.out.println(rset.getString(1) + "    " +
                      rset.getString(2) + "    " +
                      rset.getString(3));
 }
 System.out.println("");
 String ls = readEntry("Select a course: ");

 grade2 g2 = new grade2();
 boolean done;
 char ch,ch1;

 done = false;
 do {
   g2.print_menu();
   System.out.print("Type in your option:");
   System.out.flush();
   ch = (char) System.in.read();
   ch1 = (char) System.in.read();
   switch (ch) {
    case '1': g2.add_enrolls(conn,term_in,ls);
              break;
    case '2': g2.add_course_component(conn,term_in,ls);
              break;
    case '3': g2.add_scores(conn,term_in,ls);
              break;
```

```
      case '4': g2.modify_score(conn,term_in,ls);
                break;
      case '5': g2.drop_student(conn,term_in,ls);
                break;
      case '6': g2.print_report(conn,term_in,ls);
                break;
      case 'q': done = true;
                break;
      default : System.out.println("Invalid option");
    }
  } while (!done);
}
```

The query to find the courses taught in a particular term is formed and executed. The results are displayed for the user to select a course. The user enters the line number of the course, and a sub-menu is shown. The sub-menu and other functions dealing with it are defined in the **grade2** class.

5.6.2 Function add_enrolls

The **add_enrolls** function repeatedly requests the student ID from the user for a particular course and adds it to the **enrolls** table. The user may stop the loop by providing a value of 0 for the ID. This function takes as input an open connection and the term and line number for the course for which the students are to be enrolled. The function is shown below:

```
void add_enrolls(Connection conn, String term_in,
                 String ls) throws IOException,
                                   SQLException {
  String id;
  PreparedStatement stmt = conn.prepareStatement(
    "insert into enrolls values " +
    "(?,'" + term_in + "',"+ls+")"  );
  do {
    id = readEntry("Student Id (0 to stop): ");
    if (id.equals("0"))
      break;
    try {
      stmt.setString(1,id);
      stmt.executeUpdate();
```

```
    } catch (SQLException e) {
      System.out.println("Error adding student.");
      while (e != null) {
       System.out.println("Message:"+e.getMessage());
       e = e.getNextException();
      }
    }
  } while (true);
  stmt.close();
}
```

A PreparedStatement object is used to speed up the execution of the insert statement.

5.6.3 Function add_scores

The add_scores function in the sub-menu shown below takes as input an open connection and the term and line number for the course for which the scores are to be added.

```
void add_scores(Connection conn,
                String term_in, String ls)
  throws SQLException, IOException {

  String query1 = "select distinct compname " +
    "from   courses,components " +
    "where  courses.term = components.term and " +
    " courses.lineno = components.lineno and " +
    " courses.term = '" + term_in + "'" + " and " +
    " courses.lineno = " + ls;

  Statement stmt1 = conn.createStatement ();
  ResultSet rset1 = stmt1.executeQuery(query1);
  System.out.println("");
  while (rset1.next ()) {
    System.out.println(rset1.getString(1));
  }
  System.out.println("");
  String cname = readEntry("Enter a component name: ");
```

```
    String query2 =
      "select distinct students.sid, lname, fname " +
      "from   enrolls,students " +
      "where  enrolls.sid = students.sid and " +
      " enrolls.term = '" + term_in + "'" + " and" +
      " enrolls.lineno = " + ls +
      " order by lname, fname";

    ResultSet rset2 = stmt1.executeQuery(query2);
    System.out.println("");

    PreparedStatement stmt2 = conn.prepareStatement(
      "insert into scores values (?,'"+
       term_in + "'," + ls + ",'" + cname + "', ?)");

    while (rset2.next ()) {
      String pts = readEntry(cname + " Score for " +
        rset2.getString(1) + ": " + rset2.getString(2) +
        ", " + rset2.getString(3) + ": ");
      try {
        stmt2.setString(1,rset2.getString(1));
        stmt2.setString(2,pts);
        stmt2.executeUpdate();
      } catch (SQLException e) {
          System.out.println("Score was not added!");
          while (e != null) {
            System.out.println("Message:"+e.getMessage());
            e = e.getNextException();
          }
        }
    }
    stmt1.close();
    stmt2.close();
  }
```

This function performs the following steps:

- Executes `query1` to get the component names. It then displays the component names from which the user chooses one. The `Statement` object is used for this query.

- Executes **query2** to get the students enrolled in the course. The **Statement** object is also used for this query.
- For each student enrolled in the course, it prompts the user with the student ID and name and requests the score for the chosen component.
- Using a **PreparedStatement** object, it inserts the score in the **scores** table.

5.6.4 Function modify_score

The function **modify_score** takes as input an open connection to the database and the line number and term for the course in which the student's score is to be modified. The function asks the user for the student ID and the component name for which the score is to be modified. It then displays the old score and requests the new one. Finally it performs an **update** statement in the **scores** table. The function is shown below:

```
void modify_score(Connection conn, String term_in,
   String ls) throws SQLException, IOException {

 String id    = readEntry("Student's ID  : ");
 String cname = readEntry("Component Name: ");
 String query1 = "select points from scores " +
   "where sid = '" + id + "' and term = '" + term_in +
   "' and lineno = " + ls + " and compname = '" +
   cname + "'";

 Statement stmt = conn.createStatement ();
 ResultSet rset;
 try {
   rset = stmt.executeQuery(query1);
 } catch (SQLException e) {
     System.out.println("Error");
     while (e != null) {
       System.out.println("Message:"+e.getMessage());
       e = e.getNextException();
     }
     return;
   }
System.out.println("");
```

```
    if ( rset.next ()  ) {
      System.out.println("Old Score = " +rset.getString(1));
      String ns = readEntry("Enter New Score: ");
      String query2 = "update scores set points = " + ns +
        " where sid = '" + id + "' and compname = '" +
        cname + "' and term = '" + term_in +
        "' and lineno = " + ls ;
      try {
        stmt.executeUpdate(query2);
      } catch (SQLException e) {
          System.out.println("Could not modify score");
          while (e != null) {
            System.out.println("Message:"+e.getMessage());
            e = e.getNextException();
          }
          return;
        }
      System.out.println("Modified score successfully");
    }
    else
      System.out.println("Score not found");
    stmt.close();
  }
```

5.7 Database Metadata

To obtain information about the database as a whole, the interface `DatabaseMetaData` is used in JDBC. A `DatabaseMetaData` object is created by invoking the `getMetaData` method on a `Connection` object as follows:

```
DatabaseMetaData dmd = conn.getMetaData();
```

where `conn` is a previously created `Connection` object. The literally hundreds of methods that come with the `DatabaseMetaData` class retrieve all kinds of information about the database system to which a connection is made. Many of these methods return the results in a `ResultSet` object.

Some of these methods take arguments that are `String` patterns. These arguments all have names such as `xxxPattern`. Within a pattern `String`, `"%"` means match any substring of 0 or more characters, and `"_"` means match any one character. Only metadata entries matching the search pattern are returned. If a search pattern argument is set to a **null ref**, it means that argument's criteria should be dropped from the search.

An **SQLException** will be thrown if a driver does not support a metadata method. In the case of methods that return a **ResultSet**, either a **ResultSet** (which may be empty) is returned or an **SQLException** is thrown.

A few of the **DatabaseMetaData** methods are illustrated in the following Java program.

```
import java.sql.*;
import java.io.*;

class meta2 {
  public static void main (String args [])
      throws SQLException, IOException {

    try {
      Class.forName ("oracle.jdbc.driver.OracleDriver");
    } catch (ClassNotFoundException e) {
        System.out.println ("Could not load the driver");
      }
    String user, pass;
    user = readEntry("userid  : ");
    pass = readEntry("password: ");
    Connection conn = DriverManager.getConnection(
      "jdbc:oracle:oci8:"+user+"/"+pass);

    DatabaseMetaData dmd = conn.getMetaData();

    System.out.println("Database Product Name = " +
           dmd.getDatabaseProductName());
    System.out.println("JDBC Driver Name = " +
           dmd.getDriverName());
    System.out.println("Tables starting with C " +
                        "in schema BOOK are:");
    ResultSet rset = dmd.getTables(null,"BOOK","C%",null);
    while (rset.next()) {
      System.out.println(rset.getString(3));
         // print table name
    }
    int n = dmd.getMaxColumnsInTable();
```

```
        System.out.println("Maximum number of columns " +
                           "allowed in a table = " + n);

        conn.close();
    }
}
```

A session capture of a run of the above program is shown below:

```
[~book/jdbc][11:44am] java meta2
userid  : book
password: book
Database Product Name = Oracle
JDBC Driver Name = Oracle JDBC driver
Tables starting with C in schema BOOK are:
CUSTSEQ
CATALOG
COMPONENTS
COURSES
CUSTOMERS
Maximum number of columns allowed in a table = 254
```

5.8 Errors and Warnings

The JDBC API provides three classes to deal with errors, warnings, and data truncations that take place during database access: `SQLException`, `SQLWarning`, and `DataTruncation`.

5.8.1 The `SQLException` Class

The `SQLException` class provides information about errors while accessing the database. It is derived from the more general class, `java.lang.Exception`. An `SQLException` object contains the following:

- The error message as a `String` object. The message can be retrieved by using the inherited `getMessage()` method.
- The `SQLState` string identifying the exception according to the X/Open SQL specification. The `SQLState` can be retrieved using the `getSQLState()` method.

- An error code that is specific to the vendor. This value can be retrieved using the `getErrorCode()` method.
- A link to the next `SQLException` object, in case there is more than one error. The next `SQLException` can be retrieved using the `getNextException()` method.

The `SQLException` object is typically used within a `try–catch` construct as follows:

```
try {
  some JDBC statement to access the database;
} catch (SQLException e) {
    System.out.println("SQL Exception caught!");
    while (e != null) {
      System.out.println("Error Message = " +e.getMessage());
      System.out.println("SQL State = " +e.getSQLState());
      System.out.println("Error Code  = " +e.getErrorCode());
      e = e.getNextException();
    }
  }
```

5.8.2 The SQLWarning Class

The `SQLWarning` class provides information about warnings generated during database access. It is derived as a subclass of `SQLException`, thereby inheriting many of the `SQLException` methods. An `SQLWarning` object contains the following information:

- The warning message as a `String` object. The message can be retrieved by using the `getMessage()` method inherited by `SQLException`.
- The `SQLState` string identifying the warning according to the X/Open SQL specification. The `SQLState` can be retrieved using the `getSQLState()` method.
- An error code that is specific to the vendor. This value can be retrieved using the `getErrorCode()` method.
- A link to the next `SQLWarning` object, in case there is more than one warning. The next `SQLWarning` can be retrieved using the following method:

  ```
  public SQLWarning getNextWarning()
  ```

  which returns the next `SQLWarning` in the chain; it returns `null` if none.

5.8.3 The DataTruncation Class

The `DataTruncation` class, a subclass of `SQLWarning`, provides information about any truncations that happen to data that are read from or written to the database. Normally, truncation while reading from the database is reported as an `SQLWarning`, and truncation while writing to the database is classified as an `SQLException`. Since JDBC does not pose any restrictions on the size of data that are to be read from the database, data truncation does not occur during reads. However, data truncation is a real possibility while writing to the database. A `DataTruncation` object contains the following information:

- The string "`Data Truncation`" as the error/warning message to indicate that data truncation has taken place.
- The `SQLState` set to `01004`.
- A Boolean value indicating if a column or a parameter was truncated. This value is retrieved by invoking the following method:

  ```
  public boolean getParameter()
  ```

  which returns `true` if the value was a parameter and `false` if it was a column value.
- An integer value indicating the index of the column or parameter that was truncated. This value is retrieved by invoking the method

  ```
  public int getIndex()
  ```

  which returns the index of the truncated parameter or column value. This may be −1 if the column or parameter index is unknown, in which case the "parameter" and "read" fields should be ignored.
- A Boolean value indicating if the data truncation happened on a read or a write. This value is retrieved by invoking the method

  ```
  public boolean getRead()
  ```

  which returns `true` if the value was truncated when read from the database and `false` if the data was truncated on a write.
- An integer value indicating the number of bytes that should have been transferred. This value is retrieved by invoking the method

  ```
  public int getDataSize()
  ```

which returns the number of bytes of data that should have been transferred. This number may be approximate if data conversions were being performed. The value may be −1 if the size is unknown.

- An integer value indicating the number of bytes that were actually transferred. This value is retrieved by invoking the method

```
public int getTransferSize()
```

which returns the number of bytes of data actually transferred. The value may be −1 if the size is unknown.

- A link to the next `SQLException` or `SQLWarning` object.

Exercises

Grade Book Database Problems

5.1 Write a JDBC program that prompts the user for the term and line number of a course and prints a report containing the median scores for all the grading components for the course. The report should have the following format:

```
              Median Scores
          CSc 226, Programming I
         LineNo: 1231,  Fall 1996


EXAM1:  69
EXAM2:  64
HW:    126
QUIZ:   88
```

5.2 Write a JDBC program that produces a report consisting of the names of all the students in the database along with the number of A, B, C, D, and F grades earned by each student. The report should be sorted by student name. The format for the report is shown below.

```
       Grade Count Report
LNAME   FNAME   #A's  #B's  #C's  #D's  #F's
--------------------------------------------
Jones   Tony     3     0     0     0     0
Smith   Manny    1     3     2     0     0
Thomas  Tom      0     0     5     1     1
--------------------------------------------
```

5.3 Write a JDBC program that produces a report containing the 10 most enrolled students in the database. The list should be sorted according to the number of courses the student is enrolled in. The report format is shown below.

```
          Top 10 Enrollees

Rank   Name                    #Courses
-----------------------------------------
1.     Rajshekhar, Nandita      12
2.     Corn, Sydney             10
.
.
.
10.    Meyer, Malachi            2
-----------------------------------------
```

5.4 Assume that a particular course has several grading components and from these the best subset of a particular size is to be chosen for the purposes of evaluation of the grade. For example, consider a course that has five components—called `quiz1`, `quiz2`, `quiz3`, `quiz4`, and `quiz5`. Each component is weighted 10 percent of the overall grade, and the three best scores are to be used to evaluate the overall grade. Assuming that all of these components are equally weighted, write a JDBC program that accomplishes the task of dropping these components and adding new ones corresponding to the subset chosen for grading purposes, with the best scores selected among the available scores. It is assumed that after this operation is performed, the sum of the weights of the components will equal 100.

The program should prompt the user for the term and line number of the course for which the manipulation is to be done. It should then prompt the user for the number of components (in the above example, this number is 5), and the names of the components to be considered (in the above example, five quizzes). Finally, it should prompt for the size of the subset of these components that is to be used in the final grade evaluation (in the above example, 3) and the names of the new components to be added (in the above example, `bestquiz`, `secondbestquiz`, and `thirdbestquiz`). The tables to be manipulated in this problem are `components` and `scores`. Old components and their corresponding scores should be deleted, and the new components along with the best scores must be added.

5.5 Consider the following SQL query, which represents the `join` of four tables:

```
select   *
from     enrolls E, students S, components C, scores T
where S.sid = T.sid and
      S.sid = E.sid and
```

```
E.term = C.term and
E.lineno = C.lineno and
E.term = T.term and
E.lineno = T.lineno and
C.compname = T.compname;
```

The select list in the above expression is deliberately left out. Write a JDBC program that prompts the user for a subset of the columns of `join` mentioned above (number of columns and their names) and prints only those columns, instead of all the columns, in the `join`. For example, if the user entered **`term`**, **`lineno`**, and **`sid`**, only these three column values must be selected from the above `join` and printed. The final results must be formatted properly, with column values lining up with the column names. This problem requires the use of metadata objects and methods.

Mail-Order Database Problems

5.6 Write a JDBC program to process an order for a customer. The program should first prompt the user for a valid employee number. After this, it should determine whether this is a new customer. If the customer is new, pertinent information for the customer should be requested and an entry in the **`customers`** table should be made; otherwise only the customer number is obtained from the user. After this, an order number should be generated internally, using the sequence **`orderseq`**. The part numbers and the quantities for each part should then be requested from the user. One row corresponding to this order should be inserted in the **`orders`** table, and several entries that correspond to this order should be inserted in the **`odetails`** table. At the end, the program should summarize the order and print it to screen. The program should be robust and should respond to all possible error situations.

5.7 Write a JDBC program that prompts the user for an order number and prints the invoice for this order, which includes the customer and employee details, as well as the parts in the order, and their quantities and total price. The format of this report should be as follows:

```
Order Number: 1020
**********************************************
Customer: Charles        Customer Number: 1111
Street  : 123 Main St.
City    : Wichita
ZIP     : 67226
Phone   : 316-636-5555
----------------------------------------------
Order No: 1020
```

```
Taken By: Jones (1000)
Received On: 10-DEC-94
Shipped  On: 12-DEC-94

Part No.  Part Name             Quan. Price  Sum
-----------------------------------------------
10506     Land Before Time I     1    19.99  19.99
10507     Land Before Time II    1    19.99  19.99
10508     Land Before Time III   2    19.99  39.98
10509     Land Before Time IV    3    19.99  59.97
-----------------------------------------------
                                 TOTAL:    139.93
***********************************************
```

5.8 Write a JDBC program that will produce a report containing the 10 most ordered parts during a calendar year. The program should prompt for a year and then produce a report with the following format:

```
               YEAR: 1997

Rank PNO   Part Name            Quantity Ordered
----------------------------------------------
1.   10506 Land Before Time I        98
2.   10507 Land Before Time II       87
.
.
.
10.  10900 Dr. Zhivago               24
----------------------------------------------
```

5.9 Write a JDBC program that will update an incorrect zip code in the database. The program should prompt the user for the incorrect and then the correct zip code. It should then replace all the occurrences of the incorrect zip code by the correct zip code in all the tables.

To verify that the program did work, write another JDBC program that reads in a zip code and prints all the customers and employees living at that zip code. This program should be run before and after the previous program is executed in order to verify the execution of the previous program.

5.10 Write a JDBC program that reads data from a text file and updates the **qoh** column in the **parts** table. The text file consists of several lines of data, with each line containing a part number followed by a positive quantity. The **qoh** value in the **parts** table for the part should be increased by the quantity mentioned next to the part number.

Assume that the last line of the text file ends with a part number of 0 and a quantity of 0. The `PreparedStatement` object should be used to accomplish this task.

Investment Portfolio Database Problems

5.11 Write a JDBC program that caters to the following menu:

```
(1) Stock Split
(2) Merger
(3) Quit
```

The program should connect to the database and present the above menu. Under the stock split option, the program should prompt the user for the security symbol and the split ratio. It should then make the necessary changes to the database to incorporate the stock split. Refer to Exercise 2.8(d) for details of the stock split. Under the merger option, the program should prompt the user for the symbols of the two companies, the new symbol and name under which the company will trade, and fractions of the new company shares to be assigned to each share of the old companies. The program should make the necessary changes to the database to incorporate the merger. The new price of the stock should be set to the larger of the two current prices of the old companies.

5.12 If you have read Chapter 6, convert the application into JDBC and compare the relative program sizes.

5.13 Write a JDBC program to view the ratings of a particular security. The program should prompt the user for the security symbol and produce the ratings list in the same format as Exercise 3.12.

Recursive Query Problem

5.14 Recursive queries are easily expressed in rule-based languages such as Datalog or Prolog. Rules are generally of the form

```
P :- Q1, Q2, ..., Qn
```

and are interpreted as follows:

```
if Q1 and Q2 and ... and Qn then P
```

Consider the `bill of materials` (BOM) problem, a classical example of a recursive query. The problem is to find out the sub-parts at all levels of a given part, assuming that a table containing immediate sub-parts is given. Consider the following tables:

```
component(super_part,sub_part,quantity,part_type)
price(part,amount)
```

The **component** table consists of information about the immediate sub-parts of a part and the quantity and the type (basic or complex) of the sub-part. The **price** table records the cost of each basic part. As an example, consider a part called **valve** consisting of one **gasket** (a basic part) and two **hangers** (a complex part). Assuming that the **hanger** consists of 5 **screws** (a basic part) and 10 **bolts** (a basic part), this information would be recorded in the **component** table as follows:

```
insert into component values
  ('valve','gasket',1,b).
insert into component values
  ('valve','hanger',2,c).
insert into component values
  ('hanger','screw',5,b).
insert into component values
  ('hanger','bolt',10,b).
```

The following rules define the notion of sub-parts at all levels for a part and, given a complex part, compute the total quantities of the basic components required to construct the complex component.

```
sub_part(X,Y,Q,T) :- component(X,Y,Q,T).
sub_part(X,Y,Q,T) :- component(Z,Y,Q2,T),
                     sub_part(X,Z,Q1,T1),
                     Q is Q1 * Q2.
basic_parts(P,Y,Q)   :- sub_part(P,Y,Q,b).
basic_comp(P,B,sum(<Q>)) :- basic_parts(P,B,Q).
```

The **sub_part** relation contains rows of the form **(X,Y,Q,T)**, where **Y** is a sub-part (at any level) of **Z** in quantity **Q**, and **Y** is of type **T**. The **basic_parts** relation is defined to be a sub-set of the **sub_parts** relation in which the sub-part is basic. The **basic_component** relation simply aggregates the quantities of each basic sub-part for a complex part. Write a JDBC program that implements the following menu-based application for the **bill of materials** problem.

```
      MENU
(1) Given a part, find all its sub-parts at all levels.
(2) Given a part, list the quantities and total cost
    of the basic parts it contains.
(3) Given a basic part, list all the complex parts
    in which it is used.
(4) Find the cost of each complex part.
(5) Quit.
```

CHAPTER

6

SQLJ: Embedded SQL in Java

This chapter introduces SQLJ, a relatively new standard that many database vendors have already adopted. SQLJ differs from JDBC in that SQL statements can be embedded directly in Java programs and translate-time semantic checks can be performed. It is a powerful tool that complements JDBC access to databases. Programming in SQLJ is discussed in detail in this chapter, and an application program for the investment portfolio database is presented.

6.1 What is SQLJ?

SQLJ is an emerging database programming tool that allows embedding of static SQL statements in Java programs, very much like Pro*C or Pro*C++. SQLJ is an attractive alternative to JDBC since translation time syntax and semantic checking of static SQL statements is now possible. As a consequence, application programs developed in SQLJ are more robust. SQLJ's syntax is also much more compact than that of JDBC, resulting in shorter programs and increased user productivity.

The SQLJ translator converts Java programs embedded with static SQL statements into pure Java code, which can then be executed through a JDBC driver against the database. Programmers can also perform dynamic SQL access to the database using JDBC features.

6.2 Simple Example

A simple program in SQLJ is presented in this section. This program illustrates the essential steps that are needed to write an SQLJ program. These steps are:

1. **Import necessary classes.** In addition to the JDBC classes, `java.sql.*`, every SQLJ program will need to include the SQLJ runtime classes `sqlj.runtime.*` and `sqlj.runtime.ref.*`. In addition, to establish the default connection to Oracle, the `Oracle` class from the `oracle.sqlj.runtime.*` package is required. So, a typical set of statements to import packages would be:

```
import java.sql.*;
import sqlj.runtime.*;
import sqlj.runtime.ref.*;
import java.io.*;
import oracle.sqlj.runtime.*;
```

2. **Register the JDBC driver, if needed.** In case a non-Oracle JDBC driver is being used, a call to the `registerDriver` method of the `DriverManager` class is necessary. For the purposes of this chapter, an Oracle JDBC driver is assumed. Therefore, this statement is not shown in any of the examples.

3. **Connect to the database.** Connecting to the Oracle database is done by first obtaining a `DefaultContext` object using the `getConnection` method (of the `Oracle` class[1]) whose specification is shown below:

```
public static DefaultContext getConnection
   (String url,String user,String password,boolean autoCommit)
throws SQLException
```

   where `url` is the database Universal Resource Locator (URL), and `user` and `password` are the Oracle user id and password respectively. Setting `autoCommit` to `true` would create the connection in auto-commit mode, and setting it to `false` would create the connection in which the transactions must be committed by the programmer. A sample invocation is shown below:

```
DefaultContext cx1 =
  Oracle.getConnection("jdbc:oracle:oci8:@",
                       "book","book",true);
```

1. The `Oracle` class can be found in the package `oracle.sqlj.runtime.*`.

The `DefaultContext` object so obtained is then used to set the static default context as follows:

```
DefaultContext.setDefaultContext(cx1);
```

This `DefaultContext` object now provides the default connection to the database.

4. **Embed SQL statements in the Java program.** Once the default connection has been established, SQL statements can be embedded within the Java program using the following syntax:

   `#sql { ⟨sql-statement⟩ }`

   where `#sql` indicates to the SQLJ translator, called `sqlj`, that what follows is an SQL statement and ⟨*sql-statement*⟩ is any valid SQL statement which may include *host variables* and *host expressions*. Host variables are prefixed with a colon, much like in Pro*C/Pro*C++.

The following simple SQLJ program performs a query against the investment portfolio database. It reads a security symbol from the user and performs a simple query to retrieve information about the particular security. The program uses the `readEntry` method presented in Chapter 5.

```
import sqlj.runtime.*;
import sqlj.runtime.ref.*;
import java.sql.*;
import java.io.*;
import oracle.sqlj.runtime.*;

public class Simple1 {
  public static void main (String args[]) throws SQLException {

    DefaultContext cx1 =
      Oracle.getConnection("jdbc:oracle:oci8:@",
                           "book","book",true);
    DefaultContext.setDefaultContext(cx1);

    String cn;
    Double ap,bp,cp;
    String sym = readEntry("Enter symbol : ").toUpperCase();
```

```
      try {
        #sql {select cname,current_price,ask_price,bid_price
               into   :cn,:cp,:ap,:bp
               from   security
               where  symbol = :sym };
      } catch (SQLException e) {
          System.out.println("Invalid symbol.");
          return;
        }
      System.out.println("\n  Company Name  = " + cn);
      System.out.println("  Last sale at  = " + cp);
      if (ap == null)
        System.out.println("  Ask price     = null");
      else
        System.out.println("  Ask price     = " + ap);
      if (bp == null)
        System.out.println("  Bid price     = null");
      else
        System.out.println("  Bid price     = " + bp);
    }
  }
```

The program uses several Java variables (host variables) in the SQL query. It also checks to see if any of the values returned from the database are **`nulls`** or not. A **`null`** value returned by the query is indicated by a Java **`null`** reference for the host variable into which the database value is retrieved. This feature of SQLJ implies that whenever there is a possibility of a **`null`** value being retrieved into a host variable, the host variable's Java type should not be a primitive type.

6.3 Compiling SQLJ Programs

The SQLJ translator takes as input an SQLJ program file (with suffix **`.sqlj`**) and produces a **`.java`** file along with several other SQLJ profile files which contain the classes necessary to perform the SQL operations. The translator also automatically invokes the Java compiler to produce a **`.class`** file.

There are several command line parameters that can be given to the SQLJ translator. For example, if the user wanted online semantics checking of SQL statements, they can specify the command line options shown below in compiling the **`Simple1.sqlj`** program.

```
% sqlj -url = jdbc:oracle:oci8:@ \
       -user = book -password = book Simple1.sqlj
```

Online semantics checking is performed by the SQLJ translator by connecting to the Oracle database using the user id and password provided as command line parameters.

One other commonly used command line parameter is the **-warn** parameter. This parameter takes as its value a comma-separated list of options that either enable or disable certain warnings from being generated by **sqlj**. For example, the command:

```
% sqlj -warn = noprecision,nonulls Simple1.sqlj
```

will disable warnings concerning loss of precision or possible retrieval of a **null** value into a Java primitive type.

SQLJ allows the possibility of providing these command line parameters in a properties file. This is convenient when there are many command line parameters which have to be specified. By default, the properties file is called **sqlj.properties**. This default can be overridden by specifying the properties file name in the **-props=** command line option. A sample **sqlj.properties** file is shown below:

```
sqlj.driver = oracle.jdbc.driver.OracleDriver
sqlj.url = jdbc:oracle:oci8:@
sqlj.user = book
sqlj.password = book
sqlj.warn = noprecision,nonulls
```

The options mentioned in this sample file are JDBC driver name, the connect string URL, the Oracle user and password, and the warnings flags.

6.4 Multiple Connections

Application programs written in SQLJ can easily access data from several databases by creating one **DefaultContext** object for the default database connection and one nondefault connection context for each additional database connection that is required. A nondefault connection context class called **DbList** is declared as follows:

```
#sql context DbList;
```

This declaration is expanded by **sqlj** into a Java class called **DbList** which can then be instantiated in the SQLJ program as follows:

```
DbList x2 = new DbList(Oracle.getConnection(
    "jdbc:oracle:oci8:@","book2","book2",true));
```

to create a new connection context. This connection context can then be used in embedded SQL statements as follows:

```
#sql [x2] { ⟨sql-statement⟩ };
```

The SQLJ translator also supports online SQL semantics checks on multiple connection contexts at translate time through command line parameters that are optionally tagged with the connection context class name. For example, the **sqlj.properties** file for the above multiple connection scenario would be as follows:

```
sqlj.driver = oracle.jdbc.driver.OracleDriver
sqlj.warn = noprecision,nonulls
#
sqlj.url = jdbc:oracle:oci8:@
sqlj.user = book
sqlj.password = book
#
sqlj.url@DbList = jdbc:oracle:oci8:@
sqlj.user@DbList = book2
sqlj.password@DbList = book2
```

Any statements that are executed within the default connection context will be verified using the `book/book` schema connection and any statements that are executed within the `DbList` connection context will be verified using the `book2/book2` schema connection.

The following SQLJ program illustrates multiple connections:

```
import sqlj.runtime.*;
import sqlj.runtime.ref.*;
import java.sql.*;
import java.io.*;
import oracle.sqlj.runtime.Oracle;

#sql context Book2Context;

public class Simple2 {
  public static void main (String args[])
      throws SQLException {
    DefaultContext x1 = Oracle.getConnection(
             "jdbc:oracle:oci8:@","book","book",true);
    DefaultContext.setDefaultContext(x1);
```

```
      Book2Context x2 = new Book2Context(
                 Oracle.getConnection(
                "jdbc:oracle:oci8:@","book2","book2",true));

      String dbname="";
      try {
        #sql [x2] { select db_name
                    into   :dbname
                    from   db_list
                    where  db_name like 'C%' };
      } catch (SQLException e) {
          System.out.println("Error:" + e.getMessage());
          return;
        }
      System.out.println("DB name is " + dbname);

      String cn = "";
      String sym =
               readEntry("Enter symbol : ").toUpperCase();
      try {
        #sql { select cname
               into   :cn
               from   security
               where  symbol = :sym };
      } catch (SQLException e) {
          System.out.println("Invalid symbol.");
          return;
        }
      System.out.println("\n  Company Name   = " + cn);
    }
  }
```

In the above program, the `DefaultContext` object `x1` was designated as the default connection and hence it was not necessary to include `x1` in the second query. It is assumed that a table called `db_list` with a column called `db_name` exists in the schema `book2/book2`. Note that the query would fail if the `db_list` table contained more than one row with the `db_name` value starting with the letter `C`. (An SQLJ iterator, introduced in Section 6.6, is necessary to process queries with multiple answers.)

6.5 Host Variables and Expressions

Host variables and expressions can be used in SQLJ to communicate values between the SQL statement and the Java environment. Host variables are either Java local variables, Java declared parameters, or Java class/instance variables. A host expression is any valid Java expression.

A host variable must be preceded by a colon (`:`) followed by `IN`, `OUT`, or `INOUT`[2], depending on whether it is an input to the SQL statement, output to the SQL statement, or both. `IN` is the default for host variables and expressions (except in an `into` list) and may be left out. When using the `IN`, `OUT`, and `INOUT` tokens, the colon immediately precedes the token and there must be a space between the token and the variable name. When not using the `IN` token for an input variable, or the `OUT` token for an output variable, the colon can immediately precede the variable name. Two examples of host variables in SQL statements are shown below:

```
#sql {select a into :a1 from t where b = :b1};
#sql {select a into :OUT a1 from t where b = :IN b1};
```

In addition to host variables, Java host expressions such as arithmetic expressions, method calls with return values, instance or class variables, array elements, conditional expressions, logical expressions, etc. can be used in SQL statements. Complicated host expressions must appear within parentheses after the colon to ensure that they are interpreted properly by SQLJ. For example, the following embedded SQL statement updates the cash balance for a particular member to a value which is 100 more than the value of the variable `x`.

```
#sql {update member
      set    cash_balance = :(x+100)
      where  mid = :y };
```

At run time, the Java expressions are evaluated and then passed on to the SQL statement.

The host variables and expressions used in SQL statements must be compatible and be convertible to and from an SQL type. Figure 6.1 gives the mapping between commonly used Oracle data types and Java types:

The Java wrapper classes `Integer`, `Long`, `Float`, and `Double` should be used instead of their primitive counterparts when there is a possibility of a `null` value being communicated from or to the database. The use of Java wrapper classes is necessary because database `null` values are converted into Java `null` references

2. The `IN`, `OUT`, and `INOUT` tokens are not case sensitive.

Figure 6.1 Mapping between Oracle data types and Java types.

Oracle Type	Java Type
`number, number(n), integer, integer(n)`	`int, long`
`number, number(n), number(n,d)`	`float, double`
`char, varchar2`	`java.lang.String`
`date`	`java.sql.Date`
`cursor`	`java.sql.ResultSet` or SQLJ iterator objects

and vice versa and it is not possible for Java primitive types to be assigned a `null` reference.

6.6 SQLJ Iterators

Processing query results, especially when they contain more than one row, requires SQLJ **iterators**. An SQLJ iterator is basically a strongly typed version of a JDBC result set and is associated with the underlying database cursor defined by an SQL query.

An SQLJ iterator declaration specifies a Java class that is automatically constructed by SQLJ. The iterator class contains instance variables and access methods that correspond to the column types and optionally, column names of the SQL query associated with the iterator. When an SQLJ iterator is declared, programmers can specify either just the data types of the selected columns (*positional iterator*) or both the data types and column names of the selected columns (*named iterator*).

An iterator object is instantiated by executing an SQL query, and the SQL data that are retrieved into the iterator object are converted to Java types specified in the iterator declaration.

6.6.1 Named Iterators

A named iterator is declared by specifying both the data types and the column names that correspond to the select list items of the query. The syntax for declaring a named iterator is as follows:

```
#sql iterator iterName
     (colType1 colName1, ..., colTypeN colNameN);
```

where **iterName** is a name given to the iterator, each **colTypeI** is a valid Java type, and each **colNameI** is a select list item name in the query to be associated with this iterator. It is important that the names and types in the iterator match the names and types in the SQL query. The order of the select list items does not have to be in the same order as the names in the iterator, but each select list item must appear in the iterator.

As an example, consider the problem of printing a monthly report of all transactions for a particular member in the investment portfolio database. The SQL query to produce such a listing is:

```
select to_char(trans_date,'DD-MON-YYYY') tdate,
       trans_type ttype, symbol, quantity
       price_per_share, commission, amount
from   transaction
where  mid = :mmid and
       to_char(trans_date, 'MM') = :month and
       to_char(trans_date, 'YYYY') = :year;
```

where **:mmid** is the host variable holding the member id, and **:month** and **:year** are the host variables for the month and year for which the listing is to be produced. The SQLJ iterator for this query is defined[3] as follows:

```
#sql iterator TReport(String tdate, String ttype,
                      String symbol, double quantity,
                      double price_per_share,
                      double commission, double amount);
```

Notice that the SQL query select list items and their data types match the column names and types mentioned in the iterator. SQLJ automatically creates a class, called **TReport**, for the iterator. This class has methods to access the values of each of the columns mentioned in the iterator.

Once the named iterator has been declared, it can be instantiated and populated in the Java program with the following statements:

```
TReport t = null;
#sql t =
  {select to_char(trans_date,'DD-MON-YYYY') tdate,
          trans_type ttype, symbol, quantity,
          price_per_share, commission, amount
   from   transaction
```

3. The iterator declaration is typically made in the same Java source file as the application that uses it. However, since the iterator declaration defines a separate Java class, it must be declared outside of the application class.

```
    where  mid = :mmid and
           to_char(trans_date, 'MM') = :month and
           to_char(trans_date, 'YYYY') = :year };
```

The individual rows of the iterator can be accessed using the **`next()`** method. Whenever **`next()`** is called, it retrieves the next row from the iterator and returns **`true`**. If there is no next row, it returns **`false`**.

Once a row has been retrieved, the individual columns of the row can be accessed using the accessor methods that are automatically created by SQLJ. These accessor methods have the same name as the column names mentioned in the iterator declaration, which are also the names of the select list items.

The iterator is equipped with a **`close()`** method, which should be called once the iterator has been processed.

The following is the method **`printReport`** which prints a monthly report of transactions for a particular member. The member id is an input parameter to this method. The method reads the month and year from the user and generates the monthly report of transactions.

```
private static void printReport(String mmid)
    throws SQLException, IOException {

  String mmid2;
  try {
    #sql { select distinct mid
           into   :mmid2
           from   transaction
           where  mid = :mmid };
  } catch (SQLException e) {
      System.out.println("No transactions");
      return;
    }
  String month = readEntry("Month(01 - 12): ");
  String year  = readEntry("Year(YYYY): ");

  TReport t = null;
  #sql t={select to_char(trans_date,'DD-MON-YYYY') tdate,
                 trans_type ttype, symbol, quantity,
                 price_per_share, commission, amount
          from   transaction
          where  mid = :mmid and
                 to_char(trans_date, 'MM') = :month and
                 to_char(trans_date, 'YYYY') = :year};
```

```
    // Print Report Header
    writeSpaces(15);
    System.out.println("MONTHLY TRANSACTION REPORT");
    writeSpaces(21);
    System.out.println(month + "/" + year);
    writeDashes(68); System.out.println();
    System.out.print("  Date"); writeSpaces(9);
    System.out.print("Type"); writeSpaces(2);
    System.out.print("Symbol"); writeSpaces(5);
    System.out.print("Shares"); writeSpaces(5);
    System.out.print("PPS"); writeSpaces(4);
    System.out.print("Commission"); writeSpaces(2);
    System.out.println("Amount");
    writeDashes(68); System.out.println();

    while(t.next()) {
      System.out.print(t.tdate() + "  ");
      writeEntryRight(t.ttype(),6);
      writeSpaces(3);
      writeEntryLeft(t.symbol(),6);
      writeEntryRight(twoDigit(t.quantity()),10);
      writeEntryRight(twoDigit(t.price_per_share()),10);
      writeEntryRight(twoDigit(t.commission()),10);
      writeEntryRight(twoDigit(t.amount()),10);
      System.out.println();
    }
    writeDashes(68); System.out.println();
    t.close();
  }

  static String twoDigit(double f) {
    boolean neg = false;
    if (f < 0.0) {
      neg = true;
      f = -f;
    }
    long dollars = (long) f;
    int cents = (int) ((f - dollars) * 100);
    String result;
```

```
    if (cents <= 9)
      result = dollars + ".0" + cents;
    else
      result = dollars + "." + cents;
    if (neg)
      return "-" + result;
    else
      return result;
  }

  private static void writeEntryLeft(String text, int width) {
    System.out.print(text);
    for (int i = 0; i < (width - text.length()); i++)
        System.out.print(" ");
  }

  private static void writeEntryRight(String text, int width) {
    for (int i = 0; i < (width - text.length()); i++)
        System.out.print(" ");
    System.out.print(text);
  }

  private static void writeSpaces(int width) {
    for (int i = 0; i < width; i++)
      System.out.print(" ");
  }

  private static void writeDashes(int width) {
    for (int i = 0; i < width; i++)
      System.out.print("-");
  }
```

After the iterator has been populated using an SQL query, the `next()` method is used to fetch the next row. For each row fetched, the accessor methods `t.tdate()`, `t.symbol()`, etc. are used to access the individual columns of the row.

The `printReport` method makes use of a dollar formatting static method called `twoDigit`. It also uses other string formatting methods including `writeSpaces`, `writeDashes`, `writeEntryLeft`, and `writeEntryRight`.

6.6.2 Positional Iterators

A positional iterator is declared in a manner similar to a named iterator except that column names are not specified. The Java types into which the columns of the SQL query are retrieved must be compatible with the data types of the SQL data. The names of the SQL select list items are irrelevant.

Since the names of columns are not specified, the order in which the positional Java types are mentioned in the iterator must exactly match the order of the data types of the select list items of the SQL query.

The positional iterator is instantiated and populated in the same manner as a named iterator, but the manner in which the data is retrieved from the iterator is different. For a positional iterator, a `fetch into` statement is used along with a call to the `endFetch()` method to determine if the last row has been reached. The syntax of the `fetch into` statement is as follows:

```
#sql { fetch :iter into :var1, ..., :vark };
```

where `iter` is the name of the positional iterator and `var1`, ..., `vark` are host variables of appropriate types that will receive values from the select list items. These variables must be in the same order as their corresponding select list items in the select list of the query.

The `endFetch()` method, when applied to the iterator object, initially returns `true` before any rows have been fetched. It then returns `false` after each successful row fetch, and finally returns `true` after the last row has been fetched. The call to `endFetch()` must be done before the row is fetched, because the `fetch` does not throw an `SQLException` when trying to fetch after the last row.

As an example, consider the problem of printing the current, ask, and bid price of a security, given a substring of the security name. The query to accomplish this task is:

```
select symbol,cname,current_price,ask_price,bid_price
from   security
where  upper(cname) like :cn;
```

where `cn` is the substring of the security name. The positional iterator for this query is declared as follows:

```
#sql iterator PQuote(String,String,double,Double,Double);
```

Note that the Java data type corresponding to the `current_price` column is declared as `double` since this database column cannot contain `nulls`.

The method to get the price quote for a security given a substring of the company name is shown below:

```
  public static void getPriceQuoteByCname(String cn)
        throws SQLException, IOException {
    double cp=0.0;
    Double ap=null,bp=null;
    PQuote p = null;
    String sym = "";

    #sql p = {select symbol, cname, current_price,
                     ask_price, bid_price
              from   security
              where  upper(cname) like :cn};
    #sql {fetch :p into :sym,:cn,:cp,:ap,:bp};
    if (!p.endFetch()) {
      System.out.print("Symbol"); writeSpaces(12);
      System.out.print("Company"); writeSpaces(17);
      System.out.print("Last Sale"); writeSpaces(4);
      System.out.print("Ask"); writeSpaces(7);
      System.out.println("Bid");
      writeDashes(74);
      System.out.println();
      while (!p.endFetch()) {
        writeEntryLeft(sym,9);
        writeEntryLeft(cn,30);
        writeEntryRight(twoDigit(cp),10);
        if (ap == null)
          System.out.print("      null");
        else
          writeEntryRight(twoDigit(ap.doubleValue()),10);
        if (bp == null)
          System.out.print("      null");
        else
          writeEntryRight(twoDigit(bp.doubleValue()),10);
        System.out.println();
        #sql {fetch :p into :sym,:cn,:cp,:ap,:bp};
      };
      writeDashes(74);
    } else {
        System.out.println("No company matches the name");
      }
    p.close();
  }
```

6.7 Dynamic SQL using JDBC

SQLJ by nature caters to static SQL. However, there are situations when dynamic SQL is needed. The dynamic SQL API for SQLJ is JDBC, that is, an SQLJ program may contain both SQLJ and JDBC code. Access to JDBC connections and result sets from an SQLJ program may be necessary for finer control. The two paradigms interoperate seamlessly with each other.

It is possible to extract a JDBC `Connection` object from an SQLJ default connection context as follows:

```
DefaultContext cx1 =
    Oracle.getConnection("jdbc:oracle:oci8:@","raj","raj",true);
DefaultContext.setDefaultContext(cx1);
Connection conn = DefaultContext.getDefaultContext()
                                .getConnection();
```

and for an SQLJ connection context to be initialized with a JDBC connection as shown below:

```
#sql context PortDB;

Connection conn = DriverManager.getConnection(
       "jdbc:oracle:oci8:book/book");
PortDB cx2 = new PortDB(conn);
```

The following is an SQLJ program that performs dynamic SQL using JDBC. A JDBC `Connection` object is extracted from the SQLJ `DefaultContext` object and a dynamic query is performed.

```
import sqlj.runtime.*;
import sqlj.runtime.ref.*;
import java.sql.*;
import java.io.*;
import oracle.sqlj.runtime.*;

public class Dsqlj {
  public static void main (String args[])
     throws SQLException {

    DefaultContext cx1 =
        Oracle.getConnection("jdbc:oracle:oci8:@",
                             "book","book",true);
```

```
      DefaultContext.setDefaultContext(cx1);

      // get a JDBC Connection object from an
      // SQLJ DefaultContext object
      Connection conn = DefaultContext.getDefaultContext()
                                      .getConnection();

      String sym = readEntry("Enter symbol substring: ")
                   .toUpperCase();
      String query =
        "select cname,current_price,ask_price,bid_price "+
        "from   security " +
        "where symbol like '%" + sym + "%'";
      Statement stmt = conn.createStatement();
      ResultSet rs = stmt.executeQuery(query);

      while (rs.next())  {
        System.out.println("\n  Company Name  = " +
                           rs.getString(1));
        System.out.println("  Last sale at  = " + rs.getString(2));
        String ap = rs.getString(3);
        if (rs.wasNull())
          System.out.println("  Ask price     = null");
        else
          System.out.println("  Ask price     = " + ap);
        String bp = rs.getString(4);
        if (rs.wasNull())
          System.out.println("  Bid price     = null");
        else
          System.out.println("  Bid price     = " + bp);
      }
      rs.close();
      stmt.close();
    }
  }
```

JDBC result sets and SQLJ iterators can also be easily transformed from one to the other. To convert an SQLJ iterator into a JDBC result set, use the **getResultSet()** method on an iterator object as follows:

```
QueryIterator q;
#sql q = { ⟨sql query⟩ };
ResultSet rs = q.getResultSet();
```

To convert the result set back into an SQLJ iterator, use the **CAST** operator as follows:

```
ResultSet rs = ....;
#sql q = {CAST :rs};
```

6.8 Calling PL/SQL from within SQLJ

When using SQLJ with Oracle, it is possible to embed PL/SQL anonymous blocks in the Java program. For example, the following program, containing an anonymous PL/SQL block, populates a table called **squares** defined as follows:

```
create table squares (n number, nsquared number);
```

with the first ten squares of natural numbers.

```
import sqlj.runtime.*;
import sqlj.runtime.ref.*;
import java.sql.*;
import java.io.*;
import oracle.sqlj.runtime.*;

public class Anon {
  public static void main (String args[]) throws SQLException {
    DefaultContext cx1 =
        Oracle.getConnection("jdbc:oracle:oci8:@",
                             "book","book",true);
    DefaultContext.setDefaultContext(cx1);
    #sql {
      declare
        n number;
      begin
        delete from squares;
        n := 1;
        while (n <= 10) loop
          insert into squares values (n,n*n);
          n := n + 1;
        end loop;
```

```
      end;
    };
  }
}
```

It is also possible for SQLJ programs to make calls to PL/SQL stored procedures and functions. Consider the following PL/SQL stored procedure:

```
create or replace procedure latestTransactionDate
  (midd in member.mid%type, ldate out date) is
begin
  select max(trans_date)
  into   ldate
  from   transaction
  where  mid = midd;
end;
```

This stored procedure takes as input a member id, `midd`, and returns the latest transaction date for that member in the output parameter `ldate`. This stored procedure can be called in an SQLJ program as follows:

```
String m = "10000";
java.sql.Date lastDate;
#sql {CALL latestTransactionDate(:in m, :out lastDate)};
```

Note the `IN` and `OUT` qualifiers for the parameters and also the data type matching between Java types and the corresponding PL/SQL types in the stored procedure. The whole SQLJ program which makes a call to the stored procedure is shown below:

```
import sqlj.runtime.*;
import sqlj.runtime.ref.*;
import java.sql.*;
import java.io.*;
import oracle.sqlj.runtime.*;

public class Plsql1 {
  public static void main (String args[]) throws SQLException {
    DefaultContext cx1 =
        Oracle.getConnection("jdbc:oracle:oci8:@",
                             "book","book",true);
    DefaultContext.setDefaultContext(cx1);

    String m = readEntry("Member ID: ");
```

```
      java.sql.Date lastDate;
      #sql {CALL latestTransactionDate(:in m, :out lastDate)};
      System.out.println("The last transaction date is " +
                          lastDate);
    }
  }
```

PL/SQL stored functions are invoked in a similar manner as stored procedures except that the **CALL** token is replaced by the **VALUES** token and the function call is enclosed within parentheses. Also, the result of the function call is assigned to a Java variable. Consider the PL/SQL stored function, called **avgPP**, which takes as input a member id and a security symbol, and computes the average purchase price the member paid for the current shares that he or she holds in the portfolio. For all the **buy** transactions the member has for the particular security, a weighted average price is computed. Finally, a commission of 1 percent is applied to the total amount to compute the average purchase price. The PL/SQL stored function is shown below:

```
create or replace function avgPP(
    mid in member.mid%type,
    sym in security.symbol%type)
  return transaction.price_per_share%type as
  cursor c1 is
    select trans_type, quantity, price_per_share
    from transaction
    where mid = avgPP.mid and
          symbol = sym
    order by trans_date;
  q transaction.quantity%type := 0.0;
  a transaction.price_per_share%type := 0.0;
begin
  for c1_rec in c1 loop
    if (c1_rec.trans_type = 'buy') then
      a := ((q * a) +
            (c1_rec.quantity*c1_rec.price_per_share))/
           (q + c1_rec.quantity);
      q := q + c1_rec.quantity;
    else
      q := q - c1_rec.quantity;
    end if;
  end loop;
```

```
  return (1.01 * a);  -- Commission of 1%
end;
```

A call to the **avgPP** function in SQLJ is shown below:

```
String m = readEntry("Member ID: ");
String sym = readEntry("Symbol: ");
double pp;
#sql pp = { VALUES(avgPP(:in m, :in sym)) };
```

Notice the **IN** tokens, the **VALUES** token, and the assignment of the result of the function call to a Java variable. An SQLJ program which illustrates the stored function call is shown below:

```
import sqlj.runtime.*;
import sqlj.runtime.ref.*;
import java.sql.*;
import java.io.*;
import oracle.sqlj.runtime.*;

public class Plsql2 {
  public static void main (String args[])
     throws SQLException {
    DefaultContext cx1 =
        Oracle.getConnection("jdbc:oracle:oci8:@",
                             "book","book",true);
    DefaultContext.setDefaultContext(cx1);

    String m = readEntry("Member ID: ");
    String sym = readEntry("Symbol: ");
    double pp;
    #sql pp = { VALUES(avgPP(:in m, :in sym)) };
    System.out.println("The average purchase price " +
        "member " + m + " paid for security " +
        sym + " is " + pp);
  }
}
```

6.9 Investment Portfolio Database Application

In this section, an application program that interfaces with the investment portfolio database is presented. A few of the methods of this application have already been discussed earlier in the chapter. The remaining are presented here.

The program begins by presenting the following main menu:

```
(a) Member Log in
(b) New Member Sign in
(q) Quit
```

A new member can use option `(b)` to create a new account. This option prompts the new member for name, address, email, and password. It creates a new account and informs the new member of the account number.

An existing member can use option `(a)` to log into their account. The member is prompted for an account number and password. Upon successful login, the member is shown the following menu of options:

```
(a) View Portfolio
(b) Print Monthly Report
(c) Update Your Record
(d) Price Quote
(e) Buy a Stock
(f) Sell a Stock
(q) Quit
```

The `main` *and* `printMenu` *Methods*

The `main` method is shown below along with the `printMenu` method:

```
public static void main (String args[])
  throws Exception,IOException,SQLException {

  String user = readEntry("userid  : ");
  String pass = readEntry("password: ");
  DefaultContext cx1 =
      Oracle.getConnection("jdbc:oracle:oci8:@",
                           user,pass,false);
  DefaultContext.setDefaultContext(cx1);

  boolean done = false;
  do {
```

```
      printMenu();
      String ch = readEntry("Type in your option: ");
      switch (ch.charAt(0)) {
        case 'a': memberLogIn();
                  break;
        case 'b': newMember();
                  break;
        case 'q': done = true;
                  break;
        default : System.out.println("Invalid option");
      }
    } while(!done);
  }

  private static void printMenu() {
    System.out.println("\nINVESTMENT PORTFOLIO " +
                       "TRACKING SYSTEM \n");
    System.out.println("(a) Member Log in ");
    System.out.println("(b) New Member Sign in ");
    System.out.println("(q) Quit. \n");
  }
```

After prompting the user for the Oracle user id and password[4], the `main` method opens a connection to the Oracle schema for the specified user and presents the main menu. Notice that the autoCommit mode is set to `false` in the `Oracle.getConnection` method call. It reads the user's option and calls the appropriate method.

The `memberLogin` *and* `printMenu1` *Methods*

The `memberLogIn` method prompts the user for the account number and password. It then verifies that the account number exists and that the password provided is correct. This is accomplished by a simple SQL query against the `member` table using the `select-into` statement. After the account number and password are verified, a member menu of options is presented. The program then reads the user's option and processes it appropriately by calling the corresponding method. The `memberLogIn` and `printMenu1` methods are shown below:

4. Note that there are two sets of user ids and passwords. The first is the Oracle user id and password which enables the user to use the application program and the second is the member's account id and password which enables the member to access his or her account.

```
private static void memberLogIn()
    throws SQLException, IOException {
  String mmid1,pass1;
  String mmid2 = readEntry("Account#: ");
  String pass2 = readEntry("Password: ");

  try {
    #sql {select mid, password
          into   :mmid1, :pass1
          from   member
          where  mid = :mmid2 and password = :pass2};
  } catch (SQLException e) {
      System.out.println("Invalid Account/Password");
      return;
    }

  boolean done = false;
  do {
    printMenu1();
    String ch = readEntry("Type in your option: ");
    switch (ch.charAt(0)) {
      case 'a': viewPortfolio(mmid1);
                break;
      case 'b': printReport(mmid1);
                break;
      case 'c': updateMember(mmid1);
                break;
      case 'd': getPriceQuote();
                break;
      case 'e': buyStock(mmid1);
                break;
      case 'f': sellStock(mmid1);
                break;
      case 'q': done = true;
                break;
      default : System.out.println("Invalid option ");
    }
  } while(!done);
}
```

```
private static void printMenu1() {
  System.out.println("\n    MEMBER OPTIONS \n");
  System.out.println("(a) View Portfolio ");
  System.out.println("(b) Print Monthly Report ");
  System.out.println("(c) Update Your Record ");
  System.out.println("(d) Price Quote ");
  System.out.println("(e) Buy a Stock ");
  System.out.println("(f) Sell a Stock ");
  System.out.println("(q) Quit \n");
}
```

The newMember *Method*

The `newMember` method prompts the user for all the pertinent information and then performs an SQL `insert` statement. The sequence object `m_seq` is used to generate a new account number. The code for `newMember` is shown below:

```
private static void newMember()
     throws SQLException, IOException {
  String pass, fn, ln, addr, email;
  double cash;

  fn    = readEntry("Enter first name: ");
  ln    = readEntry("Enter last name: ");
  addr  = readEntry("Enter address: ");
  email = readEntry("Enter email: ");
  pass  = readEntry("Enter password : ");
  cash  = Double.valueOf(readEntry("Enter initial cash : "))
             .doubleValue();
  try {
    String mmid;
    #sql {select m_seq.nextval into :mmid from dual};
    #sql {insert into member values
             (:mmid,:pass,:fn,:ln,:addr,:email,:cash)};
    #sql {commit};
    System.out.println("\nYour Account Number is " + mmid);
  } catch (SQLException e) {
      System.out.println("Could not add member");
      System.out.println("Message:"+e.getMessage());
      return;
    }
}
```

Figure 6.2 Portfolio view output.

```
                        MY PORTFOLIO

Symbol  Shares    Current    Market     Purchase    Gain     %Gain
                    PPS      Value       Price
----------------------------------------------------------------
ORCL    100.00    23.25      2325.00    2708.06   -383.06   -14.14
SEG     100.00    30.00      3000.00    3244.62   -244.62    -7.53
----------------------------------------------------------------
  Security Value:            5325.00    5952.68   -627.68   -10.54
  Cash Balance:             94047.33
  Account Value:            99372.33
----------------------------------------------------------------
```

The `viewPortfolio` *Method*

The `viewPortfolio` method takes as input the member id and prints the member's portfolio of stocks owned, their purchase price, the current value of the stocks, and the gain or loss. A summary for the entire portfolio is also produced. A sample portfolio view is shown in Figure 6.2.

The query used to compute the current portfolio for a member is as follows:

```
select s.symbol, p.quantity, s.current_price,
       (p.quantity * s.current_price) MarketValue,
       (p.quantity * avgPP(:mid,p.symbol)) PurchasePrice
from   security s, portfolio p
where  p.mid = :mid and s.symbol = p.symbol;
```

This query uses the view `portfolio` defined in Section 2.5. It makes use of a PL/SQL stored function called `avgPP`, which was introduced earlier in Section 6.8. The `viewPortfolio` method uses a named SQLJ iterator called `PView` shown below.

```
#sql iterator PView(String symbol, double quantity,
   double current_price, double MarketValue,
   double PurchasePrice);
```

This iterator is used to retrieve all the stocks currently owned by the member, and the information retrieved is formatted and sent to the screen. The `viewPortfolio` method is shown next.

```
private static void viewPortfolio(String mid)
     throws SQLException, IOException {
  String mmid;
  try {
    #sql { select distinct mid
           into   :mmid
           from   portfolio
           where  mid = :mid };
  } catch (SQLException e) {
      System.out.println("Empty Portfolio");
      return;
    }

  PView p = null;
  #sql p =
    {select s.symbol,p.quantity,s.current_price,
            (p.quantity*s.current_price) MarketValue,
            (p.quantity*avgPP(:mid,p.symbol))
            PurchasePrice
     from   security s, portfolio p
     where  p.mid=:mid and s.symbol=p.symbol};

  double cash;
  #sql {select cash_balance
        into   :cash
        from   member
        where  mid = :mid};

  // Print Report Header
  writeSpaces(30);
  System.out.println("MY PORTFOLIO");
  System.out.print("Symbol"); writeSpaces(5);
  System.out.print("Shares"); writeSpaces(3);
  System.out.print("Current"); writeSpaces(4);
  System.out.print("Market"); writeSpaces(6);
  System.out.print("Purchase"); writeSpaces(6);
  System.out.print("Gain"); writeSpaces(7);
  System.out.println("%Gain"); writeSpaces(21);
  System.out.print("PPS"); writeSpaces(7);
  System.out.print("Value"); writeSpaces(8);
```

```
System.out.println("Price");
writeDashes(76); System.out.println();

double gainLoss, pGL;
double total_pp = 0.0, total_mv = 0.0;

while(p.next()) {
  writeEntryLeft(p.symbol(),8);
  writeEntryRight(twoDigit(p.quantity()),9);
  writeEntryRight(twoDigit(p.current_price()),9);
  writeEntryRight(twoDigit(p.MarketValue()),12);
  total_mv += p.MarketValue();
  writeEntryRight(twoDigit(p.PurchasePrice()),12);
  total_pp += p.PurchasePrice();
  gainLoss = p.MarketValue() - p.PurchasePrice();
  pGL = (gainLoss/p.PurchasePrice() ) * 100;
  writeEntryRight(twoDigit(gainLoss),12);
  writeEntryRight(twoDigit(pGL),12);
  System.out.println();
}

p.close();

writeDashes(76); System.out.println();
System.out.print("  Security Value: ");
writeSpaces(8);
writeEntryRight(twoDigit(total_mv),12);
writeEntryRight(twoDigit(total_pp),12);
writeEntryRight(twoDigit(total_mv - total_pp),12);
writeEntryRight(twoDigit(((total_mv - total_pp)/
                             total_pp)*100),12);
System.out.println();

System.out.print("  Cash Balance: ");
writeSpaces(12);
writeEntryRight(twoDigit(cash),10);
System.out.println();

System.out.print("  Account Value: ");
```

```
    writeSpaces(11);
    writeEntryRight(twoDigit(cash + total_mv),10);
    System.out.println();

    writeDashes(76);
  }
```

The `updateMember` *Method*

The **updateMember** method allows the member to make changes to his or her password, address, or email. The method first performs a query to obtain the current password, address, and email of the member. It then prompts the user for new information and issues an SQL **update** statement to make the changes. The code follows:

```
private static void updateMember(String mmid)
     throws SQLException, IOException {

  String password, address, email, answer;
  try {
    #sql { select password, address, email
           into   :password,:address,:email
           from   member
           where  mid = :mmid };
  } catch (SQLException e) {
      System.out.println("Invalid member account");
      return;
    }

  boolean change = false;
  System.out.println("password : " + password);
  answer = readEntry("Change password?(y/n):").toLowerCase();
  if (answer.equals("y")) {
    password = readEntry("Enter new password : ");
    change = true;
  }

  System.out.println("address : " + address);
  answer = readEntry("Change address?(y/n):").toLowerCase();
```

```
    if (answer.equals("y")) {
      address = readEntry("New address : ");
      change = true;
    }

    System.out.println("email : " + email);
    answer = readEntry("Change email?(y/n):").toLowerCase();
    if (answer.equals("y")) {
      email = readEntry("New email : ");
      change = true;
    }

    if (change) {
      #sql { update member
               set password = :password,
                   address = :address,
                   email = :email
               where mid = :mmid };
      #sql {commit};
      System.out.println("Updated successfully ");
    }
    else
      System.out.println("No changes made");
  }
```

The `getPriceQuote` *and* `getPriceQuoteBySymbol` *Methods*

The `getPriceQuote` method allows the member to obtain a quote on a security based on the symbol or the company name of the security. It prompts the user for the option and calls the appropriate method for obtaining the quote. The `getPriceQuoteByCname` method was presented earlier in this chapter. The `getPriceQuoteBySymbol` method prompts the member for the exact security symbol and then performs a simple SQL query using the `select-into` statement. The code for these two methods follows:

```
  private static void getPriceQuote()
         throws SQLException, IOException {

    System.out.println("(a) Look up by symbol");
    System.out.println("(b) Look up by company name");
```

```
    String ch =
      readEntry("Type in your option: ").toLowerCase();

    String sym="",cn="";
    switch (ch.charAt(0)) {
      case 'a' :
        sym = readEntry("Enter symbol : ").toUpperCase();
        getPriceQuoteBySymbol(sym);
        break;
      case 'b' :
        cn = "%" + readEntry("Enter search string: ")
                   .toUpperCase() + "%";
        getPriceQuoteByCname(cn);
        break;
    }
  }

  public static void getPriceQuoteBySymbol(String sym)
         throws SQLException, IOException {
    double cp=0.0;
    Double ap=null,bp=null;
    String cn = "";

    try {
      #sql { select cname,current_price,ask_price,bid_price
             into   :cn,:cp,:ap,:bp
             from   security
             where  symbol = :sym };
    } catch (SQLException e) {
        System.out.println("Invalid symbol.");
        return;
      }
    System.out.println("\n  Company Name  = " + cn);
    System.out.println("  Last sale at  = " + cp);
    if (ap == null)
      System.out.println("  Ask price     = null");
    else
      System.out.println("  Ask price     = " + ap);
    if (bp == null)
      System.out.println("  Bid price     = null");
```

```
    else
      System.out.println("  Bid price      = " + bp);
  }
```

The buyStock *and* buyConfirmation *Methods*

The **buyStock** method first prompts the member for the security symbol. It then obtains the current bidding price from the database. If the bidding price is **null**, it uses the current selling price. After this, the method obtains the number of shares from the user. Using this information, it computes the total cost of this transaction including a 1 percent commission on the total value. The current cash balance for the member is obtained to see if the member has enough funds to pay for the transaction. The method then asks the member for a confirmation by calling the **buyConfirmation** method. Upon confirmation, a new row is added to the **transaction** table for this transaction. The cash balance in the **member** table is also updated. The code for **buyStock** and **buyConfirmation** follows:

```
  public static void buyStock(String mid)
      throws SQLException, IOException {

    double currentprice = 0.0;
    Double bidprice;

    String symbol  = readEntry("Symbol  : ");
    try {
      #sql { select current_price, bid_price
             into   :currentprice, :bidprice
             from   security
             where  symbol = :symbol };
    } catch (SQLException e) {
        System.out.println("Stock information not found");
        return;
      }

    double quantity =
      Double.valueOf(readEntry("Quantity: ")).doubleValue();

    double price,total, cash;
    if (bidprice == null)
      price = currentprice;
    else
```

```
      price = bidprice.doubleValue();

    double commission =
      Double.valueOf(twoDigit(0.01 * (price * quantity)))
            .doubleValue();
    total =
      Double.valueOf(twoDigit((price * quantity) + commission))
            .doubleValue();

    #sql { select cash_balance
           into   :cash
           from   member
           where  mid = :mid };

    if (total > cash) {
      System.out.println("Sorry, Not enough money!");
      return;
    }

    if(!buyConfirmation(symbol,quantity,price)){
      System.out.println("Transaction was not processed");
      return;
    }

    #sql { insert into transaction values
             (:mid,:symbol,sysdate,'buy',:quantity,
              :price,:commission,:total) };
    #sql {commit};

    #sql { update member
           set    cash_balance = cash_balance - :total
           where  mid = :mid };
    #sql {commit};

    System.out.println("Successful Buy Transaction");
  }

  public static boolean buyConfirmation(
           String symbol, double quantity,
           double price_per_share) {
```

```
    double total = price_per_share * quantity;
    System.out.println("\n\t\tConfirmation:");
    System.out.println(quantity + " shares of " + symbol +
        " at $" + price_per_share + " per share.");
    System.out.println("\n");
    System.out.println("\tTotal price of shares:    " +
                       total+"\n");
    System.out.println("\tCommission:               +"
                        + (0.01 * total));
    System.out.println("\t                          " +
                       " -------------");
    System.out.println("\tTotal:                    $" +
                        (1.01 * total));
    System.out.println();
    for (;;) {
      String answer =
        readEntry("Accept?  (Y or N): ").toUpperCase();
      switch (answer.charAt(0)) {
        case 'Y': return true;
        case 'N': return false;
        default:  break;
      }
    }
  }
```

The `sellStock` and `sellConfirmation` methods are very similar.

Exercises

Investment Portfolio Database Problems

6.1 Write an SQLJ program that populates the **security** table by fetching data from the following Web address:

```
http://www.quicken.com/investments/snapshot/?symbol=XXXX
```

where **XXXX** is the security symbol. This Web page contains information about the company in detail, however, only the name of the company and the current price need to be retrieved. The **ask_price**, and **bid_price** values should be set to **null**. To solve this problem, you should import the **java.net** package and use the following Java method that fetches the HTML content of a Web page into a Java string variable.

```
private static String getHTMLContent(URL hp) throws Exception {
  BufferedReader data = new BufferedReader(new
    InputStreamReader(hp.openStream()));
  String line, sHtml="";

  while ((line = data.readLine()) != null)
    sHtml += line + "\n";
  data.close();
  return sHtml;
}
```

This method should be invoked as follows:

```
URL hp = new URL(
  "http://www.quicken.com/investments/snapshot/?symbol="+XXXX);
String sHtml = getHTMLContent(hp);
```

where `XXXX` is a string variable containing the security symbol. To retrieve data for more than one security, you should create a constant array of security symbols within the Java program, loop through the array, and for each symbol in the array, fetch data from the Web page and store it in the database.

6.2 Write an SQLJ program that updates the `security` table for the current, ask, and bid prices by fetching data from the following Web address:

```
http://www.quicken.com/investments/quotes/?symbol=XXXX
```

where `XXXX` is the security symbol. This Web page contains a variety of information about the price quotes for the company. However, only the current, ask and bid prices need to be retrieved.

6.3 Write an SQLJ program to implement the following menu for analysts:

```
(1) Rate a stock
(2) Update a stock rating
(3) Quit
```

The program should begin by prompting the analyst for the id and password. After verifying the id and password, the program should display the menu. To rate a stock, the program should prompt the analyst for the symbol and the rating. To update a stock rating, the program should prompt the analyst for the symbol, display the current rating by the analyst, and prompt the analyst for a new rating.

6.4 Implement the following two additional menu options for the `MEMBER OPTIONS` of the application presented in Section 6.9:

```
(g) View Ratings for a Security
(h) View Top Five Rated Securities
```

The program should prompt the user for the security symbol for the view rating option and then display all the ratings by analysts for that symbol. The output should resemble the following:

```
Symbol: ORCL
Company: Oracle Corporation
Ratings:  Strong Buy  (rating = 1) : *****
          Buy         (rating = 2) : **
          Hold        (rating = 3) : **
          Sell        (rating = 4) :
          Strong Sell (rating = 5) :
          Consensus:       1.67
```

The number of stars after each rating is the number of analysts rating the start with that particular rating. The consensus mean is the weighted mean of the ratings. The view top five rated securities option should display the top five securities based on the consensus mean value in increasing order of consensus mean.

CHAPTER

7

Projects

This chapter presents some project suggestions that can be developed by the reader to get a better understanding of the material presented in this book. Each project would typically go through the following phases:

- *Phase 0:* Design the database (using Entity-Relationship Diagrams).
- *Phase 1:* Create the tables, including constraints such as primary keys, foreign keys, check constraints, and **`not null`** constraints.
- *Phase 2:* Create triggers and active elements to maintain integrity of the database and to perform appropriate actions on database updates.
- *Phase 3:* Populate the database using SQL **`insert`** statements or by writing programs in Java or Pro*C.
- *Phase 4:* Write application programs in Java and/or Pro*C and/or PL/SQL.
- *Phase 5:* Document the project

The application programs would have to implement some form of user interface. The simplest user interface is terminal based and involves menus and sub-menus. However, there are several tools and languages that support the development of fancier user interfaces such as the **`curses`** package in Unix, the Java AWT toolkit, and the X-Windows libraries. The reader may choose to develop the user interfaces using these tools and languages.

The rest of this chapter discusses several application areas for which a database application can be developed. For each application area, a brief description of the application is followed by a description of the relational tables and a sketch of the application program requirements in the form of menus and sub-menus. The reader is encouraged to use the ideas presented as a starting point for the definition of the problem and to modify it according to their understanding of the problem.

7.1 Airline Flight Information System

The airline flight information database consists of information relating to the operations of the airline industry. One possible design of the database results in the following relational tables:

```
AIRPORT(AIRPORT_CODE,name,city,state)
FLIGHT(NUMBER,airline,weekdays)
FLIGHT_LEG(FLIGHT_NUMBER,LEG_NUMBER,
  departure_airport_code,scheduled_departure_time,
  arrival_airport_code,scheduled_arrival_time)
LEG_INSTANCE(FLIGHT_NUMBER,LEG_NUMBER,LEG_DATE,
  number_of_available_seats,airplane_id,
  departure_airport_code,departure_time,
  arrival_airport_code,arrival_time)
FARES(FLIGHT_NUMBER,FARE_CODE,amount,restrictions)
AIRPLANE_TYPE(TYPE_NAME,max_seats,company)
CAN_LAND(AIRPLANE_TYPE_NAME,AIRPORT_CODE)
AIRPLANE(AIRPLANE_ID,total_number_of_seats,
  airplane_type)
SEAT_RESERVATION(FLIGHT_NUMBER,LEG_NUMBER,DATE,
  SEAT_NUMBER,customer_name,customer_phone)
```

Note: The primary key columns are shown in uppercase.

Each `FLIGHT` is identified by a `FLIGHT_NUMBER` and consists of one or more `FLIGHT_LEG`s with `LEG_NUMBER`s 1, 2, 3, etc. Each leg has many `LEG_INSTANCE`s, one for each date on which the flight flies. `FARES` are kept for each flight, and `SEAT_RESERVATION`s are kept for each `LEG_INSTANCE`. Information about airports is kept in the `AIRPORT` table and about individual airplanes in the `AIRPLANE` table. `AIRPLANE_TYPE` records the information about the airplane type, and the `CAN_LAND` table keeps information about which airplane type can land in which airport.

The following is an outline for the application program to be developed for the airline reservation system. It includes a main menu of options and several sub-menus.

```
      MAIN MENU
(1) Customer Functions
(2) Reporting Functions
(3) Administrative Functions
(4) Quit

      CUSTOMER FUNCTIONS MENU
(1) Make a reservation
(2) Cancel a reservation
(3) Confirm a reservation
(4) Print trip itinerary
(5) Locate fare
(6) Quit

      REPORTING FUNCTIONS MENU
(1) Print flight roster
(2) Print flight schedule (based on several criteria
    such as airline, departure city, arrival city)
(3) Print flight performance report
    (Given airline, print on-time and delayed flights)
(4) Quit

      ADMINISTRATIVE FUNCTIONS MENU
(1) Add/drop flight
(2) Add airport
(3) Update fares
(4) Create leg instance
(5) Update leg instance (departure/arrival times)
(6) Quit
```

7.2 Library Database Application

Consider the operations of a public library system in a city. The library has many patrons who borrow books from one of its many branches. Each branch of the library holds a number of copies of a particular book. Books that are not returned on time are fined at a rate of 25 cents for each day after the due date. One possible design of a database for the public library system results in the following relational tables:

```
BOOKS(BOOK_ID,title,publisher_name)
BOOK_AUTHORS(BOOK_ID,AUTHOR_NAME)
```

```
PUBLISHERS(NAME,address,phone)
BOOK_COPIES(BOOK_ID,BRANCH_ID,no_of_copies)
BRANCHES(BRANCH_ID,branch_name,address)
BOOK_LOANS(BOOK_ID,BRANCH_ID,CARD_NO,
  date_out,date_due,date_returned)
BORROWERS(CARD_NO,name,address,phone,unpaid_dues)
```

Note: The primary key columns are shown in uppercase.

The BOOKS table records information about all the books that are available in the library system. Each book has a unique BOOK_ID. Information about the authors of books are kept in the table BOOK_AUTHORS and about the publishers in the table PUBLISHERS. The number of copies of each book in a particular library branch is recorded in the BOOK_COPIES table. The branch information is kept in the BRANCHES table. Information about the patrons of the library is kept in the BORROWERS table, and the loaned books are recorded in the BOOK_LOANS table.

The following is an outline for an application program to be developed for a library database.

```
     MAIN MENU
(1) Patron functions (ask for card number,
     then show sub-menu)
(2) Administrative functions
(3) Quit
```

```
     PATRON FUNCTIONS MENU
(1) Book checkout
(2) Book return
(3) Pay fine
(4) Print loaned books list
(5) Quit
```

```
     ADMINISTRATIVE FUNCTIONS MENU
(1) Add a book
(2) Update book holdings
(3) Search book
(4) New patron
(5) Print branch information
(6) Print top 10 frequently checked-out books
(7) Quit
```

7.3 University Student Database

Consider the data that are usually maintained by a typical university concerning students, courses, and enrollments. Students are admitted to the university, and they pursue a degree program in a particular department. The university catalog consists of courses that are offered every term. Students choose courses to take and enroll in them during registration. Instructors are assigned courses to teach, and they in turn assign grades. A possible database design results in the following relational tables:

```
COURSES(CNO,ctitle,hours,dept_id)
DEPARTMENTS(DEPT_ID,dept_name,college)
INSTRUCTORS(LAST_NAME,FIRST_NAME,
  dept_id,office,phone,email)
SECTIONS(TERM,LINENO,cno,instr_lname,instr_fname,
  room,days,start_time,end_time,capacity)
STUDENTS(SID,last_name,first_name,class,phone,
  street,city,state,zip,degree,dept_id,hours,gpa)
ENROLLMENT(SID,TERM,LINENO,grade)
```

Note: The primary key columns are shown in uppercase.

The `COURSES` table maintains the list of courses in the university catalog. Information about departments, instructors, and students is maintained in the `DEPARTMENTS`, `INSTRUCTORS`, and `STUDENTS` tables respectively. Notice that some of the columns in the `STUDENTS` table are computed columns (`gpa`, `hours`)—i.e., their values are determined by other values in other tables. The `SECTIONS` table maintains information about the schedule of classes for each term. These are the sections of the various courses that are offered each term. The `ENROLLMENT` table keeps information about the enrollment of students in sections.

The following is an outline of a possible application program for the student database.

```
    MAIN MENU
(1) Student functions
(2) Administrative functions
(3) Reporting functions
(4) Quit

    STUDENT FUNCTIONS MENU
(1) Register for courses
(2) Add/drop a course
(3) Request transcript
(4) Pay fees (get a fee report)
(5) Quit
```

```
    ADMINISTRATIVE FUNCTIONS MENU
(1) Create a new course/drop course
(2) Prepare term schedule (add sections)
(3) Add/drop instructors
(4) Alter term schedule (add/drop/update sections)
(5) Add/drop students
(6) Quit

    REPORTING FUNCTIONS MENU
(1) Print schedule of classes (for a term)
(2) Print the catalog
(3) Print the honors list of students for a department
(4) Quit
```

7.4 Video Chain Database

Consider the operations of a video rental and sales chain. Such a company purchases videos from vendors and stocks them in one of many stores. Each store has several employees who rent or sell these movies to members. Members are required to return the rented movies by the due date, otherwise a fine is imposed. Commissions are awarded to employees based on their sales volume. One possible design of a database for this application results in the following relational tables:

```
STORE(STORE_NUM,address)
EMPLOYEES(EID,name,store_num,commission_rate)
MOVIES(VID,STOCK_NUM,title,cost,category,rent_price,
       sale_price,purchase_date,vendor_name,qoh)
MEMBERS(MID,lname,fname,address,bonus_points)
RENTALS(RENTAL_TRANSACTION_NUMBER,mid,stock_num,
        vid,eid,date_out,frequency,date_in)
SALES(SALE_TRANSACTION_NUMBER,mid,stock_num,vid,eid,
      sale_date)
VENDORS(VENDOR_NAME,address,phone).
```

Note: The primary key columns are shown in uppercase.

The STORE table records the store numbers and addresses of the individual stores. The EMPLOYEES table records information about the employees and the store they are associated with. The MOVIES table contains information about all the videos in the company. The STOCK_NUM column may indicate which store the videocassette belongs to. Information about the members is kept in the **MEMBERS** table. Members are given some bonus points each time they rent a movie. The accumulated points are recorded in this table. Members are eligible for a free rental after accumulation of a certain number of bonus points. The **RENTALS** and **SALES** tables record each transaction made. For the rental of movies, the date checked out, the frequency for the checkout (how many days?), and the date returned are recorded. The **VENDORS** table records information about vendors from whom the videos are purchased.

A possible application program for the video company is outlined in the following menu/sub-menus.

```
      MAIN MENU
(1) Member functions
(2) Reporting functions
(3) Administrative functions
(4) Quit

      MEMBER FUNCTIONS MENU
(1) Video checkout
(2) New member signup
(3) List of outstanding videos
(4) Membership cancellation
(5) Video purchase
(6) Quit

      ADMINISTRATIVE FUNCTIONS MENU
(1) Video return
(2) Add/delete employee
(3) Process new shipment of videos
(4) Open new store
(5) Quit

      REPORTING FUNCTIONS MENU
(1) Print catalog (arranged by categories)
(2) Print due list of videos
(3) Print employee commission report
(4) Print rental summary
    (sorted based on frequency of rental)
(5) Quit
```

7.5 Banking Database

Consider the operations of a typical banking enterprise. A bank normally has many branches, and customers can open accounts at any of these branches. It is normal for more than one customer to have the same account and for one customer to have multiple accounts. The bank offers various types of services—from savings and checking accounts to loans. A possible design for the banking enterprise results in the following relational tables:

```
BRANCHES(BRANCH_NUM,branch_name,address)
CUSTOMERS(CUSTOMER_NUM,name,address,phone)
CHECKING_ACCOUNTS(ACCOUNT_NUM,branch_num,date_opened,
  balance,overdraft_amount,check_limit)
SAVINGS_ACCOUNTS(ACCOUNT_NUM,branch_num,date_opened,
  balance,interest_rate)
LOAN_ACCOUNTS(ACCOUNT_NUM,branch_num,date_opened,
  loan_type,interest_rate)
HAS_ACCOUNT(CUSTOMER_NUM,ACCOUNT_TYPE,ACCOUNT_NUM)
TRANSACTIONS(ACCOUNT_TYPE,ACCOUNT_NUM,TRANS_DATE,
  TRANS_AMT,TRANS_TYPE,trans_comments)
```

Note: The primary key columns are shown in uppercase.

The `BRANCHES` table keeps information about all the branches of the bank, and the `CUSTOMERS` table records information about all the customers of the bank. There are three tables for the three different types of accounts. Each has an `ACCOUNT_NUM` column, which may or may not be unique across the accounts. Hence, the table `HAS_ACCOUNT`, which keeps information about which customers own which account, has the column `ACCOUNT_TYPE` to indicate what type of account the customer owns. The `TRANSACTIONS` table records all the transactions that occur within the accounts.

The following is a sketch of an application for the banking enterprise:

```
        MAIN MENU
(1) Customer functions
(2) Administrative functions
(3) Reporting functions
(4) Quit

        CUSTOMER FUNCTIONS MENU
(1) Deposit
(2) Withdraw
(3) Transfer
```

```
(4) Loan payment
(5) Quit

      ADMINISTRATIVE FUNCTIONS MENU
(1) Process checks
    (assume a file containing checks received
     by the bank)
(2) Add/drop customer
(3) Open/close account
(4) Quit

      REPORTING FUNCTIONS MENU
(1) Print monthly statement
(2) Print loan payment schedule
(3) Print yearly tax statement (interest earned)
    (to be mailed out for each customer)
(4) Quit
```

7.6 BiBTeX Database

Consider the TeX word processing system and the way it handles bibliography information. The bibliographic entries are created in a text file in a particular format and are consulted by the **BiBTeX** program when processing the entries referenced in a document.[1] The problem is to keep the collection of bibliographic entries in an Oracle database and to allow manipulation of these entries via an application program.

The bibliographic entries are classified into various categories: **article**, **book**, **inbook**, **proceedings**, **inproceedings**, **techreport**, **manual**, **conference**, etc. An entry in each of these categories has some required fields and some optional fields. Each entry is identified by a unique **citekey**.

One possible design of a relational database results in the following tables:

```
MASTER_ENTRIES(CITE_KEY,entry_type)
ARTICLE(CITE_KEY,author,title,journal,volume,number,
  pages,month,year,note)
BOOK(CITE_KEY,author,editor,title,publisher,address,
  volume,edition,series,month,year,note)
```

1. See Leslie Lamport, *LaTeX User's Guide and Reference Manual* (Reading, MA: Addison-Wesley, 1986), for details on this format and other specifics regarding the BiBTeX program.

```
PROCEEDINGS(CITE_KEY,editor,title,publisher,
  organization,address,month,year,note)
INBOOK(CITE_KEY,author,editor,title,publisher,address,
  volume,edition,series,chapter,pages,month,year,note)
INPROCEEDINGS(CITE_KEY,author,editor,title,booktitle,
  publisher,organization,address,pages,month,year,note)
.
.
.
REQUIRED_FIELDS(ENTRY_TYPE,FIELD)
```

Note: The primary key columns are shown in uppercase.

The MASTER_ENTRIES table contains the cite key and the type of entry (article, book, etc.) for all the bibliographic entries. There is one table for each entry type that maintains all the entries under that particular category. For example, the table ARTICLE contains all the bibliographic entries that are articles. The REQUIRED_FIELDS table records information about the required fields for each type of entry. This information will have to be consulted when creating a new bibliographic entry.

An application program that manipulates the above database is sketched out below:

```
     MAIN MENU
(1) Update functions
(2) Search functions
(3) Reporting/Utility functions
(4) Quit

     UPDATE FUNCTIONS MENU
(1) Add an entry
(2) Modify an entry
(3) Delete an entry
(4) Quit

     SEARCH FUNCTIONS MENU
(1) Search based on author
(2) Search based on keyword in title
(3) Search based on multiple search criteria
(4) Quit

     REPORTING/UTILITY FUNCTIONS MENU
(1) Print summary reports
(2) Read .bib files and load database
(3) Write all entries to .bib file
(4) Write selected entries to .bib file
(5) Quit
```

7.7 Music Store Database

Consider the operations of a company that sells prerecorded compact discs and related items. The company has many outlets in several states. Each outlet has been assigned a number and has its own manager, employees, inventory, sales, and returns. Company-wide product and customer lists are maintained. Based on the above information, the following relational tables constitute one possible design of the database:

```
OUTLET(OUTLET_NUMBER,address,city,state,zip,phone)
EMPLOYEE(OUTLET_NUMBER,EMP_NUMBER,emp_name)
PRODUCT(PRODUCT_CODE,artist,title,cost,sale_price)
CUSTOMER(CUSTOMER_ID,customer_name,address,city,
  state,zip,phone)
MANAGER(OUTLET_NUMBER,emp_number)
INVENTORY(OUTLET_NUMBER,PRODUCT_CODE,quantity)
SALES(OUTLET_NUMBER,EMP_NUMBER,CUSTOMER_ID,PRODUCT_CODE,
  SALE_DATE,SALE_TIME,quantity)
RETURNS(OUTLET_NUMBER,PRODUCT_CODE,CUSTOMER_ID,
  RETURN_DATE,RETURN_TIME,quantity,reason,restock)
```

Note: The primary key columns are shown in uppercase.

The following is a sketch of an application program interface using menus and sub-menus:

```
        MAIN MENU
(1) Sale/return processing
(2) Outlet/employee/customer/product maintenance
(3) Reports
(4) Quit

        SALES/RETURNS MENU
(1) Process a sale
(2) Process a return
(3) View a sale (given date and customer id)
(4) View a return (given date and customer id)
(5) Quit

        MAINTENANCE MENU
(1) Add/modify/drop outlet
(2) Add/modify/drop employee
(3) Add/modify/drop customer
(4) Add/modify/drop product
```

```
(5) Process new shipment of products for an outlet
(6) Process returns
(7) Quit

      REPORTS MENU
(1) Produce yearly sales report for outlet
(2) Produce sales report for employee
(3) Produce the list of top 10 selling items
(4) Quit
```

7.8 Online Auctions Database

Consider the operations of an online auction company that offers members the opportunity to buy and sell computer related hardware and software items. The seller lists the item for sale. A description of the item along with the starting price and bid increments are specified by the seller. Various other information such as shipping mode and charges, category of the item, when the auction ends, etc. are also provided at the time of the listing. Buyers make bids for the items they are interested in buying. The person placing the highest bid at the time of the end of the auction is declared the winner and a transaction between the buyer and seller may proceed soon after. Buyers and sellers can leave feedback regarding their experience on a purchase or sale on the system. This feedback is available for every member to look at.

Based on the above information the following relational tables constitute one possible design of the database:

```
MEMBERS(USERID,password,name,address,phone,email)
ITEMS(INO,category,title,description,sellerID,quantity,
      startPrice,bidIncrement,lastBidReceived,closeTime)
SHIPPING(INO,SHIPTYPE,SHIPPRICE)
BID(BUYERID,INO,PRICE,QTYWANTED,BIDTIME)
RATING(INO,BUYERID,SELLERID,sComment,bComment,sScale,bScale)
```

Note: The primary key columns are shown in upper-case.

The `MEMBERS` table records information about all the members of the online auction company. These include both buyers and sellers, and the same member could be the seller of one item and the buyer of another item. The `ITEMS` table keeps track of items that are on the auction block. Each item is assigned a unique item number. The seller's user id is included in this table. For each item on auction, there could be several shipping modes and the `SHIPPING` table keeps track of this information. The bids placed by members for items are recorded in the **BID** table. The **RATING** table records the ratings placed by buyers or sellers for a transaction. The rating includes a descriptive comment as well as a numeric value (say, −1 for negative experience, 0 for neutral experience, and +1 for a positive experience).

The following is a sketch of an application program interface using menus and sub-menus.

```
    MAIN MENU
(1) Member registration
(2) Member login
(3) Quit

    MEMBER MENU
(1) Place an item for auction
(2) Bid on an item
(3) Search for items
(4) Place a rating
(5) View rating
(6) Quit
```

7.9 Oracle Data Dictionary Browser

Oracle maintains information about all the database objects in its data dictionary as briefly described in Section 2.8. The data dictionary includes the names and structures of all tables, constraints, indices, views, synonyms, sequences, triggers, stored functions, procedures, and packages. Each individual Oracle user has access to the portion of the data dictionary that pertains to their schema via pre-defined views. Some of these views are:

```
user_objects   : description of user's objects
user_tables    : description of user's tables
user_indexes   : description of user's indexes
user_sequences: description of user's sequences
user_synonyms  : description of user's synonyms
user_source    : description of user's stored
                 functions, procedures, and packages
user_triggers  : description of user's triggers
user_views     : description of user's views
```

This project involves providing a convenient and powerful way for the user to search and browse their database objects.

The following is a sketch of an application program interface for the data dictionary browser using menus and submenus.

```
      MAIN MENU
(1) Oracle user login
(2) Quit

      ORACLE USER MENU
(1) View tables
(2) View functions/procedures/packages
(3) View synonyms
(4) View sequences
(5) View indexes
(6) View triggers
(7) View views
(8) View objects
(9) Quit
```

To implement this project, the reader must get familiar with Oracle's data dictionary. Within SQL*Plus, the **`describe`** command on each of the predefined views lists the data dictionary table structure for that view.

SUGGESTED READINGS

Koch and Loney (1997) provide comprehensive coverage of all of Oracle's features, including a detailed discussion of all Oracle SQL commands and statements. This is a must have reference for any serious Oracle programmer. There are numerous books covering SQL. Among the more interesting ones are Melton and Simon (1993), Pratt (1995), and Bowman, Emerson, and Darnovsky (1996). Embedded SQL is covered in McClanahan (1996) and Melton and Simon (1993). Three widely cited and used books on PL/SQL are Urman (1997), Urman and Smith (1996), and Feuerstein and Pribyl (1997). Hamilton, Cattell, and Fisher (1997), Reese (1997), and Traub and McElroy (1997) are among the books focusing on JDBC. Relational database concepts are covered in academic database textbooks such as those by Elmasri and Navathe (2000), O'Neil (1991), Ullman and Widom (1997), and Silberschatz, Korth, and Sudarshan (1997).

Bowman, J. S., S. L. Emerson, and M. Darnovsky. *The Practical SQL Handbook : Using Structured Query Language*, 3rd ed. Reading, MA: Addison-Wesley, 1996.

Elmasri, R., and S. B. Navathe. *Fundamentals of Database Systems*, 3rd ed. Reading, MA: Addison-Wesley, 2000.

Feuerstein, S., and B. Pribyl. *Oracle PL/SQL Programming*, 2nd ed. Sebastopol, CA: O'Reilly, 1997.

Hamilton, Graham, Rick Cattell, and Maydene Fisher. *JDBC Database Access with Java: A Tutorial and Annotated Reference*. Reading, MA: Addison-Wesley, 1997.

Koch, G., and K. Loney. *Oracle8: The Complete Reference*. Berkeley, CA: Oracle Press, Osborne/ McGraw-Hill, 1997.

McClanahan, David. *Oracle Developer's Guide*. Berkeley, CA: Oracle Press, Osborne/McGraw-Hill, 1996.

Melton, J., and A. R. Simon. *Understanding the New SQL : A Complete Guide*. San Francisco: Morgan Kaufman, 1993.

O'Neil, P. *Database: Principles, Programming, Performance*. San Francisco: Morgan Kaufmann, 1994.

Pratt, P. J. *A Guide to SQL*, 3rd ed. Boston: Boyd & Fraser, 1995.

Reese, George. *Database Programming with JDBC and Java*. Sebastopol, CA: O'Reilly, 1997.

Silberschatz, A., H. Korth, and S. Sudarshan. *Database Systems Concepts*, 3rd ed. New York: McGraw-Hill, 1997.

Traub, Janet L., and David J. McElroy. *Core JDBC Programming*. Englewood Cliffs, NJ: Prentice Hall, 1997.

Ullman, J. D., and J. Widom. *A First Course in Database Systems*. Englewood Cliffs, NJ: Prentice Hall, 1997.

Urman, S. *Oracle8: PL/SQL Programming*. Berkeley, CA: Oracle Press, Osborne/McGraw-Hill, 1997.

Urman, S., and T. Smith. *Oracle PL/SQL Programming*. Berkeley, CA: Oracle Press, Osborne/McGraw-Hill, 1996.

INDEX